PLAYING GAMES

—————— AT ——————

CNN

HOW A SOFTBALL TEAM CAPTURED THE SPIRIT OF A NEWS NETWORK

5editorial

Silver Spring, Maryland U.S.A.

Playing Games at CNN
How a Softball Team Captured the Spirit of a News Network
Copyright ©2024

ISBN 978-0-9982771-3-4

Cover artwork and composition
by Jenine Zimmers, Oakhurst, New Jersey

Editing and publishing by Dennis Tuttle, 5editorial, Silver Spring,
Maryland

The book was printed in the United States of America

10 9 8 7 6 5 4 3 2 1

Barncraigio Sizkins

A combination of my extended family's last names:
Barnett, Craighill, Gregorio, Sizer and Elkins.

CONTENTS

INTRODUCTION

Thirty years of covering global events at CNN has been part of a rewarding career in news. As a journalist, I've had a front-row seat to the best and worst life has to offer. Along the way, there have been wars, terrorist attacks, riots, mass shootings, deaths, and disasters, both man-made and natural. It hasn't always been an uplifting experience. The world, at times, can be unwelcoming with its distressing images and disturbing subject matter. Viewers, of course, can tune out and change the channel at any time. But for those of us on the front lines, we can't just leave it at the office. The media reports the news whenever it happens and wherever it leads.

Yet, it can be a struggle to turn off the information spigot. We grow accustomed to the adrenaline rush, deadlines, and the pressure of getting things right and informing the public. My connection to fellow journalists and their commitment and optimism have kept me grounded during challenging times.

I was devoted to news gathering while at CNN for three decades. During an annual review, I told my supervisor that one of my most gratifying accomplishments as a broadcast journalist was going 10 years without missing a day of work. Her response? "You're supposed to come to work. That's what the company pays you to do." Blunt and on point.

I dealt with a variety of news stories every day, especially as a copy editor and producer. If I did a back-of-the-envelope calculation, I probably had a hand in at least 20,000, give or take.

I also traveled to different places on assignment and interviewed newsmakers, too many to list. I'll never forget the night I spent at the Pentagon on 9/11 and the smell of smoke throughout the dark corridors of the burning building. I was among the first non-government civilians to fly on a V-22 Osprey test flight, only after signing a waiver absolving the Marine Corps of liability if the plane crashed. I was especially proud of an 18-minute story I produced about LBJ and whether the president deserved a Silver Star. The investigative piece by reporter Jamie McIntyre was so comprehensive we had to do it in two parts to allow for a commercial break. After it aired, other news organizations picked up our reporting.

What was my favorite or most memorable story? Not easy to answer. Were it not for the fact that CNN's middle name is "news," it might be surprising to know a sports story is smack-dab near the top.

It was September 1998. I spent three days in St. Louis covering the dramatic home run race between Mark McGwire and Sammy Sosa. The two Major League Baseball sluggers were on pace to break Roger Maris' 1961 record. CNN needed a producer to help gather details and coordinate live shots. At the time, I was the coach of the CNN softball team, so they figured I knew something about the subject. I was on the field at Busch Stadium for media interviews and batting practice, standing next to my boyhood idol, Cardinals Hall of Famer Lou Brock. On Labor Day, I saw McGwire hit No. 61 to tie Maris on his way to 70. That experience was about as good as it gets.

I've always loved sports and the underdog. Like many kids in the 1960s, I listened to the radio late at night. On clear nights from my bedroom in New Orleans, my transistor radio would pick up the signal of KMOX in St. Louis, a 50,000-watt station almost 700 miles away. I would sit on the bed and keep a scorebook as Harry Caray and Jack Buck called the play-by-play.

Sports events were my relief valve, a happy place in my life, especially throughout my career in news. It still holds true.

After grad school in Boston and three years as a reporter and weekend anchor in Richmond, I began writing news at CNN in 1983 alongside Christiane Amanpour in Atlanta. We alternated writing the A and B blocks every weekend for a year for the late anchor Rick Moore.

Back then, Ted Turner owned the Atlanta Braves. One of the employee perks was getting 20 baseball coupons each season to see the home team play. I think back to one night in particular. It was July 4th, 1985. I was working the 5:30 p.m.-2:30 a.m. shift. The Braves were playing the New York Mets at Atlanta-Fulton County Stadium, a short drive from CNN. There had been a couple of rain delays. It was around 2 a.m., and I was getting off work when I realized the game, now in extra innings, had not ended. So, I drove over to the stadium and walked right in—the ticket takers were long gone, as were most of the 45,000 in attendance, and the concession stands were closed.

The Braves were losing by a run in the 18th inning and had one batter left on the bench, described at the time as the "worst-hitting pitcher in baseball." His name was Rick Camp, with a lifetime batting average of .074. Down to his last strike and with two outs, he bashed a home run to tie the game, the only homer of his 12-season career. It was around 3:30 in the morning. The game continued until a little before 4 a.m., with the Mets finally prevailing 16-13 in 19 innings in what has been called "one of the greatest, strangest, longest games in baseball history."

I watched six innings of free baseball, all after 2 a.m. And here's the piece de resistance: the Atlanta Braves went ahead with their July 4th (now July 5th) postgame fireworks show as promised for the remaining few thousand faithful. Of course, the neighbors were not too pleased about that decision.

I transferred to the CNN Washington Bureau in 1989 as a supervising producer and joined the network's softball team a few years later. It was just my speed: slow pitch, underhand, Saturday morning, and co-ed. That started a love affair with the Metropolitan Media Softball League, comprised of other like-minded journalists. I enjoyed playing and especially getting to know colleagues in a venue other than a newsroom. It wasn't long before I became the CNN coach... and team chronicler.

From the start, I focused on writing about the players in the context of world events. The two were not mutually exclusive. I used a pseudonym, Joe Baseball Jr., thinking it might engage a wider audience. Of course, it was no secret who wrote the weekly softball columns. My real name was at the top of every entry for all to read.

The softball write-ups quickly grew a following. Players liked seeing their names in print and getting recognition. Just as important, I wanted to spotlight that we all had roles in the CNN newsgathering process and shared a stake in the company's success. Writing about it was my way of acknowledging the concept of teamwork.

My mission was to pull back the curtain to report what happened on the field and provide readers with the humorous shenanigans of a team establishing its identity like the news network we represented.

I poked fun at myself, my teammates, and executives within the company. Written in wire service style (with a few exceptions), I recapped each game while also imagining what CNN employees and newsmakers might say if someone had interviewed them. Satire was my literary genre to find the humor and the occasional absurdity of the events we covered.

In the early 1990s and particularly during the Gulf War, CNN reigned supreme over the cable news kingdom, having shaken its moniker as the Chicken Noodle Network, when lack of respect, low pay, and on-air gaffes ruled the day. The broadcasting landscape was forever changed by rivals MSNBC and Fox News and the AOL Time Warner merger. After that, CNN's hold on the 24-hour news cycle was never quite as firm.

It was a tumultuous and remarkable period, from politics to pop culture. All of it was in play when I wrote about softball through the prism of irony. The summaries with concocted quotes became must-read stories on Monday mornings across CNN's many bureaus. Even those I skewered would privately embrace the ribbing and encourage me.

For this book, I have pulled together a decade of seasonal weekly write-ups, which provide a snapshot of the world, the news network, and the characters who were part of it between 1998 and 2007. Unlike the television series *Dragnet*, the names have not been changed, but the quotes are all purely fictitious.

You don't have to be a CNN Washington insider to enjoy this free-swinging look back at a wacky co-ed team of real journalists competing on Saturday mornings for bragging rights in the Metropolitan Media Softball League.

PREGAME MEETING

The Metropolitan Media Softball League might never have started in the spring of 1991 if it hadn't been for a shard of glass from a broken beer bottle.

Media teams around Washington, D.C., had been informally playing against each other for years, usually on the National Mall... or at a benefit tournament... or wherever they could find a school with an open field on weekends.

The Washington Post found such an arrangement in Rockville, Maryland, and welcomed fellow media teams, think tanks, congressional offices, and just about anyone wanting to play. WRC-TV also made the rounds, and a cluster of small newspapers—the Gaithersburg Gazette, Potomac Almanac, and Montgomery Sentinel, among others—played in suburban Montgomery County. The Washington Times, another active media-playing team, participated in the Thursday evening Publisher's League in the District neighborhood of Takoma.

Dennis Tuttle, the Times' coach, had suffered three years of fits with the D.C. Department of Parks and Recreation over lousy scheduling, intoxicated umpires, and park fields that resembled cow pastures. He vowed to find a new venue after the 1990 season when their left fielder raced in for a liner and made a diving catch, his face stopping inches from a broken beer bottle. That incident proved to be a seminal moment in Washington media history.

Tuttle, along with Lola Demma at the Montgomery Journal, pulled nine teams together in early 1991 for a co-ed media softball league under the umbrella of Montgomery County Recreation. Demma delivered the county press teams, including the Silver Spring Record and Express Papers. Tuttle recruited the Post and USA Today. He also drafted a rulebook and provided sensible structure, such as playing doubleheader games on Saturday mornings to better accommodate media work schedules instead of having a single game on weeknights.

But it wasn't all smooth sailing for the MMSL in those early years. Like D.C., ballfields were not routinely maintained, and teams often had to bring rakes, shovels, and kitty litter to make the fields playable. In some instances, they brought lawn mowers, too.

There was also the matter of autocratic umpires. Many were defiant about some of the league rules that differed from the rec department programs. And per national co-ed softball rules, Montgomery County wanted the MMSL to have five women players on the field, but the roster numbers were insufficient to make that work.

However, the biggest problem was Mother Nature. We talk about climate change today, but in the '90s, it seemed like it always rained before Saturday's games. That's an exaggeration, but only slightly. In May 1995, every Saturday was rained out, forcing teams to play tripleheaders during the wretched summer heat to catch up with the schedule.

Through the years, the league has welcomed 64 media teams from local and national newspapers, local TV stations, national and foreign networks, radio stations, news agencies, websites, and magazines. There's even an MMSL team comprised of players from clubs that are no longer around. Of the original nine teams, the Washington Post remains the only charter member to play in every MMSL season.

Lola Demma left the program after the 1992 season because she felt the league was too competitive. She wasn't wrong. Journalists are competitive by nature. But Dennis Tuttle had been playing softball since the early '70s and had built a successful media league when he was a sportswriter in Knoxville, Tennessee. He was attuned to the game on the field and administratively in ways that few in the MMSL understood.

Admittedly, The Commish ran things with an iron fist, which often irritated people, but he had some critical core values, such as playing time for all, competitive balance, and stressing the league's name meant the program was for working media players only. No outsiders or "ringers" were allowed, but teams tried anyway.

Scripps Howard was a repeat offender and had to forfeit those games when caught. The Associated Press relinquished the 1996 championship due to an illegal player. And in the ugliest scene anyone can remember, a fight broke out at the end of a 1994 game at Layhill Park, where a ringer

Coach Jim Barnett with the haul of CNN softball trophies and awards in 2008.

threw haymakers at an opponent. Three players were ejected, and Montgomery County banned the offender for life.

Tuttle preached that the MMSL must be about camaraderie and sportsmanship. That was always his goal, even if he had to cuss and threaten everyone to play nice. Suspensions occasionally happened, but for the most part, fellowship has been achieved throughout the league's long history of compatibility, sustainability, and innovation.

When CNN joined the growing MMSL in 1993, divisional play was already established, unlike the county leagues. Teams were paired against common opponents based on the type of media. For example, local TV stations were in one division, national network teams in another, large newspapers in one, and a hodge-podge of teams in a fourth.

Three years before Major League Baseball, the MMSL instituted a wild-card system that allowed more good teams to qualify for the playoffs if they didn't win their divisions. This format was hugely popular, and many important games went down to the final hour on the season's last day. No other softball program among more than 1,200 teams in Montgomery County was using this system.

Expansion was always on the league's mind. When CNN came along, the MMSL expanded from 12 teams to 16 (including America's Most

Wanted, NewsChannel 8, and CapitalView News). The MMSL would later top off at 24 teams, six divisions, and almost 450 players. There was a brief time in the mid-2000s when the league dreamed of 30 or 36 teams. But that was before the digital news explosion and attrition of local and national media advertising. With players leaving for new jobs and teams disbanding due to budget cuts or faded interest, a new reality set in: Softball was dying nationwide, and the next wave of players was not arriving.

Those 1,200 Montgomery County teams? There are now fewer than 70.

CNN's venture into the MMSL started like most others. We played like newbies, just for fresh air and recreational fun. We often played like a tee-ball softball team and rarely exhibited lightning in a bottle. In our first game, the defense was so porous that we allowed 10 unearned runs in one inning. "I spend my whole week catching errors made by news writers, and then I come out to play and have to deal with this," quibbled CNN national correspondent Gene Randall back in the day.

Good intentions aside, the road to eventual softball success would start with potholes and gravel. That first season, we produced nine wins and nine losses and missed the playoffs on the season's final day.

Joe Baseball Jr. was just a figment of my imagination in those early years. CNN softball was not something the newsroom talked about on the weekends or during the week, for that matter. The write-ups were handled by David Shuster, who later became an anchor at MSNBC. Shuster was a weekend assignment desk editor at CNN in the inaugural season and played on the softball team.

He had a flair for writing game summaries. In 1993, Shuster wrote about the CNN games to amuse employees and pass the time on slow news weekends. His biggest concern was a fear the bean counters at CNN headquarters in Atlanta would read his musings and wonder why they paid him to write about softball on company time. For that reason, he kept his powder dry so as not to wake a sleeping giant. His reports generally focused on those who showed up to play.

Here's an example: Following a rare doubleheader sweep by CNN, Shuster touted coach Brian Haefeli for his "brilliant coaching and religious vision." His write-up said, "Players noticed pitcher Jim Barnett performing a weird sort of 'voodoo' ritual before and after the game." Looking back on his game summaries, Shuster acknowledged it was pretty tame commentary.

In 1994, CNN began making modest strides between the chalk lines, starting 6-0 and flirting with the No. 1 seed for the playoffs—but then, we lost five of eight games. The vaunted Commish's Office reported the league had scored an all-time high of 394 runs the second week of the season. CNN did its part. Against UPI, we plated 18 runs in the top of the first inning.

"Eighteen runs, 7,000 hits, and three dozen errors," Shuster reported.

The team was flush with women players, a cornerstone of any good lineup. We had women pitching (Pam Benson) and playing shortstop (Carolyn Robertson), positions customarily filled by men on most teams in the MMSL. We embraced our gender diversity and finished 13-5, reaching the playoffs.

Perhaps that's why, on one occasion, nine spectators showed up to watch. It prompted Shuster to write that everyone was invited to participate and bring their resumes, cover letters, and salary requirements, including "sadists and Hollywood producers."

The team had no prima donnas or divas, even though we had occasional stars. One of our players, Dennis Baltimore, once went 9-for-9 with seven singles, a double, homer, and seven RBI in a pair of wins. When we beat C-SPAN on the last day of the 1994 season, it sealed the club's first berth in the playoffs.

Shuster documented the feat by writing that the CNN player who scored the winning run "was seen hugging the umpire after the game." We finished in third place overall with the team earning the fleeting moniker the Head-Turners. We got a taste of winning, but it was short-lived.

Joe Baseball Jr. took over the writing duties from Shuster in 1995, but real-world events like terrorism and high-profile trials, including O.J. Simpson, made that job more difficult. The Oklahoma City bombing in April put a pall on the season before it started, as work-related assignments siphoned away players.

We had one win in our first eight games. Despite all the rain and triple-headers, plus the midseason folding of United Press International's team that further muddied the soggy schedule, we bounced back for an 8-10 record and missed the playoffs by one game. "The season that wouldn't end," the MMSL proclaimed, even though CNN's turnout for the games was spirited.

The 1996 season was two steps back. Joe Baseball Jr. didn't even bother writing about the last couple of weekends as the squad limped to a 5-11 finish. It had gotten so demoralizing on the field that he recalled half the team showed up with 'Hello. My Name is _____' stickers. Every game featured new faces. Someone threatened to file a FOIA request to uncover how much money the network was budgeting for the softball team instead of newsgathering.

By 1997, CNN was no longer one of the new kids on the block. It was time to show more than just flashes of competitiveness as our fifth season rolled around. Miscues and recriminations dominated games. We started 2-0 and finished 8-10, again losing a chance to make the playoffs on the final day by allowing 13 runs to WUSA-TV in the bottom of the sixth inning of a seven-inning game. One CNN player spoke truth to power: "We're giving away games like donations to the Salvation Army."

But the team's fortunes were about to change. CNN hired reporter John King, a star player at the Associated Press. King was allowed to continue playing with AP for the remainder of the season, but his arrival on the CNN softball team in 1998 was the beginning of our most successful years in the MMSL.

Everything happens for a reason, like that Washington Times player who just missed that shard of glass in the outfield.

Erika Dimmler (top) throws out runner at second base; Lindy Royce (left) always a threat at the plate; Greg Robertson (above) pitches with an accuracy that could make a jeweler jealous.

(Top) CaNiNes celebrate another victory; (middle) Team wins its second title in 2002 against AOL; (right) Charles Bierbauer and Jim Barnett share a happy moment after the trophy presentation.

(L-R) Jim Barnett, Bill Tipper, and Howie Lutt (top) map out strategy and a lineup; (above) John Davis surrounded by Lindy Royce, Lydia Garlikov, Jessica Rosgaard, Vilinda Dickerson, Sarah Chakales, and Liz Flynn.

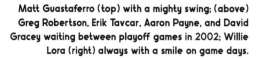

Matt Guastaferro (top) with a mighty swing; (above)
Greg Robertson, Erik Tavcar, Aaron Payne, and David
Gracey waiting between playoff games in 2002; Willie
Lora (right) always with a smile on game days.

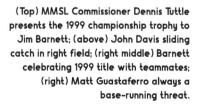

(Top) MMSL Commissioner Dennis Tuttle presents the 1999 championship trophy to Jim Barnett; (above) John Davis sliding catch in right field; (right middle) Barnett celebrating 1999 title with teammates; (right) Matt Guastaferro always a base-running threat.

(Top) Team photo circa 2010 and (above) the CaNiNes gathering for their pre-game ritual in an undated photo.

TOP OF THE 1st

Batter Up

April 16, 1998

- **Buckle up! CNN softball season set to begin bumpy ride.**
- **White House promises to give President Clinton softball updates during his trip to South America.**
- **Personal secretary Betty Currie to throw out first ball.**

By Joe Baseball Jr.
Bureau Sports Writer

WASHINGTON (UPI) — Employees at CNN's Washington Bureau have been on pins and needles for months, waiting to hear two words.

"*Inside Politics*?" shouted giddy political producer Chris Guarino.

"Free food?" grumbled a studio camera operator.

"Hail democracy?" President Bill Clinton pondered as he spoke to reporters aboard Air Force One on his way to Chile.

Not even close.

It's play ball—that time of year when a merry band of brave men and women put aside their manifestos and say goodbye to sleeping in on Saturday mornings.

"Softball, like democracy, is never perfect, but it's always perfectible," said President Clinton's speechwriter.

This weekend, CNN's reputation is on the line when the network's softball team takes the field against division foes Fox News and ABC News in a doubleheader at Aspen Hill Park.

"I know there are questions about the mental capabilities of our players, but physically, we're in good shape," gushed Washington Bureau Chief Frank Sesno.

Gone is legendary skipper Brian Haefeli, who spent five years at the helm. In his place, CNN has anointed not one but three stooges to chart a new direction: Bierbauer, Barnett, and Lynn.

"We think there'll be enough blame to go around," quipped coach Jack Lynn. "If it doesn't work out," added an insightful Charles Bierbauer, "We can always start a law firm."

There are many parts of the lineup puzzle to cobble together. A rainy preseason has forced the cancellation of several practices. Who will play what position? It's a head-scratcher. The team features six left-handers who can't all play first base.

Few want to talk about last year. CNN played like it had blinders on every game. It was so bad the CEO of Pearl Vision showed up to provide free comprehensive eye exams.

Lou Dobbs, recently named *Moneyline* executive vice president, told a Business Roundtable that Moody's will lower CNN's credit rating from AAA to D+ if the team doesn't show improvement.

If the first exhibition game is any indication, hitting won't be a problem. Look for high-scoring games and implementation of the mercy rule.

There's something else in the air at 820 First Street: unbridled enthusiasm and not settling for second-best.

Some credit the realignment of the assignment desk. Others suggest it's the incessant bitching about mandatory 7 a.m. package recuts. "I think it's just the realization that the team has a bunch of losers, and there's no place to go but up," producer Bob Waller waxed philosophically.

Sources say management has been working feverishly to get the season off to a good start. One insider opined, "If Paula Jones thinks she has a prayer of winning a retrial in her sexual harassment lawsuit, there's hope for CNN."

Even William Ginsburg, Monica Lewinsky's attorney, is holding court on CNN's softball prospects. "How often will I have to appear on *Last Word with Wolf Blitzer* before you get the message? My client has given a deposition, and I can tell you what she said about the team is not pretty."

Others speaking on the record are more direct.

"(Deputy Bureau Chief) Peggy Soucy has paid the Metropolitan Media Softball League fee," barked Sesno, simmering and unforgiving over last year's 9-11 season. "(Finance Manager) Diane Stanley has taken care of the equipment expenses, and PR has signed off on the new T-shirts."

CNN President Rick Kaplan echoed those sentiments in a blunt statement: "Heads will roll if D.C. doesn't get its act together. We have better things to do around here, like 8p specials. CNN will not keep throwing money down the toilet no matter how high Time Warner stock goes."

It's been a busy off-season at CNN's Washington office. If you think the CNN library has new faces, check out the names on this year's softball roster: Hathway, Cartwright, Dimmler, Braun, Milstein, Essex, Gratehouse, Lutt, Miller, Silver, Gold, Platinum, and Bronze. Ok, not the last two.

There are plenty of story arcs to come after the first pitch.

"It will be like reading a Dan Silva spy novel – high expectations, lots of intrigue, but in the end, unbearable ennui, disappointment, and despair," said chin-wagged Executive Producer Peter Kendall at the Eight Bells Pub in England.

"We'll know a lot more about how we do this weekend after it's over," fancied editor Michael Jackson, no relation to the pop star. It couldn't be said any better.

April 18, 1998

GAME 1		GAME 2	
CNN	9	ABC NEWS	5
FOX NEWS	4	CNN	2

- **CNN splits doubleheader as 20 employees turn out to play.**
- **Newt Gingrich's book *Lessons Learned the Hard Way* dedicated to softball team.**
- **A&E network to profile CNN players on Biography.**

By Joe Baseball Jr.
Bureau Sports Writer

ASPEN HILL, Md. (UPI) — Moving faster than a tornado outbreak with 20 supercells across Nashville, CNN's 1998 softball season got off to a whirlwind start as the team tore a hole through upstart Fox News, winning 9-4 in the muddy grass at Aspen Hill Park.

CNN humiliated Rupert Murdoch's team by scoring three runs in the first inning, two in the second, and two in the third, and never looked back on Opening Day.

"I think we taught Fox a lesson. They should stick to happy news and leave the serious news business to professionals," warned CNN D.C. Bureau Chief Frank Sesno. "By the way, (Producer) Charley Keyes will run a few game highlights on our noon show, which should double the ratings."

CNN was looking for a sweep. But their bats were colder than Pol Pot on ice, and ABC News hung on to win 5-2 in the nightcap. The games were played on a wet field resembling a Louisiana swamp.

"We came in with bathing suits and a game plan, and we played to perfection," said tri-manager Jack Lynn, who reached base six times on the day. "The big difference this year is chemistry and the fact we don't have any more dweebs in our newsroom."

President Clinton's spiritual advisor, the Reverend Jesse Jackson, speaking from his Rainbow Coalition headquarters, said, "The softball players can put dope in their veins or hope in their brains. If they can conceive it and believe it, they can achieve it. They must know that it is not their aptitude but their attitude that will determine their altitude. Keep hope alive!" He added one more rhetorical flourish, "CNN's team showed it could play *Both Sides with Jesse Jackson* from Capitol Hill to Aspen Hill."

In the opener, video editor Scott Miller led off as the designated hitter and clubbed a double, the first of several on the day. "Getting the edit decks to work at the office is much harder than hitting a softball," he said.

Cameraman Greg Robertson, who knows a thing or two about being a "Team" player, picked up where he left off last summer, smacking the ball with his trademark smooth swing and playing flashy defense. On one play, a Fox News batter hit a grounder almost through the hole to center field, but Robertson grabbed the ball and threw the runner out at first base.

It was an all-around esprit de corps. Marty Kramer had four singles, Charles Bierbauer advanced runners and got several game-sustaining RBI, and Tim Durham played errorless left field.

Additional support came from Kate Steinhilber, who delayed an out-of-town trip to play; Erika Dimmler, Elizabeth Hathway; Sheara Braun, who brought along her grace-under-pressure skills from the CNN library; Jonathan Aiken, who did a great impersonation of Oakland A's speedster Rickey Henderson, Patrick Davis, Fred Frommer, Melissa Cartwright, Suzanne Lepofsky, Michael Jackson, Ginanne Brownell, Pat Brennan, Jim Barnett and Evan Lipson, all rising stars in their own right.

There wasn't much to say about the second game. Even the umpire seemed disinterested and confused, going so far as to threaten to put CNN players in the penalty box for high-sticking, pass interference, and a three-second lane violation. CNN bats were dormant, and ABC did enough to slip out of town with a 5-2 victory.

"Two runs in a co-ed underhand softball game will usually guarantee a loss every time," said one passerby.

The pundits wasted little time commenting about the doubleheader.

Media critic Howard Kurtz wrote, "If they can get John King off weekends, this will be an unstoppable team, and that's no spin. He has a rapaciousness to become a superpower."

Arkansas businessman David Hale, whose allegations against President

Bill Clinton set off the Whitewater investigation, raised his right hand and said, "The softball team is a lot more credible than I ever will be, and I don't think they'll be intimidated."

Even supporters of convicted murderer Samuel Sheinbein, who dismembered another man, cheered the performance from his Israeli prison cell. "It was masterful the way CNN dissected Fox limb by limb."

Next week, CNN will try to end its losing skid when it faces WJLA-TV in Game 1 and WRC-TV in Game 2 at Norwood Park.

April 25, 1998

GAME 1		GAME 2	
CNN	11	WRC	14
WJLA	7	CNN	6

- CNN 2-2 splits another doubleheader.
- Softball team aspires to become cultural touchstone of this generation.
- Independent counsel to probe whether players are using performance-enhancing drugs.

By Joe Baseball Jr.
Bureau Sports Writer

BETHESDA, Md. (UPI) — It was a weekend to dream about opportunities, sustainable growth, and working together. But enough about the G8 summit next month in Birmingham, England.

Let's talk softball.

There was no doubt about who was the better team in Game 1 as CNN turned in a sparkling performance and beat WJLA, 11-7. The smell of spring and a sweet sweep was in the air for a while, but CNN ran out of gas in the nightcap, losing to WRC, 14-6.

"It was a gutsy effort," said a red-faced, finger-wagging Russian President Boris Yeltsin.

The weather was a feast for the eyes. The field conditions at Norwood Park were superb. Everyone in the red and white CNN T-shirts had smiles on their faces. "Not a Debbie Downer in sight," hedged one CNN player, who refused to give his name.

Make no mistake about it: CNN came out with white-hot intensity.

With the addition of a half dozen new faces (Gary Krakower, Michael Watts, Jeff Milstein, Ann Curley, Darren McInerney, and Pete Hartogs), the team was ready to claim broadcasting rights as king of the hill.

CNN did not dampen the spirits of its followers, as everyone got to play. Greg Robertson's bat continued to sizzle as he hit for the cycle. It was contagious as Patrick Davis, Scott Miller, tri-manager Jack Lynn, Marty Kramer, Tim Durham, tri-manager Jim Barnett, Patrick Brennan, Erika Dimmler, Milstein, and Curley all got on base.

Curley, sporting a scar the size of Texas on her leg, stood in the batter's box while Suzanne Lepofsky did the running. The buddy system worked so well CNN D.C. Bureau Chief Frank Sesno is reportedly considering "pairing up everyone" in the Washington office. "Who wants to work with Bob Franken?" he asked in front of a suddenly quiet newsroom.

Senior White House Correspondent Wolf Blitzer said, "Sources believe WJLA and CNN matched up pretty evenly, but privately, those sources said they didn't know enough to talk publicly about anything private."

In the second game, WRC tried to ratchet up the stakes by wearing freshly-pressed color-coordinated uniforms. In a fit of pseudo-analysis, the umpire, who had just arrived via the Hale-Bopp comet, chided the local news station for its "snarly attitude."

Elizabeth Hathway, Sheara Braun, Cybele MacHardy, and her cocker spaniel Tobey helped keep the score close when everyone else was ready to head to Cap City Brewery. "If we can find a Pam Olson package on a 1984 edit master, I thought we could find a way to win," said the library contingent when the game was clearly out of reach.

CNN's repugnant effort didn't fare well with plugged-in executives in Atlanta. President Tom Johnson released a short statement: "I am prepared to swap out the entire Washington Bureau with the Dallas Bureau unless the team does better. I may throw in the Southeast Bureau while I'm at it."

There are no games next Saturday. CNN will be back in action on May 9 when it plays U.S. News and the Washington Post at Aspen Hill.

What's in a Nickname?

In the early years, the CNN softball team was nicknamed the Head-Turners for its good play and a nod to founder Ted Turner. Then came the Ted and Janes when Turner married actress Jane Fonda. While these were passing attempts, it wasn't until 2003, our 10th year in the league, that CNN decided it needed something catchier.

Nicknames in the MMSL have a funny history. Not every team has a moniker, and it can take a while for some clubs to establish identities. League nicknames are earned; other times, they are given. Most had to go through the somewhat fictional "MMSL Properties and Licensing Division" for approval, which was a prickly challenge—for good reason. Many of the suggested nicknames were dumb and summarily rejected...

- CBS News: Rather's Raiders
- WashingtonPost.com: The Arlington Army
- Associated Press: Copperheads
- ABC News: Mice (since Disney owned them)

Now, this seems silly until you realize a good nickname is your branding, and league history shows a team with a good nickname has a better chance of winning championships.

If you were the WRC-TV Peacocks, Comcast SportsNuts, Bloomberg Moneyballers, CNN CaNiNes, USA Today Gannetoids, Gaithersburg Gazette Green Machine, America's Most Wanted Manhunters, WashingtonPost.com Bucketheads, Washington Rag Times, and the National Public Radio Microphones, you know the power of your nickname. Those teams have a combined 27 MMSL titles.

At CNN, we had long searched for the right name. We liked the idea of a "canine" theme but wanted something catchy. While staring at the word canine, I enlarged the letters C, N and N. Our graphic artists added red and black Pantone to the logo, and the rest is CaNiNes history.

Along the way, nicknames have been a fun part of the league. WTTG-Fox 5 was dubbed the Fox Trotters. WUSA-TV was called the One and Onlies, based on their popular slogan, "The One and Only Channel 9." They won a title in 1995. The Washington Times held an office contest for a nickname. The winning entry of Rag Times emerged, and the Rags won the 1998 championship. The Alumni team, comprised of players who lost their jobs, became the Pink Slips. They won it all in 2021.

No team went through more nickname angst than Discovery. At one point in 2003, they had 29 nickname options they were considering, including *Discover This!* They liked the name Crocodiles, settled on Ducks, and later switched to Sharks, thanks to their popular Shark Week programming.

Digital news upstart Post.com also struggled for a name during the '90s. MMSL Properties rejected their fantasy league suggestions and finally anointed them as the Bucketheads. The young team and players hated it. They didn't know the Buckethead was an old pre-IT term for computers (bucket of bolts) and the intelligent people (heads) who worked on the systems. Since Post.com shockingly won the 2005 championship as the 10-seed, Buckethead Fever continues to live in those players' hearts.

The MMSL has had some great nicknames, but most took quite a bit of time. The Associated Press became the Flash for its legendary breaking news alerts over teletype machines. National Geographic Channel was the Explorers, Dow Jones the Bulls, and America Online the AOLiens. NewsChannel 8 was the Crazy Eights, who didn't win many games, and when they merged with sister station WJLA-Channel 7, they cleverly became the 78ers.

What's in a name? As William Shakespeare wrote in *Romeo and Juliet*, "A rose by any other name would smell as sweet." But when it comes to the MMSL, some might argue it's the difference between winning and losing.

May 30, 1998

GAME 1		GAME 2	
CNN	11	CNN	15
WASHINGTON POST.COM	0	GAZETTE	2

- **World on brink of Armageddon after CNN execs insist anchors pronounce Pakistan PAWK-istan.**
- **CNN softball team unleashes secret intern, sweeps two games.**
- **Convicted Whitewater investor Susan McDougal breaks silence and becomes permanent host of *Talk Back Live*.**

By Joe Baseball Jr.
Bureau Sports Writer

LAYHILL, Md. (UPI) — The game ball Saturday went to CNN Human Resources Manager Ginny Umrani, as far-fetched as that might sound.

She never played, didn't show up, and didn't even know that when you get three strikes, you're out.

So, how did Ginny Umrani single-handedly help CNN blank the Washington Post.com by the score of 11-0 in Game 1 and demolish the Gazette, 15-7, in the nightcap?

It turns out she does more than organize intern seminars and edit Bureau Buzz, the D.C. monthly newsletter. She also selects the interns for the Washington intern program.

Meet Shana Eagle. She's the newest intern working for Charles Bierbauer, one of the skippers of CNN's softball team. Shana (pronounced like banana) showed up Saturday at Layhill Park with hand spasms after transcribing a Bierbauer interview with Georgian President Eduard Shevardnadze. She was immediately put in the starting lineup. Not only did the Wake Forest law school student hit the stitches off the ball, but she also filed for radio.

It was a David Wells-like performance in the opener as Jim Barnett pitched the club's first shutout since the team joined the league five years ago. To be fully transparent, the New York Yankees pitcher tossed a perfect game on Saturday. Barnett was far from perfect, but good enough.

"My wife said I might end up like (the late comedian) Phil Hartman if I came home without winning," divulged Barnett.

CNN is 4-4 on the season.

It was also a moral victory for CNN after several weeks of desolation and despair in the newsroom.

The network recently announced it was laying off 70 employees.

That prompted Representative Dan Burton to release a batch of secretly recorded intimate phone conversations between Associate Attorney General Webster Hubbell and CNN producer Sol Levine.

Now comes word that CNN President Rick Kaplan has named a blue-ribbon panel headed by Supervising Producer Tom Dunlavey and Indonesian businessman James Riady, a key figure in the Democratic fundraising scandal that funneled foreign money to President Clinton's 1992 election campaign. They will look into why Mrs. Lee charges so much for a plain bagel at the coffee shop downstairs at CNN's Washington Bureau.

CNN began with two quick runs in the first inning. Darren McInerny, Bierbauer, and Eagle did most of the damage. The team made it 6-0 in the third with timely at-bats by Ralph Marcus, Sue Bennett, first-timer Amy Silver, Patrick Brennan, and Tim Durham. After adding two more runs in the fifth, CNN censured what was left of Washington Post.com with three more runs in the sixth inning, thanks to opportune hits from Pete Couste, Ann Curley, Elizabeth Hathway, and Greg Robertson.

"It felt like I was in a Fellini movie," said Durham. "We played like a well-oiled calibrated film projector."

Added Bierbauer, "There was none of that blatant foot-dragging and outright obfuscation you frequently see on The Rim, where all the senior decision-makers in the newsroom sit."

In the second game against the Gazette, CNN continued its intensity and virulence as players showed no sign of their usual mystifying torpor.

By all accounts, the 15-2 demolition was sorely needed after weeks of self-flagellation. The final would have been even higher, but nine-year-old Andrew Bierbauer was keeping the scorebook and said, "I felt sorry for the other team, so I stopped counting."

CNN D.C. Bureau Chief Frank Sesno said, "If the team continues to blow out their opponents, I'll order Diane Stanley to scrounge up enough petty cash to buy an actual working black-and-white TV set for the 11th-floor break room."

Meanwhile, sources say D.C. Deputy Bureau Chief Peggy Soucy is kicking around an alternative money-generating idea, requiring employees to use quarters to operate all TV sets in the office.

"I saw passengers doing that at airports a long time ago," a parsimonious Soucy mused.

Next Saturday, CNN is back in action when it plays WUSA-TV and NewsChannel 8 at Aspen Hill Park.

June 6, 1998

GAME 1		GAME 2	
WUSA	7	CNN	14
CNN	6	NEWSCHANNEL 8	11
	9 innings		*10 innings*

- **Extra! Extra! Read all about it! CNN claws way to split.**
- **Team shows true grit as both games go extra innings.**
- **Players use laughing gas between contests to calm nerves.**
- **Trial lawyer William Ginsburg fills in for producer Judd Ginsberg at State Department, and no one notices.**

By Joe Baseball Jr.
Bureau Sports Writer

ASPEN HILL, Md. (UPI) — If you watched the 130th running of the Belmont Stakes, in which Real Quiet lost by a nose to Victory Gallop in a photo finish, you would know how close CNN came to upsetting one of the best teams in the Metropolitan Media Softball League on Saturday.

Just ask Elizabeth Hathway, Jack Lynn, Chris Guarino, Kate Steinhilber, Patrick Davis, Patrick Brennan, Shana Eagle, Jim Barnett, Pete Hartogs, Greg Robertson, Darren McInerny, Marty Kramer, Michael Watts, Charles Bierbauer and Ralph Marcus.

They'll tell you if you don't believe it. They're all witnesses and have the Drudge Report bookmarked on their computers.

"I don't have time for commenting about sissy stuff," said CNN Vice President Sid Bedingfield in a snippily written read-me. "I'm busy trying to run *NewsStand*. Did you see we got a point three on Sunday night? We tied with *Time & Again* and *Petticoat Junction* on TBS. Fantastic."

CNN fell just short in the opener against WUSA, which walked away with a 7-6 win in nine innings. But the good guys secured Game 2, coming back in dramatic fashion despite being short-handed. CNN topped upstart NewsChannel 8 in 10 innings, 14-11. CNN is 5-5 at the midway point of the season.

How did CNN find the energy to pull out a victory from the jaws of defeat? "It was quite elementary," cogitated Bierbauer. "We pretended we were the Bulls and NewsChannel 8 was the Jazz.

"I don't mean to be a heartless vulture, but those teams played like roadkill," said first-timer Guarino, who was suffering from butterflies in his stomach. "I think it was the Malt-O-Meal Toasty O's I picked up at Safeway. I didn't know they were part of a recall."

Neither game was for the timid. "I thought CNN was left for dead," stammered CNN founder Ted Turner, who personally called medical reporter Andrew Holtz to make sure the news was not passed on to Headline News.

"Been there, done that. I'll never forget how close we came to reporting that President Bush had died in Japan during a state dinner," Turner reflected.

As it happened, both softball contests went into extra frames where the rules were simple. If a game is tied after seven innings, batters get one pitch. They either get on base, or they're out— no foul ball exceptions.

"Wow, that sounds like fun," laughed Jann Connor from a poolside phone at a four-day Human Resources retreat in Braselton Georgia. "By the way, if anyone needs their Metro cards, tell them to wait."

Greg Robertson once again spurred a CNN comeback by slamming two taters in the nightcap (he's got eight on the year) and helped push across six runs in the final inning. "Maybe one of these days, Frank Sesno will thank me for saving CNN from being the laughingstock of the MMSL," stewed the center fielder.

"Indeed," said Wolf Blitzer.

The road to victory was not easy. In Game 2, the team was gender challenged because it did not have enough women players, so it received an automatic out.

"Now you know what we go through when booking Mary Tillotson's show," carped Jill Neff. "I have to fill those boxes with real women, not the kind you see on Jerry Springer."

The bookers for *Burden of Proof* made haste chiming in. "We have the same problem. It's not easy to get Michael Zeldin or Henry Hudson. Last month, we only had them on 23 times," said one booker. "We also were damn lucky to snag George Terwilliger."

CNN President Rick Kaplan refused to comment on the softball team's effort, but he did say Ted Turner is close to signing off on a new project, the Funeral News Network, with hosts Bob Cain, Mark Leff, and Jeff Flock. The channel would also replay *Moneyline* shows on the weekends.

The rugged schedule on the diamond continues this week with another doubleheader. It's a make-up day for an earlier rainout. CNN plays U.S. News and the Washington Post at Aspen Hill.

June 20, 1998

GAME 1		GAME 2	
CNN	6	USA TODAY	9
WASHINGTON TIMES	5	CNN	8
	10 innings		

- **CNN is first team to knock off Washington Times this year.**
- **Club suffers Three Mile Island meltdown in nightcap.**
- **Disgraced Boston Globe journalist Patricia Smith hired as senior writer for *NewsStand*.**

By Joe Baseball Jr.
Bureau Sports Writer

ASPEN HILL, Md. (UPI) — With one dramatic victory already in its back pocket on the day, CNN's softball team was looking to make a significant move toward postseason play by beating another contender, except for one untimely problem: the clock.

Leading 8-3 against USA Today, CNN let down its guard when opposing players on the so-called McNews team started handing out backstage passes to the upcoming Spice Girls concert. In a blink, USA Today scored six runs in the fifth inning to steal a win as time ran out in the nightcap.

"What a colossal blunder! What a disgrace! How pathetic can a group be?" belched retired Maj. Gen. Perry Smith from his yacht on Lake Lanier just outside Atlanta. "The team inhaled too much sarin if you ask me."

When pressed for additional comment, the former CNN military analyst said he didn't serve in the military but added, "I did watch *Combat* on Tuesday nights on ABC when I was a kid."

CNN played well enough to win but came up short on a roller-coaster weekend. They had to settle for a doubleheader split on Saturday at Aspen Hill Park, where hellish temperatures reached what felt like 135 degrees on the field.

In the opener, CNN came through in the clutch against the undefeated Washington Times by pushing across the winning run in the bottom of the 10th inning. It was CNN's third straight extra-inning game. Pete Hartogs singled in Jim Barnett from second with the game-winner, 6-5.

"It was one for all and all for one," said Marty Kramer, who defended his propensity to read the Washington Times seven days a week."

CNN's record now stands at 6-6, but what happened in Game 2 may come back to haunt this gutsy team.

"Highway robbery," frothed D.C. Bureau Chief Frank Sesno. "The CNN players need a little pep talk. Mellonie, get me Admiral Moorer and April Oliver at once, and while you're at it, call Ginsburg, too, Bill, not Judd."

Blame it on the umpire if someone is looking for a scapegoat. Or the MMSL. The rulebook says no game can last beyond an hour and five minutes unless it's for extra innings. It was only the bottom of the fifth when the man in blue gesticulated it was time for his midday snack of three double-cheese Whoppers with fries but "no apple pie."

"He ordered us to take off our watches at the start of the game," meowed newcomer Carey Bodenheimer. "For Christ's sake, how did he expect us to know what time it was, stare at the sun? The last time I forgot to meal a crew was September 1995. I think I know a little something about keeping an eye on the clock."

No one was more saddened than seven-year-old Latia Robinson, the bubbly and precocious District girl who drove herself to the games in her parents' Honda Accord to show off her citation from Washington D.C. Mayor Marion Barry.

Observers say it was a blatant move by the second-grader to be a guest on *Larry King Live*. Said show producers, "What's the big deal about a little girl whose legs can't even reach the accelerator driving her unconscious father to the hospital and saving his life? Besides, Carol Channing and Mel Torme are already booked. She's just a little twerp."

"I once drove in the Indy 500," said little Latia. "I would never lie about that. You can ask my stepmother, Patricia Smith. Can you get me autographs with Pete Couste, Charles Bierbauer, Jack Lynn, Darren

McInerny, Patrick Davis, John Davis, Shana Eagle, Ann Curley, Ralph Marcus, Elizabeth Hathway, Kate Steinhilber, Michael Watts, Sheara Braun, Erika Dimmler, Brenda Elkins and Fred Frommer?"

There are six games left in the softball season, weather permitting. The brutal June schedule continues next Saturday at Aspen Hill, where CNN plays division contests against America's Most Wanted and Fox News.

CNN will likely play two additional games the same day for a quadruple-header to make up for earlier rainouts.

(Update Note: As of this book's publication, the MMSL says CNN's three consecutive extra-inning games on June 6 and 20 remain the only time it has happened in league history.)

June 27, 1998

GAME 1		GAME 2	
AMERICA'S MOST WANTED	10	CNN	14
CNN	7	FOX NEWS	0
GAME 3		GAME 4	
CNN	5	CNN	10
U.S. NEWS	4	WASHINGTON POST	6

- **CNN wins three games during Saturday marathon, bringing credibility back to network.**
- **Air Force Major Gen. Perry Smith defects to Baghdad after MSNBC announces joint cable venture with Iraq.**
- **Vietnam veteran Van Buskirk goes berserk, tells *NewsStand* he once had a thing for anchor Donna Kelley but repressed his memory.**

By Joe Baseball Jr.
Bureau Sports Writer

ASPEN HILL. Md. (UPI) — With an unwholesome cloud of despair hanging over CNN since early June and the world's attention riveted on whether the network was going to hire former Congresswoman Susan Molinari as a talking head, executives at Time Warner were praying for a revelation on Saturday, and they got it.

For the first time this year, standout slugger John King showed up to play softball thanks to the White House schedulers who sent President

Bill Clinton to Beijing to eat eggrolls with Chinese leader Jiang Zemin.

"I know a little something about taking things to completion," winked the correspondent, who did two early morning live shots and then went full tilt to Aspen Hill with his earpiece still in place.

CNN won three out of four games in a marathon quadruple-header and improved to 9-7.

With just two games left in the regular season, the team is on the verge of making the playoffs. Only nine teams qualify, and CNN is ranked eighth. CNN has to beat ABC on July 11 to clinch.

"I knew it was going to be a scorcher out there," explained Kate Steinhilber. "But given the choice of playing in the heat or swimming in an E. coli-infected water park with Jane Maxwell in Atlanta, I decided to play. I can always do Six Flags White Water next summer."

In Game 1, CNN gave up four first-inning runs to AMW and then outscored the bad guys the rest of the way. But the team couldn't overcome the hole it dug for itself, losing 10-7.

"It was a pretty lame effort," Carey Bodenheimer jibber-jabbered when reached for postgame comment at the Chi-Chi Lounge. "We played like the Washington Mystics instead of like a bunch of sleazy journalists."

CNN sources say the level of play early on was so alarming that company attorney Dave Kohler immediately flew to Washington, fired everyone on the Monica Lewinsky scandal team, and named Linda Tripp the starting pitcher.

The move was lauded by the players who showed up: Charles Bierbauer, Pete Hartogs, Darren McInerny, Patrick Davis, Shana Eagle, Jack Lynn, Ralph Marcus, Ann Curley, John Davis, Jim Barnett, Michael Watts, Sheara Braun, Elizabeth Hathway, Pete Couste, Scott Miller, Kate Steinhilber, Carey Bodenheimer, John King, Brenda Elkins and Ingo the intern.

D.C. Bureau Chief Frank Sesno, who was on vacation but called in to get the results, promised a celebration if the winning ways continued.

"I have decided for each game CNN wins from here on out, we'll rent one playback machine for every five package producers. And if we go all the way, I'll put Vito Maggiolo back in the slot."

A spokesman for Team Video had no immediate comment.

In the meantime, all of Washington is abuzz about CNN going into the final weekend.

"We now know who is buried in the Tomb of the Unknown Soldier," certified U.S. Defense Secretary William Cohen, "The only thing undecided is whom CNN will name as its next military warmonger."

Sources close to Political Director Tom Hannon reported seeing retired Navy Admiral Thomas Moorer in the facilities area of the ninth floor at CNN's Washington Bureau last week getting a photo ID. Then again, so was Susan Molinari.

July 11, 1998

GAME 1		GAME 2	
ABC NEWS	13	CNN	17
CNN	9	AMERICA'S MOST WANTED	6

- **Season comes to ignominious end as team misses playoffs.**
- **Loss to ABC News ends pipe dream of postseason play.**
- **Legendary war correspondent Peter Arnett admits he's never been to Vietnam but likes the food.**
- **Eds: Note language in 3rd graph.**

By Joe Baseball Jr.
Bureau Sports Writer

ASPEN HILL, Md. (UPI) — Anyone old enough to remember what happened on May 6, 1937, at Lakehurst, New Jersey, will know how CNN's softball team played in the most critical game of the year on Saturday.

A win against division rival ABC News would have guaranteed a trip to the playoffs. A loss would mean a free Saturday morning next week.

Can you say the Hindenburg disaster? Oh, the humanity of it all. The hopes of the CNN team exploded like a dirigible in the final inning of Game 1. With the score tied at six, ABC was handed seven runs, a lead that proved too much for CNN to overcome.

But with a mathematical chance to slip in the postseason back door, CNN demolished playoff-bound America's Most Wanted in the nightcap, 17-6, only to have their worst fears realized. ABC won three of its last four games to wind up with an 11-7 record.

CNN finished the regular season 10-8, 10th place overall in the 20-team league. Last year, CNN was 9-11.

Ted Turner immediately called Time Warner CEO Gerald Levin. "If I could bring back *World Championship Wrestling* on TBS, I would do it. Nothing has agitated me more except perhaps when I managed the Atlanta Braves in 1977 when the team lost 16 straight games."

Turner, who founded the news network in 1980, went on to say, "I would do anything. Buy ABC News? Done. CBS News? Easy-peasy. NBC News? No problem. You can tell Joe Baseball he doesn't have to make up hypothetical quotes."

It was a particularly glum defeat at the hands of ABC because it was played before CNN's largest crowd of the year, including Virginia Nico-laidis, Nancy Lane, and Lisa Durham.

This reporter could dredge up Tailwind fodder and a network retraction to wrap things up, but in the interests of putting forgettable news in the rearview mirror, the Joe Baseball column will now go on hiatus until next spring.

A special thanks to Charles Bierbauer and Jack Lynn for their counsel throughout the season, the faithful readers around the network, and the players who showed up on Saturdays.

That's what it's all about.

CNN's 1998 team missed the playoffs but the best was yet to come.

TOP OF THE 2nd

We Are the Champions

March 15, 1999

- **Start of softball season is month away, tempers flare.**
- **Bureau chiefs gather in Atlanta to map strategy.**
- **Intern program under investigation after coordinator caught recruiting ringers.**
- **Eds: Note language in 6th graph.**

By Joe Baseball Jr.
Bureau Sports Writer

WASHINGTON (UPI) — The CNN Washington Bureau softball season is in jeopardy even before the first pitch. There are many questions and no known answers.

"You mean like whatever became of reporters Patricia Ochs and Pam Olson?" seethed CNN founder Ted Turner. "Or the more pressing issue about what kind of softball team are we going to field this year?"

Industry sources are tight-lipped following unconfirmed reports that CNN's sagging ratings have forced the fledgling news network to consider replaying old *NewsNight* programs anchored by Patrick Emory and Beverly Williams.

On top of that, softball players are threatening a boycott.

Several unidentified players said the team was in a funk about missing the playoffs last year. They're calling for a complete newsroom overhaul and the appointment of David Schechter as an ombudsman, Richard Griffiths as a mediator, and Diane Stanley as the caterer.

"I predict the odds of us fielding a competitive team about as good as the Rim getting another senior producer," lamented tri-captain Charles Bierbauer, returning to play in his 138th consecutive softball season. "I also strenuously object to the copy editors taking out the phrase 'albeit surreptitiously' from my latest script."

An anonymous post on CNN's All Politics web page urged a write-in campaign to form a team of *Burden of Proof* staffers and commentators, including Michael Zeldin, Henry Hudson, Stuart Rothenberg, Jamie Rubin Amanpour, Tucker and Margaret Carlson (no relation), Henry Kissinger, Donna Shalala, Arianna Huffington, and Hugh Sidey.

"It's either produce or kiss the new CNN T-shirts goodbye," Deputy Bureau Chief Peggy Soucy stated. "Frank (Says No) and I will not tolerate

Spoiler alert! CaNiNes win it all in 1999 for the team's first championship. Back row, (L-R) James Knott, Jack Lynn, Greg Robertson, John Davis, Carey Bodenheimer, John King, Chris Guarino, Lesley Gold, and Erika Dimmler; middle row, Marci Starzec and Jim Barnett; front row, Paul Miller, Ari Perilstein, Patrick Davis, Ralph Marcus, Charles Bierbauer, and Virginia Nicolaidis.

frivolous expenditures as long as Time Warner stock falters."

The first Metropolitan Media Softball League game is scheduled for April 17. A practice is set for Saturday at 10 a.m. in Bethesda. The team is at its wits' end for quality players, so the guest bookers on *Talk Back Live* are begging the audience to show their allegiance by wearing name tags upside down in an act of civil disobedience.

"We're doing everything we can to field a team the network can be proud of. Pardon the dangling preposition," fretted Jack Lynn, another of the tri-coaches. "We're chewing over letting John King play every position and benching everyone else. That's how desperate we are."

CNN finished last year 10-8, good enough for 10th place out of 20. Two new teams are joining the league: PVC (Potomac Video, not polyvinyl chloride) and NBC News Channel.

Dennis Tuttle, the MMSL commissioner, met with coaches over the weekend to go over rule changes and remind players it's okay to bribe umpires. Another addition is a web page devoted to tracking the highs and lows of every team.

CNN Washington Bureau Chief Frank Sesno is weighing a season-ending incentive if the softball team makes the payoffs. "I promise to get the Time Warner brass to drop the Propecia ads."

Bierbauer, albeit surreptitiously, misty-eyed from watching CNN's coverage of the NATO conflict in Bosnia Herzegovina, summed up his team's potential for this season, "If not now, when?"

Start oiling those gloves and breaking in those cleats. Time to play ball.

April 17, 1999

GAME 1		GAME 2	
CNN...13		CNN..7	
MONTGOMERY JOURNAL...........6		WASHINGTON POST.COM...4	

- **Holy Cow! CNN wins first two games.**
- **Superior play overshadows allegations of Serb atrocities in dugout; NATO summit delayed.**
- **Astonishing softball performance under review by war crimes tribunal and IOC.**

By Joe Baseball Jr.
Bureau Sports Writer

ASPEN HILL, Md. (UPI) — If CNN wins the Metropolitan Media Softball League title in July, sports lovers may look back at the opening weekend in April and say the real hero was an Atlanta firefighter. They'll be talking about Matt Mosely, who plucked a construction worker off a burning crane last week.

"We knew if Mosely could do the impossible, our team could, too," said a psyched Carey Bodenheimer. "Everyone who works at CNN knows from personal experience what it's like to be left hanging without anyone backing them up."

There were 22 other reasons why CNN did so well. Close to two dozen players, a rare blend of interchangeable weapons turned out. Each walked away proudly wearing a CNN T-shirt after helping the news network sweep a doubleheader, 13-6 against the Montgomery Journal and 7-4 versus Washington Post.com.

"It's amazing to think so many people showed up on a Saturday morning instead of staying home to watch the 'Ask Bob Franken' segment on *Weekend Edition*," exuded a confident D.C. Bureau Chief Frank Sesno, who immediately put a freeze on hiring any more ABC employees "for at least another week."

It all began against the Montgomery Journal with a seven-run second inning by CNN, which squeezed the ink right out of the scribes by exposing their glaring deficiencies.

There were timely contributions from Pistol Pete Hartogs, Jumpin' Jack Lynn (who went six for six), Crazy Horse Charles Bierbauer, Lively Lesley Gold, Manly Marty Kramer, Journeyman John King, Raucous Ralph Marcus, and Merry Marci Starzec. The big hit came from the dependable bat of the other "Great One," Greg Robertson, who "only" had a homer and a couple of triples on the day.

By the end of the game, the lineup featured a number of new and old faces, including Jammin' John Davis, Enthusiastic Elizabeth Hathway, Tenacious Tanya Littlejohn, Gleeful Glenn Davis, All-purpose Ari Perilstein, Versatile Vince Goodwine, Powerhouse Pete Couste, Jovial James Knott, Rookie Ron Couvillion and Sensational Sue Bennett.

"We oozed with synergy," concluded Senior Washington Correspondent Bierbauer, who played a flawless game at first base.

Another standout, John King, spent much of Friday traveling with the president. In the fourth inning of the second game, he told one colleague he thought he was still in Michigan or Massachusetts. "One of those states that begins with an 'm.' I'll gladly keep working my typical 20-hour day if it means I can stay off weekends," he promulgated.

Speaking of the White House, Jim Connor made his presence felt. Reached at home for postgame comment, he pledged to "cut down on the live shot requests so King can brush up on the strike zone."

In a related development, Senior White House Correspondent Wolf Blitzer told viewers on *Late Edition with Wolf Blitzer* in a candid admission, "I welcome more exposure. Did you hear we got Lanny Davis AND David Gergen for next week's show?"

The nightcap against Washington Post.com was strictly a defensive affair. Tied at four after four innings, CNN pushed across three big runs with the help of a screaming line drive single by Robertson to make it 6-4 and an RBI single by Davis. In the last frame, the Post.com loaded the bases with two outs. Pitcher Jim Barnett shrugged off the effects of the Melissa virus and lucked out by getting the batter to tap a soft grounder back to the mound to end the game. It was a relief for Barnett, the only player in the MMSL who wears shin guards under his socks.

"I'm so damn proud of our team," phoned in CNN Executive Eason Jordan, who promised to include the doubleheader sweep in this week's

International Insights, where employees can get the real scoop.

The gaiety was short-lived when Rick Davis, executive vice president of news standards and practices, said his department would conduct an internal audit of how the team acquired T-shirts.

In two weeks, CNN will be back in action for another twin bill on May 1 against its nemesis, ABC News, and rival Fox News. The games will take place at Wheaton Forest starting at 10 a.m.

May 1, 1999

GAME 1		GAME 2	
CNN	13	CNN	6
ABC NEWS	9	FOX NEWS	4

- **CNN remains unbeaten; players inspired after call from Yugoslav leader Slobodan Milosevic.**
- **Voice of an Angel singing sensation Charlotte Church named team mascot.**
- **MSNBC's Laurie Dhue begs to return to CNN and promises to read scripts ahead of time.**

By Joe Baseball Jr.
Bureau Sports Writer

WHEATON, Md. (UPI) — CNN executives had good reason to celebrate this past weekend after getting a double dose of good news.

Within the span of 24 hours, the cable news network got word it finished for the first time ahead of Serbian TV in head-to-head Nielsen ratings. Then, as if that wasn't enough, the CNN International Desk reported the scoop that the softball team had swept its second straight doubleheader this season.

"I was on the edge of my seat," said a bewildered Brent Sadler in a beeper from his demolished hotel room in downtown Pristina. "I watched the first game on my sat phone but missed the second after NATO bombed the last TV tower standing in Belgrade."

Unlike the first weekend, when CNN (4-0) waltzed past its opponents, the games at Wheaton Forest Park Saturday against crosstown rivals ABC News and Fox News were nailbiters, full of discord, rancor, finger-pointing, petty jealousy, back-stabbing, and that was before the first pitch.

CNN's talented starting lineup played with the moxie of a British nanny and spanked ABC in the opener, 13-9. Roone Arledge's squad took a 2-0 lead in the top of the first inning, but CNN answered back with five runs in its half. The big smash was a two-run double by John King.

Eight of the first nine players got hits: Ari Perilstein, Jack Lynn, Greg Robertson, Charles Bierbauer, Carey Bodenheimer (2 for 3 in Game 1), Jim Barnett and Vince Goodwine.

"I kept hearing a little voice inside my head say 'R-E-S-P-E-C-T,'" an elated Goodwine said. He reportedly put a note about his hitting accomplishment in his own Human Resources personnel file.

Undaunted after ABC regained the lead in the fifth inning, CNN zoomed ahead by putting six consecutive batters on base (Robertson, Marci Starzec, Bierbauer, James Knott, Bodenheimer, and Marty Kramer) and pushing across six more runs.

The nightcap against the David Shuster-led Fox News squad was a bit like World War Two when the nation turned to its young to carry the heaviest burden.

Pete Hartogs, Patrick Davis, and Michael Watts played critical roles in keeping the game close as the CNN bats fell silent.

"Those guys made all the difference," thundered the home plate umpire, who refused to take off his trench coat during the game. He also ordered the opposing team's outfielders to stay in the outfield and not move closer when CNN had women hitting.

"Normally, the guys move up so close when I'm at bat, I can see whether they have on briefs or boxers," crowed Kelli Arena, who didn't go to the games but would have blurted out the previous observation if she had been there.

It had little practical impact on CNN because only two women showed up. "The games are debilitating enough as it is," grumbled half a dozen men on the team, who offered to provide CNN women Saturday wake-up calls, breakfast in bed, and even $10 Starbucks certificates to encourage a better turnout next time.

As for the details of the contest against Fox News, the hitting stars included Watts (2-2), Hartogs, King, and Perilstein, with defensive kudos to Starzec.

Assignment Desk Manager John Towriss is credited with much of the team's recent success. Last week, he ordered the installation of a dozen more TV monitors in the newsroom. "I was hoping the players would absorb massive amounts of radiation and play with some energy," he hummed.

Meanwhile, Facilities Manager Kim Linden denied accusations the extra monitors were bought to augment the building's unpredictable heating system. "If you truly want to know, we got them to replace the aging microwave oven in the breakroom," he exclaimed.

This Saturday, CNN is back in action at Aspen Hill against the Associated Press and the National Press Club.

May 8, 1999

GAME 1		GAME 2	
AP	9	CNN	12
CNN	8	NATIONAL PRESS CLUB	10

- **CNN bogs down in mud, loses first game of year, but bounces back to win Game 2.**
- **Serbs accuse weatherman Flip Spiceland of botched Balkan seven-day forecast.**
- **Time Warner executives sell softball team to Jeff Milstein.**

By Joe Baseball Jr.
Bureau Sports Writer

ASPEN HILL, Md. (UPI) — As the fog lifted Saturday morning and the sun poked its soft rays through the low-hanging clouds, the CNN softball team knew it was an omen. Clearing skies could mean only one thing. There would be no rain out. The games were going to be played on a muddy field by an undefeated team missing its core lineup.

Outmanned by a robust Associated Press squad in the opener, CNN battled through three extra innings of one-pitch play before losing 9-8. With the optical illusion of an undefeated season shattered, CNN picked up the pieces and staved off the National Press Club in the second game, 12-10, to improve its record to 5-1, second-best in the 20-team Metropolitan Media Softball League. Gaining a split helped assuage some of the sour taste of losing a tough first game.

"The entire softball experience is like a future's meeting," convulsed Tim McCaughan, the lone spectator. "At first, you think the agony will never end, and then there's a sense of relief, and you get back to doing normal things like interviews for the San Fran bureau and nutrition unit."

The team's power hitters may have been on the road with the president in Oklahoma, but that didn't deter the Dirty Dozen, who showed up ready to play. Behind by three runs in the third inning of Game 1, CNN put four hits together, including a bases-loaded double by dependable Jack Lynn. CNN pulled ahead 6-5 after Lesley Gold knocked in two runs on a ground out.

The AP tied it, and the two teams went into extra frames, where under MMSL rules, each batter faces one pitch – either an out or the runner gets on base. The wire service guys got a leadoff triple in the ninth inning and scored the winning run with a single.

Former CNN war correspondent Peter Arnett took the softball team's first loss in stride. "While I didn't see the game or talk to anyone who was there, I know it must have been discouraging. It was a lot like covering the Tet Offensive."

Paul Miller went 3-5 against the Associated Press. Marty Kramer got two hits in four at-bats. Lynn had two doubles in five trips and three RBI. Charles Bierbauer impressed his son Andrew by getting dirty sliding around the basepath. Marci Starzec and Patrick Davis played heads-up defense all day long.

Discouraged by the defeat and the fact there was no time before the next game to call Wendy Walker-Whitworth to check and see who would be hosting *Larry King Live* this week, the umpire yelled, "Play ball."

Game 2 began on an ominous note when Carey Bodenheimer avowed that she once survived an F-6 Fujita scale tornado with winds greater than 318 miles per hour. "It was freaky because I heard what sounded like a freight train just before the storm hit. As it turned out, an Amtrak Metroliner just missed my house."

The anecdote about close calls had nothing to do with the game, but the team appreciated Bodenheimer's attempt to buck up everyone's morale and inject some fundamental silliness.

It worked because, in the nightcap, James Knott hit a three-run homer in a seven-run third inning to put CNN ahead and give it a lead it would never surrender. Other standout performances were turned in by Elizabeth Hathway, Sheara Braun, Lynn (3-3 with three RBI), Kramer, and Bierbauer, who all went 2-4.

CNN's doubleheader split leaves the team atop the Aspen Hill Division, two games ahead of ABC, Fox News, and America's Most Wanted.

CNN is back in action this Saturday at a new location, Layhill Park.

May 15, 1999

GAME 1		GAME 2	
CNN	10	WASHINGTON POST	9
U.S. NEWS	9	CNN	3

- **CNN shows split personality, wins opener, then plays like Little Leaguers in nightcap.**
- **Executives at FN respond by promoting everyone to rank of vice president.**
- **Johnny Chung and Connie Chung to join Wolf Blitzer on revamped 10p newscast.**
- **Person "in the back row" on *Burden of Proof* has crush on Roger Cossack.**

By Joe Baseball Jr.
Bureau Sports Writer

LAYHILL, Md. (UPI) — Playing for a team in the Metropolitan Media Softball League takes effort, much like watching CNN's popular afternoon gabfest *Talk Back Live*. It's often entertaining and exhausting and lacking in relevance.

It also depends on how one defines "team." Editors at Merriam-Webster say it's a group of animals or persons associated with an activity.

"Our team is many things to many people, but there are no swine on our squad," Charles Bierbauer pointed out. "Metaphorically speaking, when it came to our offense today, we incontrovertibly stunk like pigs."

Seventeen people showed up Saturday morning at Layhill Park to enjoy the sun, and all were itching to play some competitive softball. As it turned out, CNN players did better at the former (showing up) than the latter (playing).

They came out ahead in the first game despite a scare from U.S. News, 10-9. But then CNN suffered from muscle memory loss against the Washington Post and went down to defeat 9-3 in Game 2.

Taking a page from the Post's new advertising slogan, "If you don't get it, you don't get it," CNN didn't get it.

For those keeping score, CNN is 6-2 after its second straight doubleheader split, good enough to stay in first place in the Layhill Division.

Washington's normally unflappable Bureau Chief Frank Sesno blew a gasket when contacted for postgame comment. "Don't you know I hate being disturbed while watching *Voices of the Millennium*! Nancy Kerrigan is on right now," he bristled.

In Game 1, CNN skated to a three-run lead by stringing together five hits, beginning with Paul Miller (who aggravated his hamstring and sat out after his single), John King (who was just plain aggravated), Greg Robertson, Pete Hartogs, and Ralph Marcus. They padded the lead in the second inning with timely hits from Bierbauer, James Knott, Tanya Littlejohn, Brad Wright, Jim Barnett, and King. Somewhere along the way, CNN bats went silent.

U.S. News, which is no Time Magazine, never gave up and pulled within one at 10-9 and had the go-ahead runs on base before their last-inning rally fell just short. "It was not a game for the faint of heart nor for that matter wimps, weasels, or worrywarts," uttered Tim Durham.

In an announcement figuratively out of left field between games, World Affairs Correspondent Ralph Begleiter informed everyone he was leaving CNN after a USA Today column revealed that Kyoko Altman was returning to work with him at the State Department. "That wasn't it," he complained. "The clincher was when Peggy Soucy ordered me to pay for the steak tartar at my going away party."

As for the second game against the Washington Post, CNN went up 2-0 in the first inning when Ari Perilstein blasted a triple to the gap, followed by singles from King, Robertson, and hot-hitting Marci Starzec (3-3 in Game 2). That was the sum and substance, besides a couple of hits from Patrick Brennan and good defensive work turned in by Lesley Gold, Vince Goodwine, Erika Dimmler, and Kelli Arena, who left after the first game. Still, this reporter couldn't figure out a way to include her name until this paragraph.

The information technology (IT) manager, Joe Murphy, explained that he couldn't make it to the games because he was too busy reading everyone's emails using the new Microsoft Outlook program. "There's some neat stuff here," he added.

CNN has its work cut out next Saturday with another doubleheader scheduled at Norwood Park in Bethesda against NewsChannel 8 and America's Most Wanted.

May 22, 1999

GAME 1		GAME 2	
CNN	13	AMERICA'S MOST WANTED	20
NEWSCHANNEL8	12	CNN	8

- **CNN remains in first place as team continues to amaze itself.**
- **Network salutes outstanding effort by adding "softball" to "Themes & Beats."**
- **Two producers suspended after recuts of Bob Franken packages go over 1:45 trt.**
- **Bureau tightens security; employees to wear ankle bracelets.**
- **Eds: SUBS 2nd graph to CORRECT number to $300, sted $30 million.**

By Joe Baseball Jr.
Bureau Sports Writer

BETHESDA, Md. (UPI) — Life is good at CNN's D.C. Bureau.

The antiquated BASYS newsroom computer system hasn't crashed since last Wednesday. Hard-working package producers will be relocated to the FERC Building to make room for a coat closet. Company brass endorses a $300 spending spree. And the softball team is solidly in first place. What could be better?

"Your squad could be undefeated," interjected CNN President Tom Johnson, who nevertheless hailed the team's performance by announcing a week-long moratorium on Power for Living commercials.

On Saturday at Norwood Park, there was plenty of power as CNN confronted NewsChannel 8 and America's Most Wanted in a double-header. CNN had a lot of punch in Game 1, but none of it in the night-cap. Despite the third consecutive split, players walked away knowing they had witnessed something special in the first game.

The umpire was a no-show for the opener, apparently miffed at the way anchor Lou Waters repeatedly stumbles over the pronunciation of John Demjanjuk's last name. The coaches got together and took a vote about who should call balls and strikes.

On the first ballot, there was a tie between Tim Durham, Stacy Jolna, and the HR guy responsible for enforcing the network's PTO policy. The second ballot came down to Durham and the lackey who has to order food for the staff of *Moneyline Newshour with Lou Dobbs* when they visit Washington. By a slim margin, players selected Durham in what presciently turned out to be the play of the game.

NewsChannel 8 went ahead with three runs in the top of the first inning. CNN stormed back with four in its half. The big hit was a double by Lesley Gold, who knocked in two runs.

"I had a feeling I would do it," said Gold. "I called the Paula Jones psychic hotline just before I left home."

CNN padded the lead in the second inning by scoring five runs, including a monster grand slam by John Davis, who went 3-4 in the game with five RBI and just missed hitting for the cycle. The so-called Crazy Eights kept chipping away with a run here and a run there and got close until serendipity struck.

A NewsChannel 8 runner was called out sliding into second base as John King applied the tag. Team captains huddled at the pitcher's mound to review umpire Durham's unbiased decision. Given the years of experience of CNN employees holding meetings and deciding very little, the call was upheld, and the runner was out.

Trailing 11-10 in the last inning, NewsChannel 8 scored two runs to take the lead. Only a rocket throw from Jack Lynn to Jim Barnett to nail a runner at home plate prevented a bigger inning.

CNN had one last trick up its sleeve to snatch victory from defeat and get home in time to catch Gene Randall's hard-hitting Q&A with Frank Newport on the latest Gallup Poll about whether Americans believe Uranus has 18 moons.

Lynn led off with a single (2-3, 1 RBI), followed by Davis, who belted a triple to tie the score. King hit the game-winning RBI. The 13-12 final was CNN's third one-run game this season.

There were standout performances: Virginia Nicolaidis, who supervised the scoring book; Carey Bodenheimer, who graciously moved aside to allow the pitcher to get a mouthful of dirt on a bang-bang play at home; Howie Lutt who changed his schedule and offered to work Saturday night to help the team; and Chris Guarino who regaled players between innings by reading aloud excerpts of the Cox report.

Details of Game 2 could not be released due to strict censorship rules. The Metropolitan Media Softball League prohibits reporting about the graphic nature of CNN softball.

Despite an early end to the game, there were a few highlights against America's Most Wanted, including good hits and nice catches from Marci Starzec, Elizabeth Hathway, Erika Dimmler, Ralph Marcus, Charles Bierbauer, James Knott, Pete Couste, Ari Perilstein and Chip Herzel.

CNN is now 7-3, three games ahead of ABC News in the Layhill Division, and tied for third best in the 20-team league.

CNN will get a much-deserved week off for the Memorial Day holiday but will return on June 5 against WJLA and WUSA at Norwood Park.

June 5, 1999

GAME 1		GAME 2	
WJLA	11	CNN	13
CNN	9	WUSA	11

- **Gutsy CNN team overcomes eight-run deficit to gain split; nine players have RBI.**
- **Mad Cow Disease apparently to blame for strange behavior on the Rim.**
- **D.C. Bureau hires Spelling Bee champion to help the control room spell fonts correctly.**

By Joe Baseball Jr.
Bureau Sports Writer

ASPEN HILL, Md. (UPI) — It was a classic showdown: David versus Goliath, truth against evil, Jean Valjean opposite Javert. CNN face-to-face with body bag journalism.

Call the match-ups what you want. The softball games on Saturday against local affiliate stations WJLA and WUSA were a Battle Royale. By the time the infield dust settled, CNN had lost one and won the other. But what a game the Ted and Jane's pulled out of their back pocket in the nightcap: a spine-tingling, sometimes stomach-churning victory.

CNN is 8-4, a whopping four games ahead of second-place ABC News. CNN could clinch a playoff spot next weekend.

You should have been there.

Sometimes, in the news business, as some correspondents like to say, the stories write themselves. This is one of those rare cases when the facts say it all. Channel 7 ambushed CNN in the opening game, 11-9. Before

Bob Waller could squawk, "Get me scripts!" the team was laced into by Channel 9 in Game 2, 11-3, and it was only the second inning.

PBS anchor Jim Lehrer did not lose a minute reacting to CNN's poor play. "Now you know why public television plans a second national news program. The American people are turning off CNN and tuning out because it's embarrassing," he discerned. "I'm talking about the softball game and the Play of the Week on *Inside Politics*."

Slowly but surely, CNN clawed its way back with five runs in the third, one in the fifth, two in the sixth, and two in the dramatic last inning to win.

Not one WUSA player crossed the plate after the second inning, thanks on balance to Patrick Davis, Jack Lynn, John King, John Davis, James Knott, Charles Bierbauer, Carey Bodenheimer, Marci Starzec, Marty Kramer, Ralph Marcus, Tanya Littlejohn, Ari Perilstein, Ann Curley, Elizabeth Hathway, Sheara Braun, Jim Barnett and Tim Durham.

Nine different CNN batters displayed athleticism and had at least one run batted in. The go-ahead and winning runs came with two outs, helped by bases-loaded walks in the one-pitch sudden-death extra inning.

Everyone was a hero, but special kudos go to Lynn (4-5, who got a gigantic raspberry scrape on his leg diving for the last out), Perilstein, who first wrenched his back then tried to catch a pop foul with his mouth, resulting in a nasty gash and a trip to Kaiser Permanente, Davis (3-4 with 4 RBI), Kramer, who interrupted his three-week vacation long enough to run the basepaths and Starzec (2-4, 1 RBI), who played despite a humongous hangover. "I'm glad I remembered to soak my mouthpiece in beer last night," she slurred.

The team appeared to have had one too many and was out of sync when the day started. "No question CNN lacked fighting power," observed one NATO pilot following a briefing in Brussels. "We can only yearn for a Serbian ceasefire like the one I witnessed on the ballfield."

CNN missed a great chance to win Game 1 against WJLA.

"The entire team played like an overturned flatbed truck full of gunpowder — plenty of dynamite but no oomph," nit-picked Vito Maggiolo by walkie-talkie while monitoring a fender bender on I-95. "I got goosebumps last week when I heard about a five-mile backup on the Beltway. Mini Six, take a meal break."

Channel 7 sucked all the life out of CNN in the opener, but the day wasn't a total loss, thanks to Game 2. The players didn't pull off the dramatic finish in the nightcap alone.

The year's largest crowd, three people, Tim McCaughan, Kristen Williams, and Amy Silver came out to rev up their friends.

Those in attendance also signed a petition calling on D.C. Bureau Chief Frank Sesno to designate June as "CNN Comeback" month.

"Forget it, maybe next year," Sesno said. "Does anyone want discount coupons for area amusement parks, including the brand new Six Flags?"

CNN has another Aspen Hill doubleheader against the undefeated Washington Times and formidable USA Today this week.

June 26, 1999

GAME 1		GAME 2	
CNN	15	ABC NEWS	18
NBC NEWS	14	CNN	8

- **CNN clinches first place and automatic playoff bid with come-from-behind win.**
- **D.C. Bureau takes closer look at Bruce Springsteen ticket scam; Frank Sesno goes into hiding.**
- **Jeff Milstein joins Railroad Killer Resendez-Ramirez on Ten Most Wanted List.**

By Joe Baseball Jr.
Bureau Sports Writer

BETHESDA, Md. (UPI) — It was the Abbott and Costello show at Norwood Park on Saturday, as just enough players showed up for a steamy, sticky, and stifling morning of softball featuring a comedy of errors and unforgettable performances.

There would have been a larger turnout at the ballpark, except some players stayed home to protest "Lou Dobbs Day." It was a day to celebrate because CNN sealed first place in its division.

The team played like it had the Midas Touch—diving catches, successful rundowns, memorable homers, and body blocks into opposing players. But there were also bonehead pitches and errant throws—and that was just during the pre-game warmups.

When it counted, CNN came out on top, and the team snagged a dramatic victory in Game 1, 15-14, in eight innings, against a relentless NBC News Channel.

Never mind that NBC had won only three times in 14 tries coming into the game. CNN's defense was so porous Andrea Mitchell and Alan Greenspan could have gotten on base. The power couple did just that during an unannounced visit in the fifth inning, as did an unidentified supporter of the Symbionese Liberation Army.

In Game 2, ABC News trounced CNN, 18-8, leaving many questioning if the Mickey Mouse club was taking out its frustration over Rick Kaplan's sudden decision over the weekend to preempt the first half of *The Moneyline Newshour* with ABC's *World News Tonight*.

"It's either that or make the highly rated Ask Bob Franken segment into a daily half-hour show," bemoaned CNN President Tom Johnson.

CNN is 11-5 after splitting its fifth doubleheader this season. Eight of their wins have been by three or fewer runs. "If this keeps up, I might repeal my ban on Control Room tours," railed a dumbfounded D.C. Deputy Bureau Chief Peggy Soucy.

Here's how the day unfolded.

NBC went on top by scoring four runs in the first inning. CNN stormed back with five runs on seven straight hits. NBC went ahead with seven runs in the third to make it 12-7. It was 14-11 in favor of NBC when John King stroked a three-run homer in the bottom of the sixth.

"While waiting to ask my question at Friday's presidential news conference, I had a vision I would hit one over the right fielder's head," said the soon-to-be senior White House correspondent, who denied a USA Today story he would also report from the State Department, Capitol Hill, and the Pentagon.

The game went into extra innings. Neither team scored in the seventh. In the bottom of the eighth, King (4-5 with 5 RBI) swung at a pitch three feet over his head to get a bloop single, bringing in Ari Perilstein with the winner.

Said one CNN player, "I haven't seen a hack job like that since Tom Farmer ripped one of Frances Hardin's scripts to shreds."

Dependable Jack Lynn also went 4-5 (4 RBI and two-run homer), and work-horse Charles Bierbauer went 3-4 (2 RBI), including a triple and two doubles.

Every other player got on base during the doubleheader: Paul Miller, James Knott, Erika Dimmler, Pete Hartogs, Chris Guarino, Jim Barnett, Elizabeth Hathway, and Rebecca Ratliff.

Meanwhile, ABC News sat in the shade, drinking lemonade, waiting for the CNN game to end. Its opponent in the opener forfeited. CNN led 4-0 in Game 2, but a rested ABC came back with six runs in the first and then scored in every inning after that: two in the second, two in the third, five in the fourth, and three in the fifth before the game was called because of the mandatory time rule of 65 minutes.

That wasn't the only bad news. In a mind-bending ripple effect, anchor Catherine Crier broadcast she was not going to *Court TV* after all. Instead, she would return to CNN to co-anchor a current events game show with Bernard Shaw. Soon after, Shaw reportedly hit the roof and told CNN founder Ted Turner he was going to MSNBC and join anchor Laurie Dhue. Dhue, like a bat out of hell, called her agent and got rehired at CNN to work alongside Gene Randall, who harrumphed and said he was immediately moving to Puerto Vallarta to raise pigs and export pork chops to the United States.

The regular season ends with a doubleheader at Aspen Hill Park on July 10 against NBC News Channel again and Fox News. The following weekend, a double-loss elimination playoff tournament begins, featuring nine teams vying for bragging rights as the best in the 20-team MMSL.

July 10, 1999

GAME 1		GAME 2	
CNN	7	CNN	15
FOX NEWS	0	NBC NEWS CHANNEL	5

- **CNN marches to playoffs with doubleheader sweep to close out regular season.**
- *Scooby Doo* **episodes to replace** *Inside Politics* **during summer lull.**
- **Political Director Tom Hannon, furious, reportedly pushed for** *The Jetsons.*

By Joe Baseball Jr.
Bureau Sports Writer

ASPEN HILL, Md. (UPI) — It was a heavenly end to CNN's most successful softball season. As first baseman Ralph Marcus squeezed his glove around the ball to get the final out against NBC News Channel and seal CNN's victory, Carey Bodenheimer ripped off her jersey and ran around the field with her arms raised in triumph.

"I saw Brandi Chastain do it after she made the penalty kick at the World Cup," clamored Bodenheimer, who failed to mention that the soccer star was also wearing a black sports bra at the time.

No one on the team seemed to mind the startling public display of fanaticism as players went bananas with whoops and hollers. The regular MMSL season was over. Now, the fun begins.

CNN is heading to the double-loss elimination playoffs next Saturday at Wheaton Regional Park, where the crème de la crème will battle for bragging rights.

You can feel the fever. You can hear the buzz. There hasn't been this sort of electricity in the air since Jim and Jann Connor sold their car top carrier. "You're smearing my good name," griped Jim Connor, who let out a stream of invective and said, "It was good for a change to see CNN players stop their maddening process toward relapse and debasement."

The weekend sweep of Fox and NBC gave the CNN a record of 13-5 (third best in the 20-team league) and a No. 3 seed as they steel themselves for the postseason. Give credit where credit is due. In one of those roll-of-the-dice scenarios, CNN was greatly helped when Fox forfeited the opening game after only a few of their players showed up.

"We heard you guys were going to replay the memorable *Talk Back Live* show about oral sex, so most of our team stayed home to watch," said Fox captain David Shuster. "We never get to cover fun topics like that, only boring stuff like Kosovo, capital gains taxes, and Medicare."

The twin wins also came with backing from Ari Perilstein, Paul Miller, James Knott, Greg Robertson, Charles Bierbauer, Marci Starzec, Patrick Davis, Bodenheimer, Jim Barnett, Rebecca Ratliff, Marty Kramer, Ralph Marcus, Chip Herzel and his dog, plus the scouting of Virginia Nicolaidis, who lounged in the shade all day warbling out defensive alignments.

"It beats watching disgusting pornographic talk shows," Nicolaidis raged. "We need more wholesome stories by Jonathan Aiken in short pants."

CNN had reason to play hard. Just before the games started, D.C. Bureau Chief Frank Sesno sent assistant Mellonie Saunders to Aspen Hill with a message.

After saying, "Frank Sesno, please call your office, Frank Sesno, please call your office," Saunders added, "Frank says if the softball team goes all the way, he will let any CNN employee with a valid ID use the freight elevator instead of having to wait."

As for what happened at the games, CNN held a scrimmage with the few Fox players who bothered to come out. Against NBC, eight different CNN batters had at least one RBI. Bierbauer went 4-4, including a triple and five runs batted in. *Crossfire* intern Kirsten White made her first appearance and went 2-2 with 2 RBI.

The sweep by CNN came despite the absence of three vitally important players: John Davis, Jack Lynn, and John King, who denied they stayed home to watch *Talk Back Live*.

Management has promised to adjust next weekend's schedules to ensure the softball team has its big guns available. But one department head was overheard later in the women's restroom saying that sports was soaking up "too much oxygen."

After a closed-door meeting among representatives from guest bookings, the assignment desk, Team Video, *Burden of Proof*, Skip the make-up artist, the Rim, and anyone affiliated with ABC (which left only two people unaccounted for), they concluded the softball team is the best thing to happen to CNN since the Sunrise Café opened on the weekends.

The playoffs begin next week. This could be it.

July 17, 1999

GAME 1		GAME 2	
CNN	17	CNN	14
NEWSCHANNEL	8	GAZETTE	3
	GAME 3	GAME 4	
WASHINGTON TIMES	12	CNN	19
CNN	11	ASSOCIATED PRESS	4
GAME 5		GAME 6 (CHAMPIONSHIP)	
CNN	8	CNN	8
WASHINGTON TIMES	7	WASHINGTON TIMES	4

- **CNN wins five of six games to claim softball championship!**
- **Team takes one small step for Washington Bureau, one giant leap for cable television.**
- **Only thing more perfect this weekend was New York Yankees pitcher David Cone.**
- **Players pass up invitation to Hyannis Port, opt for The Dubliner.**

By Joe Baseball Jr.
Bureau Sports Writer

WHEATON, Md. (UPI) — There was something beautiful to see as CNN employees in Washington got off the 11th-floor elevators on Monday morning.

Was it the latest FTD bouquet of roses for guest booker Jill Neff?

No, it was a gleaming trophy awarded to a softball team comprised of selfless players who, for months, sacrificed their Saturday mornings, rearranged schedules, endured scorching heat and oppressive humidity, and suffered assorted injuries.

This wasn't just your average group of weekend warriors. It was CNN's team, the best cable news network, and now the Metropolitan Media Softball League champions.

"Cut the crap," cussed Rick Kaplan, who was in no mood to celebrate. "I'm shelving all Apollo 11 programming after discovering that my deputy Sid Bedingfield believes the moon is made of green cheese."

Bedingfield was unavailable for comment but issued a finely honed

Bedingfield Notes in read-me, which said, "Diligence."

In a development unrelated to softball or lunar landings 30 years ago this week, CNN executives refused to confirm or deny that Office Depot would become the network's new supply vendor. Time Warner stock dropped to five dollars a share before rebounding to $189 on news of the softball team's success.

In what has to be the most jaw-dropping news to hit the network since CNN used a milk graphic on a story about MLK, the softball team put the hurt on its opponents over the weekend in the double-loss elimination tournament. Do you want heroes? Forget Neil Armstrong and Buzz Aldrin. Don't look to the heavens. Look around. Some 34 people representing a cross-section of the CNN Washington Bureau played during the year. Half that group was there at the end to sip champagne.

Here's how the action unfolded on Saturday. At 9 a.m., precisely four hours after John King returned from Iowa on the press plane, he and the mighty mice of CNN were taking the field at Wheaton Regional Park. CNN won the coin toss against NewsChannel 8 to determine the home team, and the Albritton crew would have done better staying in bed.

CNN sent 14 batters to the plate in the first inning, scoring nine runs. Ari Perilstein and Jack Lynn each had two hits in the inning. CNN stretched the lead to 15-0 by the third. The Crazy Eights were so zealous in their pursuit to get back in the game they urged their local viewers to boycott the new Wolf Blitzer show. "You have our word. We won't do any counter-programming against *Street Sweep* and *NewsStand*," pledged their coach.

CNN won going away, 17-9. Perilstein went 4-4 (3 RBI), Greg Robertson 3-4 (2 RBI), including a home run over the 260-foot sign in right field. John Davis (3-4, 5 RBI) also homered.

Next up. Gazette. It was the first meeting between the two teams this year. CNN had only two hits through the first three innings. Chip Herzel led off with a called third strike. Lynn hit a scorcher in the gap, but the umpire called him out when he said Jack took too long putting out his cigarette butt on the back of the catcher's neck. Gazette scored three runs in their half of the first, but that was all she wrote. CNN's defense shut them down, and the offense tacked on 14 unanswered runs. Davis hit for the cycle, Robertson went 3-4 and pitched a masterpiece. The number three, four, and five hitters went 11 for 12. Final: CNN 14, Gazette 3.

Between Games Two and Three on Saturday, the heat/humidity index rose to somewhere near 155 degrees. The ump threatened to call the game not because of the Code Red conditions but because of the frenzy created when approximately 17 beepers simultaneously went off, calling people into work. Searchers off Martha's Vineyard had found debris from the missing plane piloted by John F. Kennedy Junior.

A bunch of players reluctantly answered the assignment desk's call to duty but did not go home and shower. "It was our way of protesting the decision," blabbed one sweaty player. CNN would have to carry on with a depleted roster. That's the news business. Next person up.

The opponents for Game 3 were the bad boys from the Washington Times, the same undefeated team before CNN knocked them off their pedestal last month. Trailing 9-5, CNN tied the game in the fifth inning when Carey Bodenheimer (3-4) smacked an RBI single after the Times intentionally walked the man in front of her. "What a bone-headed move," cursed Body, who immediately used her cell phone from first base to call Patti Kloehn to cut off the delivery of the Washington Times. "I just read it for the comics, anyway," she added.

CNN took the lead but wilted like a Georgia peach on a vine in the last inning, giving up three runs and losing its first game of the tournament, 12-11. King went 4-4 (4 RBI) and got credit for phoning in 14 wires.cnn updates between batters while playing shortstop. Perilstein went 4-4, and Davis 3-4 (3 RBI). This was the second one-run game against the Times and wouldn't be the last. Keep reading.

Sunday morning dawned, and CNN returned to the battlefield. A new day, a fresh start. With one loss already, it was win or go home. Everyone came ready to finish the job. The team was as perky as Bill Hemmer tossing to a Jeanne Moos package about a talking iguana.

CNN never looked back against the Associated Press, scoring four runs in the first inning, three in the second, three in the fifth, and nine in the sixth on its way to a double-digit lead. The umpire invoked the mercy rule to spare the opponents any further ignominy. Final: CNN 19, Associated Press 5. It was the most runs scored by CNN this season.

Lynn was 3-4 (6 RBI), including two homers, a solo shot in the first, and a three-run poke in the sixth. Charles Bierbauer's game-winning triple galvanized the AP to file an appeal with the Supreme Court charging CNN with using corked bats. King went 3-4, Davis 3-4 (3 RBI). The AP had beaten CNN by a run earlier in the season. Revenge is sweet.

Then, there were just two teams left: the unbeaten Washington Times from the winner's bracket and CNN, the winners of the loser's bracket.

The Times led for the first three innings. CNN led for the next three. The Times tied the score at seven in the top of the seventh, but the heart of the batting order was due up. Lynn led off with a single. King singled him over to third. Robertson sealed the victory with a single. It was the third game between these two teams decided by a run. CNN 8, Washington Times 7.

Now, each team had a loss. It was down to the last game for all the marbles. Everything was on the line. It was time to go for broke. Give it your all. Win one for the Gipper.

Facing the Washington Times for the third time in 24 hours, CNN players knew more about the opposing team than they did about the colleagues who work in D.C. Feeds.

Virginia Nicolaidis, producer extraordinaire, kept meticulous notes about where the Times' players hit every ball. She waved and hollered to move CNN players into better defensive positions. "We had 'em by the cojones," growled Nicolaidis.

The two teams went mano a mano, with CNN taunting them with shouts of "Moonies." The Times responded in kind by spelling out T-A-I-L-W-I-N-D in the infield dirt. For half the game, the score was tied at four runs apiece. It was only natural that the championship game would go into extra innings.

CNN took command in the eighth when Lesley Gold doubled, Bierbauer knocked in the go-ahead run with a two-bagger, designated hitter James Knott doubled in two more, and Bodenheimer put the finishing touches on the uprising with an RBI double of her own.

Then came the celebration. CNN players, including Erika Dimmler, Chris Guarino, Patrick Davis, Ralph Marcus, Marci Starzec, Jim Barnett, and Paul Miller, rushed onto the field and participated in a group hug. Several players from Saturday who couldn't make it back were missing but not lost in the dust, including Howie Lutt, Rebecca Ratliff, Elizabeth Hathway, and Herzel.

CNN wrapped up 1999 at 18-6, 12 games above .500... number one out of 20 teams.

Need more stats? Perilstein went 11-12 in the first three games of the playoffs (13-21 overall); King 16-25, Robertson 14-19; Davis 18-23 and 19 RBI. Batters three, four, and five collectively went 48-67 in six games.

Back in mid-April, Joe Baseball Jr. presciently wrote that if CNN ended up winning the championship, sports enthusiasts could say the true driving force all season long was Atlanta firefighter Matt Mosely, who put his life on the line and rescued a construction worker from a crane on fire.

Well, thanks again, Matt.

If readers of this column see any of the three dozen people who played this year on the CNN softball team, congratulate them for leaving an indelible mark on a memorable season.

And check out the trophy!

Day of Infamy: The "JFK Jr." Game

RICHARD THOMPSON FOR U/N&WR

Please hold while I shag flies

Washington cellphonemania now has a face: CNN White House correspondent **John King**. We're not talking annoying calls at fancy restaurants or in church. Picture this: King plays shortstop for CNN in Washington's Metropolitan Media Softball League and often handles plays *while* interviewing White House aides. "I'm trying to reach people who are very busy," he explains. Once, he was part of a double play "and I almost threw the phone instead of the ball." Says league commissioner **Dennis Tuttle**, "It's amazing how often his cellphone goes off during a game." Few other marquee names play in the league for networks, big papers, and major magazines. The exceptions: CNN's **Charles Bierbauer** and Fox's **David Schuster**. But of the three it's King who plays it like **Pete Rose**. "I like to win," says the reporter who once took a red-eye flight from California to play. He'd better try harder: CNN is the defending league champion but approaches this month's playoffs with a .500 record. "Everyone's gunning for us," says King.

John King gets a shout-out in U.S. News & World Report for his ability to play shortstop and call sources at the same time during games.

The playoff games on the weekend of July 17, 1999, were unlike any others because of breaking news. On the Friday night before the playoffs, a single-engine, six-seat Piper piloted by John F. Kennedy Jr. disappeared in hazy conditions off the coast of Massachusetts on a flight from New Jersey to Cape Cod. He was headed to a family wedding with his wife, Carolyn Bessette, and her sister, Lauren Bessette.

As dawn broke on Saturday, there was a massive air and ground search by planes, helicopters and boats. Aircraft debris started washing ashore just after noon. Right about that time, CNN and the Washington Times began to play the winner's bracket final at Wheaton Regional Park. Not only were spectators and players glued to the coverage as playoff games were being held on three adjoining fields, but beepers and cell phones were going off like pinball machines.

Players were pulled away from the games throughout the day to work on the story. WJLA-TV coach Dale Solly was immediately sent to Hyannis Port. Like other coaches and players, Solly had tried to ignore the 911 messages that arrived while he was stationed in right field.

The CNN assignment desk blasted urgent messages to every pager for employees to come into the Washington Bureau. Seven CNN players responded to the breaking news and went to work in their softball jerseys. Many pleaded to stay and finish the game. Fortunately, there were enough players to field a team.

Reporter John King wasn't scheduled to be at the office but worked sources while playing shortstop. Fifty minutes after CNN's last game, he was on the air from the White House. "And that included going home to take a shower," King said.

The image of King holding a cell phone in one hand and a glove and ball in the other was captured in a watercolor published in U.S. News & World Report. CNN won the game and went on to become MMSL champions.

TOP OF THE 3rd

Take No Prisoners

April 10, 2000

- **New season, new faces; CNN hopes to repeat as softball champs despite naysayers.**
- **Players predict more pleasure than a Carol Buckland romance novel.**
- **Eds: Note language in 6th paragraph.**

By Joe Baseball Jr.
Bureau Sports Writer

WASHINGTON (UPI) — Faster than a Red Phone call from producer Terry Frieden, more powerful than a read-me edict from CNN President Rick Kaplan, able to reach a rating of .3 in a single night, it's time for the start of the Metropolitan Media Softball League season.

Last year, CNN bulldozed its way to the crown, besting 19 other teams and forcing the facilities department in the D.C. Bureau to find somewhere other than the mail room to show off the championship trophy.

"I pledge to use my $9 million stock option bonus to build a display case," boasted Time Warner Chairman Gerald Levin. "Furthermore, starting Monday, in a tribute to all the players, we will run twice as many of those catchy 'We are the Champions' commercials."

It will be another fun-filled and exciting year with returning veterans, a sprinkling of new faces, and the usual complement of out-of-shape wannabees ready to push the envelope. CNN, which finished with an 18-6 record a year ago, is 66-68 (.493) since entering the MMSL in 1993.

Even the CNN public relations department in D.C. took time out from selling unused tickets from last week's Radio and Television Correspondents' dinner at the Hilton Hotel to issue a short and sweet statement: "In honor of the team's recent success, we are going to hand out movie vouchers good for any AMC Theatres for those who are interested."

"It's outrageous," spewed Gene Randall, bristling over an Atlanta writer's script error linking the veteran weekend anchor to the recent decoding of the human gene. "I spent an hour arguing with him. Not that Gene, you idiot."

There's no question about the makeup of this year's softball squad and a possible return to the mountaintop with a group of ascendant superstars and a new front office.

Tri-captains Jack Lynn, Charles Bierbauer, and Jim Barnett have promised to stitch together a competitive amalgamation of players. When asked to assess the team's future after a splashy offseason, distinguished baseball scholar and journalist George Will said succinctly, "I think the head coaches are a salad and an appetizer short of a fine dining experience. They should have cleaned house when they had the chance."

When little Elian Gonzalez throws out the ceremonial first pitch next Saturday, the players promise to put the backstabbing aside and knuckle down on winning back-to-back titles.

"Yeah, enough already about the White House unit," said correspondent John King. "There's more tension around here than in a room full of hardliners from Taiwan and China, more in-fighting than a gaggle of Chechen rebels, more incriminating faces than a breakroom full of Team Video employees."

Despite the uncertainty, the turnout for four energetic practices this Spring has been good. Greg Robertson, Carey Bodenheimer, James Knott, Ari Perilstein, John Davis, Howie Lutt, Paul Miller, Marty Kramer, Ralph Marcus, Tim Durham, Pete Hartogs, Rebecca Ratliff, and Chip Herzel appear in tip-top shape.

Fresh faces include Darrin White, Heather Shaw, Hunter Waters, and Dick Uliano. Team scouts hope the schedule will allow the recently transferred Major Garrett and Kelly Wallace to appear in a supporting role and become part of CNN lore.

"The fact is they can use all the help they can get," said an unidentified D.C. bureau chief. "Hell, I might even show up for a laugh," the executive sniveled. "I told Mel to put it on my calendar. I'll try to make the opener, but it depends on how much fun I'm having at the World Bank protests."

The first pitch this Saturday is at 10 a.m. against WJLA at Capitalview Park. In game two, CNN faces NewsChannel 8.

April 17, 2000

GAME 1		GAME 2	
CNN	9	CNN	21
WJLA	5	NEWSCHANNEL 8	8

- **Team sweeps to opening victories with potent offense.**
- **Juan Miguel Gonzalez shows up to give CNN the finger.**
- **Softball commissioner warns players to stop throat-slashing gestures and dugout gyrations.**

By Joe Baseball Jr.
Bureau Sports Writer

KENSINGTON, Md. (UPI) — Poet and playwright T.S. Eliot once wrote, "April is the cruelest month." He did not have CNN's softball team in mind when he composed that opening line in his poem, "The Waste Land."

On Saturday, the only wasteland scholars and sportsaholics could identify was the debris left behind after Cable News Network's softball team demolished WJLA and NewsChannel 8.

CNN took time from its saturation coverage of little Elian and the World Bank protests over the weekend to leave a calling card for the rest of the Metropolitan Media Softball League in the misty morning season opener at Capitalview Park.

The sturdy team pulverized its two thoroughly overmatched broadcast opponents and taunted them for using film.

"That was one of the most memorable things I've ever witnessed except for the time Bob Novak lost his teeth during a taping of Crossfire," CNN executive Rick Davis said while rolling on the floor in hysterics.

CNN stopped local affiliate WJLA in the first game, 9-5, and then racked up the first 17 runs against forlorn NewsChannel 8 in the nightcap, scoring the equivalent of three touchdowns and winning 21-4.

"And they call themselves a news channel," scoffed Osama bin Laden from his mountain hideaway in Pakistan.

The umpire ordered a stop at the end of the fifth inning in Game 2 and came forward to say CNN's mauling had made him sick to his stomach.

"I haven't seen that kind of affront since the 8p show led with a Jeanne

Moos package about brassiere straps," grumbled the ump, whose face was a poster child for erectile dysfunction. "Hey, when will you guys do a story about Flomax rebates?"

Shame is nothing new to CNN.

"There was that time last week when anchor Bobbie Battista tossed to Justice correspondent Pierre Thomas and called him Pierre Salinger," recalled Charles Bierbauer, who went 2-2 with 3 RBI against WJLA.

Reached for comment in Atlanta, Battista said in a prickly but catchy retort, "At least I got the Pierre part right. So, get off my Talkback back."

CNN catapulted to an early 3-0 lead in the first inning when Bierbauer clubbed a 20-foot dribbler with the bases loaded, bringing home two runners. CNN then added four in the third. In keeping with a sequence of scoring only in the odd number innings, the team rung up two more runs in the fifth to take a commanding 9-2 lead and never looked back.

There were many heroes in the first game. Fresh off the campaign trail and with his kids in tow, John King knocked in three runs with a couple of hits. John Davis also went 2-3 with an RBI. Carey Bodenheimer, aka the Mudflap Madam, officially had one hit, but she also collected two walks and played stellar defense, as did Rebecca "Scrap Iron" Ratliff, who made the highlight reel with a back-handed flip for a force out.

"Our women showed more class out there than a room full of enigmatic Darva Congers, the former *Who Wants to Marry a Multi-Millionaire* winner, but what kind of name is Darva?" asked Pilar Keagy from her perch in the legal department.

Everyone on the squad saw action in the opener except for Jim Barnett, who sources say was in a funk after losing out on playing the part of "Stuart" on the TD Ameritrade commercials.

The fun began in the second game after CNN President Rick Kaplan rolled out of the Lincoln bedroom and showed up in his pajamas to perform a snake-charming ritual. "We have a new campaign slogan, guys. 'You are what you eat.'"

"I thought it was *Play Like a Man, Win Like a Woman*," said Executive Vice President Gail Evans during a book signing event at Politics and Prose.

The new-and-improved CNN came out swinging for the fences, with every batter using two-handed slashes like Marty McSorley of the Boston Bruins. Darrin White, Paul "Hound Dog" Miller, James "Dizzy" Knott, Marty "The Rimster" Kramer, Howie "The Hacker" Lutt, Elizabeth "30 Day It" Hathway, Jack "No Relation to Loretta" Lynn and Dick "The

Sleeper" Uliano shrugged off apathy and indifference and played with typical newsroom swagger.

"We came looking for a fight," snorted Ralph "The Rattle Snake" Marcus, who pitched brilliantly. "I've been ticked off since last week when the CNN interns cut in line and ate all the good stuff at the free lunch."

Bill Schneider, known to occasionally expend political capital, rejected outright bribes to choose the doubleheader sweep as the Play of the Week. "Sorry, I already picked Getty, CNN's out-of-work parking attendant with a master's degree."

Building managers Dewey, Cheatum & Howe had no comment before towing away three dozen illegally parked cars, then ripping up the surface parking lot in front of the bureau to make way for another half-occupied government office building.

There were heroes aplenty in Game 2, which featured 29 base hits by CNN against NewsChannel 8.

Davis — celebrating his birthday but not feeling his age — just missed hitting for the cycle. His performance included a grand slam, a three-run homer, and a bases-loaded triple. King, Miller, and White had three hits, but in what could augur the beginning of a memorable year, Ratliff went 4-4, attributing her success to getting knocked in the head three weeks ago by one of those exploding manhole covers.

The two wins on Saturday get CNN started on the right foot to repeat as champions and evens their overall record since joining the MMSL seven years ago at 68-68. The team is idle next week for Easter. Batting practice using dyed hard-boiled eggs is optional. League action resumes on April 29.

April 29, 2000

GAME 1		GAME 2	
AMW	20	CNN	19
CNN	14	WUSA	6

- (Stations: This version replaces earlier writethru, which moved at 8:35 a.m., to delete vulgarities and offensive material and CLARIFY 15th graph)
- CNN gains doubleheader split after playing too fast and loose in opener.
- Bureau chief punishes team by tripling vending machine price for Twizzlers.
- Facilities to build underground tunnel from K Street lot if employees stop complaining.

By Joe Baseball Jr.
Bureau Sports Writer

KENSINGTON, Md. (UPI) — Faster than you can say, "Open up, Lazaro, this is the INS," CNN gave up 10 runs to America's Most Wanted in the opener at Capitalview Park on Saturday — an underwhelming way to start the game.

After AMW compiled an insurmountable 17-2 lead, CNN realized the other team's coach was "Mafiaboy," the bratty high school student and hacker who brought down the Internet two months ago. By then, it was too late. Talk about denial of service.

The pesky gang from First Street made it interesting with a 10-frame in the fourth inning to get within striking distance, but back-to-back homers by the Manhunters put a cork in the bottle, and time ran out after just five innings. League rules say games can only last 65 minutes. The final score was 20-14, CNN's first loss of the year... and the first defeat going back to last July.

Said a tearful Marisleysis Gonzalez, "My relatives in Cuba could play better than you pushovers. Give me the damn boy, or I will run for Miami city manager in November."

One fan with knowledge of the situation giggled after the first game. She hadn't seen that much turmoil since Nancy Ambrose ordered David Schechter to stop calling the Rim and asking for package description updates.

"Amateur hour, plain and simple," said Keith McAllister from his new office in the graphics department, where efforts are underway to determine why every CNN map shows Saigon instead of Ho Chi Minh City.

Mercifully, CNN gained some salvation in Game 2 when Sister Jean showed up in a tank top to provide motivation. CNN scored in every inning against the Eye-witless news team at WUSA, suffocating the CBS affiliate 19-6.

Everyone got to play: Darrin White, Chip Herzel, John Davis, John King, Greg Robertson, Jack Lynn, Howie Lutt, Carey Bodenheimer, James Knott, Jim Barnett, Rebecca Ratliff, Marty Kramer, Heather Shaw, Ari Perilstein, Dick Uliano, Arthur Hardy, Brad Wright, Tiffany, and Eric.

"We had more players turn out than an early-morning raid in Little Havana," said Virginia Nicolaidis, who dutifully kept track of the score and implied she once went on a double date in college with a guy named Donato. "He took me to the Wye River Plantation and kept whispering 'Pescador' in my ear."

Game 1 was a disaster from the get-go for CNN.

"Reports of them being brain-dead were not that far off," said a spokesman at Children's Hospital.

Jack Lynn muttered, "(Pitcher) Barnett threw so many gopher balls the folks at the National Zoo dropped by and offered him a full-time job manning their new metal detectors."

It wasn't all exasperation in the first game. James Knott was 3-3 with 4 RBI. In addition, he booked 17 guests for Monday's *Larry King Live*, including Bob Smith, Ileana Ros-Lehtinen, April Oliver, Ernie, and Bert. "I was so lucky to get April," he shrugged.

John King also played well, going 2-3 with 2 RBI. Jack Lynn was 2-2 and John Davis 2-3.

"Utter disgrace. A debacle," stammered Charles Bierbauer, now under the federal witness protection program in the wake of his reporting on the Boy Scout case before the Supreme Court. "I didn't go to the game, but from what I heard, everyone on the team played like impostors. It was like a bad episode of *To Tell the Truth*."

Editor's Note: To Tell the Truth was a popular television program that aired on kinescope before most of the players were born.

There was a second game to be played. CNN led from start to finish. The news junkies scored in every inning, prompting Alan Greenspan and

Andrea Mitchell to issue an unusual weekend advisory: "First, it was all about the economy, then our marriage. Now, CNN players are red hot as well. We hereby raise interest rates one-quarter percent."

John Davis had four hits in the nightcap (12-15 on the season), Jack was 3-3, Brad smashed a solo homer, and power-hitting Carey went 2-3 with one RBI.

The split leaves CNN 3-1 for the year and tied for first place with ABC. CNN is off next week, and the 18 teams that make up the Metropolitan Media Softball League are back in action on May 13.

May 13, 2000

GAME 1		GAME 2	
CNN	17	CNN	11
ABC NEWS	5	NBC	6

- **CNN sweeps past commercial networks in remarkable style.**
- **Team institutes Los Alamos scorched earth policy, destroys everything in its path.**
- **Cash shortfall prompts D.C. Bureau to sell old Supreme Court sketches by artist Peggy Gage.**

By Joe Baseball Jr.
Bureau Sports Writer

KENSINGTON, Md. (UPI) — They're all smiles at CNN headquarters in Atlanta this week, and for good reason.

For starters, Kathleen Koch scooped all other reporters with the breaking news there were not a million mothers protesting at the Million Mom March in Washington on Sunday. "It felt good to be out in front on this one," she trumpeted to colleagues.

The good luck continued when CNN's softball team won big on Saturday, not just once but twice, thereby scuttling plans by the Board of Directors to close down *Showbiz Today* and CNNfn "for the time being."

CNN lowered the boom on division rival ABC News 17-5 in the opener at Capitalview Park. In the nightcap, CNN tuned out NBC News Channel, 11-6, upping its record to 5-1 for the season and good enough for first place. The largest crowd of the year (one fan) turned out to see the games.

"It was purely serendipitous," conceded Jim Connor, the lone fan, who showed up wearing bike tights. "I had a flat tire on my three-speed Schwinn just a block away and stumbled upon some cheap entertainment."

Washington D.C. Bureau Chief Frank Sesno couldn't resist piling on. "It's frustrating to be out of town when big games happen. It's also oddly gratifying to be as far away as possible. That's why I'm moving to the 6th floor as soon as Facilities packs up my White House photos."

The day started on a sour note. Kids from a Pee Wee League were playing on the field for which CNN had a permit, and their coach and players refused to leave. Someone threatened to call the Montgomery County police and run the little urchins off.

CNN players had to hold back Charles Bierbauer after several children made a pinky swear that they had never heard of him, but they *could* name every justice on the Supreme Court. A settlement was reached when a second field became available.

All the pregame melodrama unsettled CNN, which straight away fell behind ABC by three runs in the first inning. The smell of defeat, the look of despair, the angst of desperation—it was all on display. The mood was as somber as an excavation cult site in Uganda.

"It takes our offense longer to get going than getting an 8p script approved," shouted one person identified only as "Mr. Todd."

Things got worse between innings. *Dateline* producer Mark Feldstein uncovered a secret carrot and stick plan by Keith McAllister to pay the Row and the Rim a $25 stipend every time producers make a single decision about anything. It's more carrot than stick. (Last week, the Rim made $50 compared to $10,300 taken in by Richard Griffiths.) A spokeswoman for *The World Today* could not decide whether to return our phone calls.

There were so many slip-ups at the start of the game. One watcher blathered to no one in particular, "I hadn't seen that kind of disorganization since the graphics department used a St. Louis Cardinal baseball logo during the funeral coverage of a Roman Catholic Cardinal last week."

CNN regrouped and put the kind of choke hold on ABC that would make even Indiana University basketball coach Bobby Knight smile. John Davis went 3-3 with four RBI, including a two-run homer. John King smashed three doubles and drove in three runs.

In addition to the manly hitting, there was ample estrogen in the air as well. Carey Bodenheimer, Rebecca Ratliff, and Erika Dimmler batted a collective 6-9. "Take your trigger lock and shove it," they chorused.

After falling behind 3-0, CNN wiped the floor against ABC by a run margin of 17-2 the rest of the way, forcing the umpire to head for the showers in the fifth inning.

Unlike the opener, Game 2 was a team effort. All 19 players got PT (playing time), including Ari, Brad, Howie, Ralph, Jim, Kate, Dick, Arthur, Chip, Paul, Tim, and Darrin. Greg Robertson was the star, coming within a single of hitting for the cycle. John Davis was 3-4 and is now a remarkable 18-22 for the season. Carey went 2-4 and was robbed when she hit a liner off the pitcher's glove right to the second baseman.

Beating two network teams in one weekend was too much for some. CNN President Rick Kaplan, who has publicly acknowledged stumbling in the early going with *NewsStand*, reacted cautiously.

"I've come up with a sure-fire way to goose the team and our ratings, which lag behind the Oxygen Network. Starting June 1, we're replacing the morning show with '*Where in the World is Bill Hemmer*.' At the very least, we get Hemmer out of the newsroom, where he belongs," gloated Kaplan. "If that doesn't work, we'll try Ralph Wenge."

CNN won't have to wait long to see its team in action again. Another doubleheader is set for this Saturday at Wheaton Forest against the Washington Post and U.S. News.

June 3, 2000

GAME 1		GAME 2	
WASHINGTON TIMES	19	WASHINGTON TIMES	8
CNN	9	CNN	4

- **CNN swept by Washington Times in 'piddling display of talent.'**
- **Doubleheader loss is biggest flop since *Inside Politics* expanded to one hour.**
- **Flamboyant bandleader Tito Puente, who died on Tuesday, showed more energy on Wednesday than softball team.**

By Joe Baseball Jr.
Bureau Sports Writer

BETHESDA, Md. (UPI) — CNN's ragged and vulnerable softball team did something Saturday that it hasn't done in over two years. It came up empty in a doubleheader and dropped out of first place. But it wasn't just a pair of stinging defeats against the Washington Times, 19-9 in Game 1 and 8-4 in Game 2. It was HOW it happened. And WHY.

You couldn't blame it on the first-class weather, the pristine field at North Chevy Chase Park, or the tremendous turnout (20 players). Just a few remained hung over following the 20th-anniversary celebrations at Union Station the night before.

There was something amiss from the start. They were down early and could never recover.

It was an all-around putrid performance. So bad that Operations Manager Mark Sweet ordered spectators to wear gas masks left over from the World Bank protests.

D.C. Chieftain Frank Sesno threatened to put the softball team's future at the top of his "to do" list when he releases what he promises will be a "coherent memo" on various pressing issues facing the bureau.

On Monday morning, C. Shelby Coffey III, president of CNNfn, stunned viewers of *Street Sweep* when he arrived at work wearing a Motley Fool's hat. He had lost a bet with Lou Dobbs on last week's MMSL games. "I'll stick to predicting Qualcomm's earnings," he said.

In the opener, before you could even say Condoleezza Rice, CNN fell behind 4-0 against the Rags, as they're sometimes called, who were hotter than a rush-hour Metro train on fire at Foggy Bottom. CNN clawed its way back to tie the score. But the floodgates opened in the fourth inning when the Times knocked in six runs.

"We all stood around with a deer-in-the-headlights look," said a flustered Virginia Nicolaidis, the first to ironically spot two deer when they strolled out of the Bethesda woods for a visit with right fielder Jack Lynn.

There were plenty of other excuses to go around.

The Reverend Jesse Jackson, the host of *Both Sides with Jesse Jackson*, admonished himself. "It's my fault. I told the team to 'Keep Bob Hope alive,' and one of the players misunderstood me."

John and Patsy Ramsey told Larry King, "It was a feed room problem. We'll take a polygraph test if you don't believe us."

"Bullshit," snapped Tom Johnson, who promised additional blue-flamed phrases in the days to come. "CNN won't be intimidated by anyone."

Except for John Davis, who was 4-6 with five RBI, Darrin White, 3-4, and Charles Bierbauer, 2-2, the rest played like they had blinders on.

In a related development and what some outsiders say was a long overdue dressing down, Eason Jordan, CNN International president, was taken to the woodshed for his handling of last January's Winter Storm Jam in Atlanta.

"While it's true we had employees sleeping on dormitory-style cots, sharing pillows, and soap-on-a-rope, I did not authorize using the left-over eye shades during Saturday's games," Jordan wrote in this week's International Insights.

CNN's two losses were viewed as payback by the Washington Times, a team CNN defeated twice last year to win the MMSL championship. CNN now stands at 5-3 for the year, one game behind ABC.

"At this rate, by the end of next week, there'll be more hurricanes in the Atlantic than softball victories," smiled weatherman Flip Spiceland, who predicted he would be at CNN when the company celebrates its 50th anniversary in 2030.

The two losses took some of the steam out of a fun-filled weekend party, which began on Friday night with appearances from David French, Ed Turner, Diane Stanley, Bill Headline, Ralph Begleiter, Frances Hardin, and Lisa Driver.

There was a stirring video montage featuring photos of the softball team and every D.C. employee except for Susan Toffler, who turned in her ID badge and said she was quitting. "C'est la vie. Laissez les bons temps rouler."

In an effort to snap the CNN Bureau out of its doldrums, IT manager Joe Murphy promised to remove Solitaire on all desktops for the sex-obsessed alien video game Panty Raider.

Reached for comment at home, former CNN producer Larry Blasé sighed, "Talk about rotten timing."

The reverberations from Saturday's dismal showing were also felt on the West Coast. Los Angeles reporter Anne McDermott said CNN couldn't beat her daughter's Sherman Oaks softball squad even with "our corrupt police department's help."

All day long, CNN gave the Washington Times too many good pitches to hit. One opposing player was heard cackling, "It's like shooting fish in a barrel."

At the end of Game 1, the sagacious umpire bellowed he hadn't heard so much whining since he turned on CNN and watched that annoying American Express commercial about the woman who had her wallet stolen at the beach.

"I'm thinking about writing my popular 'one in an occasional series' notes about what it means to be a team player," said Assignment Desk editor David Schechter. "In the meantime, my congratulations to Howie, Heather, Jim, Erika, Brad, Ralph, Jen, Dick, Greg, Ari, Elizabeth, Eric, Arthur and Pete as well as the others."

CNN has only a few days to plug the holes in its leaky defense and get its offense back in gear. This Saturday, the team has another doubleheader at Veirs Mill Park against the undefeated Gazette (8-0) and the National Press Club (2-6).

June 10, 2000

GAME 1		GAME 2	
GAZETTE	19	**CNN**	15
CNN	10	**NATIONAL PRESS CLUB**	12

It's a clammy and humid mid-June morning in Washington, D.C. The setting is CNN's 11th-floor newsroom. The Bureau is already in overdrive, and it's not even 9 a.m.

Judge Thomas Penfield Jackson has arrived 15 minutes late for a live interview because Guest Bookings forgot to pick him up at the side entrance of Metro, and he had to walk three blocks. On top of that, there's no make-up artist on duty.

National Security Advisor Samuel Berger is ranting in the Green Room because his earpiece hasn't been cleaned, and there are no bagels. In the office space next door, a vial of "influenza virus" is unearthed in medical reporter Jeff Levine's old mailbox.

Making matters worse, CNN has decided to run the MSN Internet access commercial (the one with the guy in the front yard yapping at people) five times an hour for the rest of the year.

(Curtain rises.)

(People are hustling and bustling in the CNN newsroom.)

MELLONIE SAUNDERS: *(Voice offstage)* Frank Sesno, call your office. Frank Sesno, call your office.

FRANK SESNO: *(He enters stage left to thunderous applause fitting for a Broadway star.)* What's up, Mel? Sounds urgent. I was in the newsroom cleaning up another mess on the Rim.

MELLONIE SAUNDERS: *(She looks concerned, her knuckles pressed to her face.)* Sorry, but Rick, Tom, Sid, Eason, and Ted are ready for the conference call. Do you want me to get Joe Baseball in here?

FRANK SESNO: *(He makes a circular motion with his hand.)* Yes, tell him to hurry up. I wanna get this over with. If our softball team doesn't turn its season around, the whole bureau's gonna go down with it.

MELLONIE SAUNDERS: I'll call him now. *(Mellonie picks up the phone.)* Joe? This is Mel. Frank wants to see you immediately in his office. *(pauses)* He says he doesn't care if you're working on an 8p spot. No one watches that show.

FRANK SESNO: *(He grabs the phone and growls.)* Let Guarino do it. *(pauses)* What about Ambrose? *(sounding incredulous)* How long has she been in Italy? Never mind. *(He starts pacing.)* You better hustle in here.

JOE BASEBALL: *(Joe enters stage right.) (slightly out of breath)* Hi Frank, I got here p.d.q. Sounds like an emergency? It can't be Assad. He's already dead. Is it Reagan? Strom? Hope? Another E. coli outbreak? Is Charlie Caudill coming back? Don't tell me the Girl Scouts will not sell Thin Mints and Do-si-Dos this year.

FRANK SESNO: *(He motions toward an empty chair in front of his desk.)* Sit down. We have a serious matter to discuss.

JOE BASEBALL: We?

FRANK SESNO: Yes. *(He motions to the phone.)* Rick Kaplan, Tom Johnson, Sid Bedingfield, Eason Jordan, and Ted Turner are on the phone. Gentlemen, Joe has joined us.

TED TURNER: Heh, yew dewin', Joe?

JOE BASEBALL: Huh?

FRANK SESNO: Ted wants to know how you are doing.

JOE BASEBALL: Fine, Mr. Turner. What's this about?

RICK KAPLAN: Cut the 'playing dumb" routine, Joe.

SID BEDINGFIELD: Rick, please, let me handle this situation. I'm your deputy. I know Joe. Hey, that rhymes. Know Joe.

TOM JOHNSON: He's right, Rick. Stay out of this.

EASON JORDAN: Hey, guys. Settle down. No need to panic. This reminds me of the time when I started working here 17 years ago. I was making $3.25 an hour and eating Kraft Macaroni and Cheese.

FRANK SESNO: *(He suddenly bounds to his feet with his arms flailing.)* We're getting off message. Joe, I'll cut right to the chase. We're in big trouble. The network is in turmoil. We've just gotten a read-out from the McKinsey & Co. survey, which says our average viewer is 93 years old, watches for 19 seconds every hour, and then falls asleep. They recommend we cut out 20 hours of daily programming and let Greta Van Susteren fill the rest of the time.

SID BEDINGFIELD: She's already on the air more than Regis.

JOE BASEBALL: What's this got to do with me and the softball team?

FRANK SESNO: *(He is briefly distracted by a breaking news story on MSNBC.)* I'm getting tired of it, Joe. We need your help. And that's why we've asked you to be part of this conference call. We've all enjoyed your insidious softball notes, your screwball humor, and your audacious disregard for management, but things have gotten way out of hand.

RICK KAPLAN: For all your guile and cunning, you stepped over the line last week with that crack about Tailwind. You're an arrogant snot.

TOM JOHNSON: The blurb on Bill Hemmer, Rick Sanchez, and Pam Olson was character assassination.

SID BEDINGFIELD: I have to admit, Tom, I thought the one about Hemmer was pretty funny. But, Joe, you went too far when you said Bernie Shaw fell asleep on the set during a Jonathan Karl package about soft money.

TED TURNER: Gentlemen, argh, did that actually happen?

FRANK SESNO: Yes, but that's not why we're having this meeting. You've got to come clean, Joe. Stop lying. The whole CNN Bureau is suffering. It's beset by vicissitudes—just one example. Last week, Sol Levine wanted a hot roll, and the OA brought him a Pillsbury croissant.

JOE BASEBALL: What about the time the graphics department used a logo of the St. Louis Cardinals during Cardinal O'Connor's funeral?

KEITH MCALLISTER: *(He makes a cameo appearance as some in the audience hiss.)* Get me a name.

RICK KAPLAN: Not now, McAllister. We're trying to save the network and our asses.

FRANK SESNO: *(He continues to pace, stops, and looks directly at Joe.)* People in the newsroom are saying you're a traitor to the cause, a turncoat. Your attacks about CNN's entrenched bureaucracy, the political infighting, the unauthorized disclosure of our strategy to increase viewership with contest giveaways, the plan by Facilities to install fare meters in our shuttle vans, our decision to bring back Video Newshound as well as the two-minute week-in-review with Eric Gershon. All of it. When will it end?

JOE BASEBALL: *(He makes eye contact with Frank.)* These are times that try men's souls. I swear I haven't said a word about your broken promise to get a graphics suite six months ago, your pledge to let employees use all eight elevators in the building, or that Wolf Blitzer and Toni Tennille are teaming up to do a re-make of Muskrat Love.

EASON JORDAN: You see. That's my point. The next thing you know, Joe will poke fun at Keating Holland and his holiday traffic trip notes to Delaware that he puts in the computer for everyone to read.

TED TURNER: Aargh. Screw Delaware. Montana is the place to be. I own half the state and every buffalo.

FRANK SESNO: *(He ignores the comment.)* So, you see, Joe, the team needs you, and we need you now more than ever. Over the weekend, you let the Gazette beat you 19-10. The Gazette?! Sure, they're undefeated, but who reads that paper? Then you barely get past the National Press Club in the nightcap, 15-12. I heard they had the bases loaded with two outs in the last inning, and you almost blew it to a team that's only won twice in 10 games.

JOE BASEBALL: Not my fault. Blame Team Video. What can I do?

FRANK SESNO: You can begin by telling the truth. What's honestly going on out there on the softball diamond every Saturday? Are things as bad as you describe? Should we call Rick Davis to discuss news standards and practices? You never have enough women. The guys can't hit. I can only do so much. I hired John King from the AP, but he can't do it all.

SID BEDINGFIELD: We're sick of your exaggerations, Joe. It's got to stop. How can Charles Bierbauer possibly keep pace with the young stallions? And the way you inflate the statistics for people like Jack Lynn, John Davis, Howie Lutt, Becky Brittain, Jim Barnett, Virginia Nicolaidis, Darrin White, Chip Herzel, Jenn Powell, Ralph Marcus, Paul Miller, Alex Dermanis, and Brad Wright. They're journalists. Not athletes. Give me a break. We want the truth.

JOE BASEBALL: But that part is true. I swear. Look what happened on Saturday. It was Code Red at Veirs Mill Park. The temperature was 105 degrees. King was the first to confirm Assad was dead. He spent the entire third inning making calls on his cell phone while playing shortstop, AND he filed for radio.

KEITH MCALLISTER: I want a name.

JOE BASEBALL: We gave it our best shot. At least we won the second game. The season is halfway through, and we're in the playoff hunt. We're only one behind ABC.

RICK KAPLAN: Don't ever mention that network again.

TOM JOHNSON: Hey, ya'll. The VP is on the other line. I've got to drop off.

RICK KAPLAN: Oh, Jesus. Bush is pissed at CNN. He thinks Crowley is getting too close to The Shrub, hanging out at Kennebunkport. We gotta give Al equal time.

EASON JORDAN: Tell Wendy Walker to get Gore on King tomorrow. That should do it.

SID BEDINGFIELD: No can do. She's got Larry doing an entire hour on arthritis again.

FRANK SESNO: *(He breaks a Coke bottle on the edge of his desk and slowly advances toward Joe while holding a jagged piece of glass.)* Please, everyone. I just sent out my State of the Bureau note. Nobody cares about broadband convergence, feasibility studies, David Bernknopf, or Democracy in America.

JEFF MILSTEIN: *(He knocks on an open door and pops in.)* Busy, Frank?

FRANK SESNO: Perfect timing. Come in, Milstein. Hey guys, I've got an idea. What if Jeff Milstein does a Boys on the Bus nat sound piece about the CNN softball team? He could sell free *(He makes air quotation marks with his hands.)* tickets to the games and the playoffs. That will be a good kicker for the noon show, put money back in our coffers, and nurture morale—a triple play.

TED TURNER: Aaarrgh.

MELLONIE SAUNDERS: *(She sticks her head in Frank's office.)* Peggy says we need $2 million just to cover the costs of moving Jim Connor's stuff to the 6th floor.

JOE BASEBALL: How 'bout we charge admission to our softball games next week against the Washington Post and U.S. News?

FRANK SESNO: Now, you're thinking, guys.

JEFF MILSTEIN: It's doable. I also have some Diana Ross tickets left over from her canceled concert. I'll put a note in bureau.wx.read-me.

FRANK SESNO: Fine. *(He shakes hands as Jeff walks off stage.)* *(Frank looks at the speakerphone.)* Gentlemen, we're off to a good start. I'll keep you posted. *(He pushes the disconnect button.)*

Frank and Joe give each other high fives.

Lights fade, and music swells.

Curtain comes slowly down.

June 24, 2000

GAME 1		GAME 2	
FOX NEWS	17	USA TODAY	17
CNN	16	CNN	7

"News Survivor"

Eighteen current and former CNN employees, plus a multitude of other characters, are forced to abandon ship in the middle of the South China Sea, marooned for 39 days. They must work to build shelter, find food, figure out a way to salvage a softball season sinking faster than Al Gore's ratings, and stack a newscast on the tiny island of Pulau Tiga.

But ultimately, it's everyone for themselves. (Eds: Isn't that always the case in a network newsroom?) Every hour, the castaways will hike deep into the jungle to participate in the tribal council, where they must vote one of their own off the island.

Ultimately, only one person will remain to decide what packages will be above the line on The World Today with Wolf Blitzer, Joie Chen, and Jim Moret, who are "all on assignment" and once again unable to anchor together.

This is a story full of intrigue and suspense, more drama than a Chris Black script about hospital medical costs, more news than a Carolyn O'Neil package on Brussels sprouts. It's about conflict and self-preservation.

Who will be voted off, who will survive, and what, if anything, should be done about the softball team?

(Curtain rises.)

(Orchestra plays "The Ballad of Gilligan's Isle.")

(In center of stage, a man is hunched over a satellite phone.)

PETER ARNETT: CNN? Hello? Atlanta, can you hear me? This is Peter Arnett. *(Pause)* Arnett. *(Pause)* You know, Tailwind? Listen, we're on a deserted tropical island in the Pacific near Borneo. There are a bunch of us. We're fine. I'm using a flyaway and can do a beeper if you're ready.

(Scene switches to television control room in Atlanta.)

BOB FURNAD: I don't hear him, Earl. Where's the audio? You're ----ing me! You're ----ing me. *(Screaming)* Tell Hemmer to toss to Flock.

(Camera switches accidentally to anchor Daryn Kagan, who's smiling, oblivious she's on the air live.)

BILL HEMMER: We're obviously having some technical difficulties.

Let's bring in Roger Cossack, our crack legal whippersnapper, who can fill some time for us until the cue tone. That was some execution the other night, huh, pal?

JEFF FLOCK: Uh, this is Jeff, Flip.

BOB FURNAD: *(Expletive)* Not ----ing Flip, Flock. Damn it.

JEFF FLOCK: I'm here at Veirs Mill Park in Silver Spring, Maryland, where another disaster is unfolding. As you can see from this camera perched atop our dirigible, next to a camera attached to a crane, right below the 14 other cameras spread around the field, it's a scene of absolute carnage out here. CNN's softball team was swept by Fox News and USA Today, putting a severe crimp in CNN's dream to make the playoffs. Kenny, if you could pan around the basepath while I … Yes, Bobbie? *(He puts his index finger to his ear and gives the famous CNN Salute.)* You're cutting out.

BILL HEMMER: It's Bill here. Would you say the team stunk worse than the sewage spill in Biscayne Bay that Pat Neal just reported on last hour? Or the tomato truck in Dover carrying the 58 space aliens? *(No response)* Well, we'll check back with you, Jeff. We've now re-established contact with the island castaways. Joining us is Sid Bedingfield, right-hand man to Rick Kaplan. What's the latest, Sid? Is it anything like *"Lord of the Flies* where you are?" Pig heads on sticks, that sort of thing? Do you feel like the Skipper, the Professor, or Thurston Howell?

SID BEDINGFIELD: Bill, it's all about integration and convergence. Thanks to TV, the computer, wireless devices like this cell phone, and my super-duper interactive beeper, we heard about Saturday's languorous performance by the CNN softball team in real-time. No delays. No waiting for the Rim and the Row to approve notes.

MELLONIE SAUNDERS: *(She enters stage left.)* Frank Sesno, call your office. Frank Sesno, call your office.

FRANK SESNO: *(Frank is looking frazzled as he tries to build a sand castle.)* Two days ago, Steve Case did a drop-by in the D.C. newsroom. I told him we're the network of record and how we've raised the bar under my watch. I listened while he talked about tectonic and tactical issues facing us in the New Economy. I even wore the same color shirt. I never left his side. What do I get for all that? A mortifying loss to Rupert Murdoch's team, 17-16. How do you lose a game to a baffling collection of second-rate minions but score 16 runs? Don't even get me started about USA Today.

KEITH MCALLISTER: Amateur hour. I want some names.

JOE BASEBALL: It was my fault, Keith. You can cannibalize me if you want. Or you can put a note in read-me. Either way, I'm going to stab myself with these bamboo stakes *(He holds up sharp-pointed poles in a traditional Shiite display of martyrdom.)* I've already voted myself off the island. *(He exits stage right.)*

STEVE CASE: *(He puts down his Palm Pilot and personal GPS-in-a-bag.)* Good news, everyone. Shareholders approved the merger. Now we'll finally get some genuine softball players and not a bunch of know-it-all ass-kissers. Trust me. Competition can be vicious. But it would be best if they learned to cheat and backstab. Forget noble aspirations. This is the real world. *(He exits stage left.)*

CISSY BAKER: That's right, Steve. I know what it's like to work in a dysfunctional newsroom, and we don't even have a softball team at Tribune. Just ask anyone on this island. That's why I left CNN because of all the weenies in Atlanta. *(She exits stage right.)*

MRS. LEE: No hotdogs today, but I have a mystery meat special. Tastes good. Grilled. You can try it at the Friday cookout. It's better than the turkey burger at Sunrise Café. It comes with chips. *(She exits stage left.)*

EASON JORDAN: May I have your attention, please? It's my turn to vote the next person off the island. But before making the announcement, if anyone is interested, I've put my schedule for the next 18 months in International.Insights. *(He clears his throat.)* Now, without further ado, I say Peter Arnett must go.

PETER ARNETT: *(He exits at the back of the stage.)* You'll pay for this, Eason. I hope Jeanee von Essen shows up on your doorstep one day and stays for a month.

EASON JORDAN: What do you take me for, some kind of wimp like the people on the softball team? Jeanee hired me. We do Instant Messaging all the time. *(He exits stage right.)*

JEANEE VON ESSEN: *(She enters stage right carrying several bags of groceries.)* Hi guys, I've been on Pulau Tiga for the past few years. I'm bureau chief. I started my own foreign desk.

FRANK SESNO: I'm sorry, Jeanee. You said, "foreign." That's an automatic expulsion from the island. You'll have to leave. I can give you a lift. I'm on my way to London and Paris. *(Frank exits first, then Jeanee exits stage left carrying Sutton Place Gourmet grocery bags.)*

SUSAN ROOK: I've got an idea. What if we bring back CNN & Company? We could replay embarrassing highlights from the CNN softball games on our show. That would fill a half hour just recounting the exploits of Greg, Ari, Howie, John D., John K., Jenn, Arthur, Jim, Alex, Dick, Ralph, Carrey, Darrin, Chip, Eric, Tim, Virginia and Susan *(She exits stage right.)*

THE RIM: *(Telephone rings 10 times, then finally stops.)* Did anyone hear that Red Phone?

UNIDENTIFIED LIVE PRODUCER: Robert Hager has the NTSB report on JFK Junior.

THE RIM: We called Rochelle. He says it's old news. Have we got anything on Los Alamos? *(Entire Rim exits stage left.)*

NANCY AMBROSE: We're getting killed on this story. We haven't done squat. I've got to go to the future's meeting, and then I need to talk to Frank about the election packages. Someone call David Schechter and Charlie Hoff and let them know. *(She exits stage right.)*

KEITH MCALLISTER: Does anyone have any names? *(He exits through a hole in the stage floor.)*

WEN HO LEE: *(He appears wearing a white lab coat.)* I can help. I know what it takes to survive on the island in this Digital Information age—rule number one. Keep fingerprints off hard drives. Is anyone up for a scavenger hunt? *(He exits stage left.)*

BILL RICHARDSON: Talk about lost standing, supreme arrogance, and contempt. I was sickened, outraged, and ashamed when I heard what was going on. *(He exits stage right.)*

SID BEDINGFIELD: Are you referring to the 8 o'clock show, the softball team, or both? Does anyone want to join my flotilla? *(He exits stage left.)*

KEATING HOLLAND, PETER KENDALL, VITO MAGGIOLO: We do! We do! *(They all exit stage right.)*

(Scene switches back to chaotic control room in Atlanta.)

BOB FURNAD: *(He's shouting.)* Go to State. Where's Begleiter? Take the White House! Get Blitzer up! Cue Greta! Where's her mike? Go to Hemmer! Go to Hemmer!

BILL HEMMER: For those of you now joining us, let me recap. There are only four more games left on the softball schedule. Just eight teams will compete in the postseason. With the two losses on Saturday, CNN is tied for the last playoff spot at 7-7. The next games are scheduled for July 8. We're also following another breaking story—this one in the South China Sea. For the latest, we go to *(He pauses, then someone yells in his*

IFB to toss to Ben Wedeman, but Hemmer misunderstands.) Ben Franklin.

BOB FRANKEN: *(It's dusk. Waves are gently lapping against the rocks along the shoreline. There's a gorgeous sunset.)* Bill, it's Bob Franken. As you can see, I'm all by myself. Sources in White House Counsel Greg Craig's office have confirmed what many have envisioned for quite some time. Everyone has been voted off the island except for me. The good news is my package on Dick Army and Barney Frank will run in the 8p. I've already done a 7a recut by taking out a sot. The bad news is I can't get off this island anytime soon.

(The closing theme song from Gilligan's Island begins.)
(Lights fade.)
(Curtain comes down.)
(Applause.)

July 8, 2000

GAME 1		GAME 2	
CNN	27	CNN	7
NBC NEWS CHANNEL	7	CBS NEWS	0

- **CNN takes giant step toward playoffs, sweeps anemic network opponents.**
- **Carol Buckland files $6 billion defamation lawsuit against Harry Potter publisher, claims she wrote *The Goblet of Fire*, not J.K. Rowling.**
- **World Today ratings drop below point one; Sprint ads draw more viewers than newscasts, according to Nielsen.**

By Joe Baseball Jr.
Bureau Sports Writer

KENSINGTON, Md. (UPI) — Imagine what was going through the minds of every CNN softball player on an absolutely radiant Saturday at Capitalview Park. Losers of three in a row, in danger of not making the playoffs, and wondering if Andrea Koppel would get lost driving to Camp David for the Mideast Summit, CNN fell four runs behind NBC News Channel after just a half inning.

NBC in the lead? Their only wins this year were by default. Was this someone's idea of a joke? Was that Irving R. Levine at first? Jessica Savitch at second, Hugh Downs at short, and Dave Garroway on third? Chet Huntley, David Brinkley, and Frank McGee in the outfield? Andrea Mitchell pitching and Robert Hager behind the plate? CNN was flirting with disaster, the likes of which hadn't been seen since Jeff Flock's three-camera live remote of a missile silo destruction in the middle of nowhere.

What a difference a year makes, from champions to Metropolitan Media Softball League doormat.

Then it happened. Carey Bodenheimer's phone rang.

"This is Keith," said a disaffected voice on the other end. "I want names! This is unacceptable. I've had it with all of you effete muggles. I can understand screwing up a wires.cnn note, but a softball game? You, morons, stumble more than Lou Waters does in a 20-second copy story. Hell, the Aflac insurance duck has more talent. Heads are going to roll, you hear me? I want names!"

"How about David Bernknopf?" replied one unidentified player.

"Who's David Bernknopf? What does he do around here?" asked another. Before anyone could come up with an answer, the umpire ordered play to resume.

With the season teetering on the brink of failure, CNN snapped out of its funk, shook off the rust, and demolished NBC in-depth. The final, 23-7, was not as close as the score indicates. It would have been 93-7, except the umpire invoked the mercy rule after five innings so he could get home to watch Venus Williams win in straight sets at Wimbledon.

CNN sent 20 batters to the plate in the bottom of the first... Fifteen scored. The biggest hit came off the bat of Rebecca Ratliff, who leveled a based-loaded double halfway to Silver Spring. She would have made it to third base if she hadn't stopped to answer an Avstar question from the second baseman. CNN was at bat so long TBS constructed and dedicated its new $1.2 billion Turner Tower.

"Awesome," raved official scorer Virginia Nicolaidis between sips of a Starbucks double espresso with two scoops of Ben and Jerry's Coffee, Coffee BuzzBuzzBuzz.

"Sort of like Pamplona. Stop. That's no bull. Stop," cabled D.C. Bureau Chief Frank Sesno, who was on a European vacation. "I passed up a midnight cruise on the Seine so I could hang out in the bar, watch the National Missile Defense launch on CNNI, and get the softball results. Unlike the noon show, I wasn't dismayed by either result."

There were big assists from Ari (4-4, 2 RBI), Jack (3-3, 3 RBI), John

Davis (3-4, 3 RBI), John King (3-4, 4 RBI), Greg (2-3, 3 RBI), Jenn, Eric, Ralph, Carey, Paul, Dick, Arthur and Jim.

CNN's (9-7) obliteration of NBC (4-12) in the opener was too painful for its next opponent, CBS (1-15), which lickety-split forfeited. They opted to attend a Buddhist temple potluck cookout. One eyewitness said it was "like watching that ship get broadsided by hundred-foot waves in *The Perfect Storm*."

"More frightening than a first draft of a Bob Franken script," added a smug package producer. "And twice as exciting as watching the Rim fight over a Dave Adhicary note."

Another onlooker countered, "More like a blind date with Roger Cossack, one of People Magazine's most eligible bachelors."

"I'd put CNN's softball performance right up there with the always scintillating *Inside Politics* segment featuring E.J. Dionne and Bill Kristol," floundered Political Director Tom Hannon.

Whatever the comparison, CNN's pair of character wins push the team back into the Elite Eight. Only two games remain in the regular season, including another against CBS and ABC. A split will guarantee CNN one of the eight playoff slots and force this writer to spend another week finding more ways to poke fun at CNN management and keep his job.

"Your job is safe, Joe. Trust me," snapped Rick Kaplan. "I will not allow us to lose anything except the millions we will flush down the toilet at the upcoming political conventions in Philly and LA. Thank goodness we have the Internet to keep the company afloat."

"I'm rolling in dough," bragged Scott Woelfel, vice president extraordinaire of CNN Interactive in Atlanta, where 1,200 people were hired on Friday, and another 46,000 cnn.com slots were advertised on the Web. "Tell (D.C. Deputy Bureau Chief) Peggy Soucy, I'll pay for a trophy case if the softball team repeats as champions. Also, I'll fix all the soap dispensers in the men's bathrooms on the 10th and 11th floors. My treat."

You can feel the buzz in Washington.

July 22, 2000

GAME 1		GAME 2	
WASHINGTON POST	9	CNN	10
CNN	5	USA TODAY	9
GAME 3		GAME 4	
CNN	9	WASHINGTON TIMES	12
WASHINGTON POST.COM	8	CNN	9

- **CNN softball season comes to a close with gutsy effort.**
- **Team pulls off two upsets before running out of gas.**
- **Players break bones, use inhalants, then feast on beer and pizza.**
- **Eds: Note language in 7th paragraph.**

By Joe Baseball Jr.
Bureau Sports Writer

WASHINGTON (UPI) — If you're a romantic and prefer not to know how some love stories end, stop here. You're about to learn how CNN's softball team fared over the weekend in the Metropolitan Media Softball League playoffs. This is the only warning—spoiler alert. Don't read the following sentence.

CNN finished in fifth place, losing to the Washington Post, 9-5, and the Washington Times, 12-9. The two losses were sandwiched around dramatic one-run wins against USA Today, 10-9, and Washington Post. com, 9-8.

Having become the darlings of the 18 teams in the MMSL, CNN showed up on Saturday morning to begin its quest to repeat as champions in the double-loss elimination tournament. Lose twice and go home.

"Break a leg," the fans shouted as they tried but failed to start a wave. Admittedly, only one spouse, a Cocker Spaniel, and a Team Video crew were on hand. They just happened to stumble across the games at Colmar Manor Park, deep in the woods off 38th Street, some 53 miles from the nearest 7-11, a zig-zag from Bladensburg, and reachable only with the help of a GPS. We're talking remote.

For devotees of the sport, there's nothing like the smell of a leather glove and the crack of a bat hitting a ball. Unfortunately, in Game 2, when CNN players heard a snap, crackle, and pop echo across the rolling hills, they instantly knew it didn't come from a bowl of Rice Krispies.

Instead, it was poor CNN radio reporter Dick Uliano's left ankle, fractured at second base during a wicked slide to avoid a tag. His teammates did not let him down. Three immediately filed for radio, and the others forced him to crawl to the sidelines on his hands and knees. Two ambulances showed up, and one of the drivers, Dr. Bob Arnot, took one look at Dick's leg and told him, "Walk it off. I don't see any bones poking out."

CNN had already lost its first game and was trailing prohibitive favorite USA Today, 4-3. CNN was six outs away from going home when it happened.

But that's jumping ahead in the story. Let's back up to the opener.

The No. 8 seed in the playoffs versus the No. 9 seed in the form of the Washington Post. Two wild card teams by the dawn's early light. The winner would get the dubious honor of facing the No. 1 seed and eventual champion, Gazette, with a record of 14-2. "No thanks," said every player on CNN: Ari, Jack, Greg, John, Brad, Chip, Jenn, Charles, Shannon, Heather, Jim, Pete, Paul, Ralph, Dick and Eric.

"We'd rather sit at our desks all day and watch Mickey Rooney in those Garden State Life Insurance ads than play the Gazette," said one player on the bench.

"I'd prefer to have the West Nile Virus, be exposed to Anthrax, and then drive cross-country in a Chevette with Kareem Abdul-Jabbar (formerly Lew Alcindor," said another.

It didn't matter because CNN came out flat against the Washington Post.

"They looked more deflated than Larry Register did after he heard he would have to pull another all-nighter in the trailer with Vito Maggiolo in the Catoctin Mountains," blustered a staffer at Camp David, "but not for attribution."

Pitcher Greg Robertson struck out two of the first three batters. Nothing good happened after that. "We were more disorganized than the CNN D.C. Bureau's library return shelf," said a team spokesman, who fessed up he once put all of Clinton's inaugural tapes in the degaussing room as a practical joke.

CNN's play was so wretched in Game 1 that CNN pollster Keating Holland offered to revise his "GOP Convention Travel Tips to Delaware" just to get a rise out of the softball squad. Andrew Holtz, former medical correspondent, suggested the team was infected with either mad sheep or mad cow disease. "One thing is certain: Bush is dead," he reiterated.

The Post thwarted CNN, 9-5. CNN never had more than three hits in an inning. So, it was off to the loser's bracket, and it was only 10 a.m.

With a look that could wilt cabbage, Charles Bierbauer told the opposing coach, "At this rate, I'll be home in time to watch the last half hour of *CatDog* on Nickelodeon.

USA Today was the next stop—the No. 2 seed. The Gannetoids, as the Neuharth bunch is affectionately known, had already beaten CNN during the regular season, 17-7. It was not looking good. It was 4-3 in the fifth inning; CNN was down by a run when things literally broke in their favor.

Dick Uliano started the rally with his fateful encounter at second base. The team, ignoring his plea for painkillers, scored five runs in nothing flat to take an 8-4 lead, with big hits from Brad and Ralph. They got a couple more insurance runs thanks to Peter, Greg, Ari, and Jenn and held a 10-6 lead as USA Today came up for their last at-bat. USA Today scrounged together three runs before CNN closed the door.

Faster than you can download the latest Santana CD using Napster, CNN was back on the field for a third game, this time against Washington Post.com, not to be confused with the first team. In less time than it takes to hang up a Red Phone call before the operator says, "Your conference controller has been disconnected. Please hang up to end this conference," CNN fell behind, 6-0.

But the day was far from over. Trailing 7-5 and the fat lady itching to sing, CNN scored four runs in the top of the seventh inning, the big tie-breaking hit coming with two outs by Chip Herzel. Post.com had its final turn at bat. They scored one run to make it 9-8, but with the tying run at first, Pete Hartogs sprinted in to catch a sinking fly ball off his shoe tops and fire to first base to complete the breath-taking game-ending double play. CNN would survive again.

"Tell those folks at *Inside Politics* with their wimpy T-shirts, we are the true survivors," bragged one player who spoke on the condition of anonymity but later said he bought 25 of the shirts from the IP unit.

CNN had to play again before anyone could look for Kevin Bohn's lost sandal or figure out their after-tax gains from the latest AOL-Time Warner earnings statement. The time was 1 p.m., hour four of the softball marathon, longer than a Mideast summit.

"It was like a M.A.S.H. unit out there. Bodies sprawled everywhere. We had two players using inhalants to breathe," said one eye-witness.

Exhibiting the conviction of Israeli Prime Minister Ehud Barak's Likud Party, with the heat index at 110, humidity virtually visible, and a kettle of vultures flying above, CNN prepared to face its fourth opponent of the day, the Washington Times.

Never mind, the Times had already beaten CNN twice this year and held clandestine practices after work every night for the past two weeks. CNN was ready to prove its mettle under pressure. CNN would have won if the game had ended after the first inning, but the games go seven innings.

Ahead 3-1, CNN allowed the Times to bat around and score eight runs in the second inning to take an overwhelming advantage. There was more confusion in the outfield than in George W. Bush's vice-presidential selection process. CNN closed the gap to 12-9 and had two runners on base, but their luck ran out.

Their season, which started in March with pre-season practices, included some 24 players at various times and got a mention in U.S. News & World Report, was over. There is no Tiger Woods ending here.

TOP OF THE 4th

Close but No Cigar

April 14, 2001

- **MMSL season begins Saturday with new faces and uniforms.**
- **CNN team ready despite offseason of mass layoffs, less news, more fluff, and hanging chads.**
- **Lou Dobbs to host *The Lou Dobbs Hour*, opposite *Wolf Blitzer Reports*; management to simulcast with big box/little box.**

By Joe Baseball Jr.
Bureau Sports Writer

WASHINGTON (UPI) — The looming question facing CNN executives in Atlanta this week is not the future employment status of White House Correspondent John King, or what makes the Super Desk super, or whether to force correspondent Lisa Rose Weaver to pay for the $25,000 videophone she handed over to the Chinese on Hainan Island. The front office wants to know how good CNN's softball team will be this year.

"The days of softball detritus are long gone. We have a new foundational philosophy," said Eason Jordan, CNN's president of news gathering and international networks, in a statement released over the weekend. "We have our competitors in a tizzy. I may not be able to afford Jeff Milstein's Jimmy Buffett tickets at Merriweather Post Pavilion, but I will personally book every uplink from here to Guam and integrate and converge every platform in our company to put our Washington softball team back on top."

When we last checked in, it was late July. Flip Spiceland was doing the weather, Carl Rochelle was doing live shots, and Arem Roston was doing whatever he did.

Since then, CNN has hired the Gadget Guy (his actual name) and started a weekly gabfest called *Take Five*, with ratings lower than the Celebrex commercials. What a difference a merger makes. Despite the turmoil and revamping of the network, the softball team is intact, and it's the paragon of virtue everyone has come to expect.

"In many ways, it will be a new CNN, softball players full of swagger and style, with our usual motley crew of oddballs," Tom Johnson, the news group chairman, said in an interview on Fox News Channel's *The O'Reilly Factor*. "I tried to get on CNN, but *Larry King Live* booked Ann

Compton and Hugh Sidey every night this week, and they didn't have time for me."

"Amateur hour," said a wigged-out New York Bureau Chief Keith McAllister. "I want names."

All of this uncertainty follows a newsroom visit a few weeks ago on Ash Wednesday from Ted Turner, who took one look at some of the employees in the Washington bureau and called them "a bunch of Jesus freaks." His version of a pep talk did little to spearhead excitement and erase the memory of last season. The Catholic League immediately announced it would boycott this year's games.

CNN (10-7) finished in fifth place out of 18 teams last year, a step back from its championship season in 1999 but still a respectable showing.

The 2001 Metropolitan Media Softball League has mushroomed to 20 teams this spring with the addition of National Geographic (featuring ex-CNNers Rebecca Ratliff and Kevin Enochs) and AOL, a neophyte squad equipped with Blackberrys so they can instant message one another during the games.

The stakes have never been higher for CNN. First, the MMSL increased its annual entry fee to $495. Then, players stormed into the office of D.C. Deputy Bureau Chief Peggy Soucy and demanded new uniforms to replace the old worn-out T-shirts. Management opened its petty cash drawer and came up with the money to avoid a sartorial controversy.

"We had no choice but to step forward," salivated D.C. Bureau Chief Frank Sesno, "But I will not apologize. The newsroom was like a roiling Hell broth of suppressed melancholy. Besides, the FERC garage will be closed again this weekend for power washing. I was boxed in."

CNN's softball team will be ready for its first doubleheader on Saturday against perennial doormat Fox News in Game 1 and last year's division winner ABC News in Game 2. The coaches say they will shine HMI lights into the eyes of opposing hitters if the situation warrants.

"Whatever it takes to get a competitive edge," complained one CNN photographer.

It's unclear who will be in the starting lineup on Opening Day, but CNN has veterans and rookie players ready to go.

Names like Bierbauer, Lynn, Lutt, Marcus, and Hartogs. There's also King, Davis, Roberston, White, Tavcar, and colts such as Kyle Johnsen, David Gracey, Willie Lora, Lindy Royce, and Beth Lewandowski.

April 21, 2001

GAME 1		GAME 2	
CNN	9	CNN	10
FOX NEWS	8	ABC NEWS	4

- **CNN opens season with big wins against Fox and ABC.**
- **Star player breaks right hand but stays in the game.**
- **Faster than walking out of the LA Bureau with a TV set, CNN bats come alive to pull off two come-from-behind victories.**

By Joe Baseball Jr.
Bureau Sports Writer

KENSINGTON, Md. (UPI) — CNN's dramatic doubleheader romp on Saturday came with a considerable price tag. Coach Jack Lynn broke his right pinky knuckle while tagging out a runner in the first game. His status is day-to-day. In any event, he can still type in Avstar using his little toe.

"The worst part is, it's my drinking hand," sighed Lynn. The team's trainer also reported several other players had colorful bruises, abrasions, and sore muscles.

Credit CNN's unwavering determination as the season got off to a glorious start.

Trailing 8-3 against pesky Fox News, CNN was down to its last nine outs in the MMSL home opener at Capitalview Park.

"Fox was sandbagging us worse than what I saw the folks doing along the Mississippi River in Davenport," smirked reporter Jeff Flock between live shots for CNN, Newsource, CNNI, and radio.

By most accounts, the mindset on the field was as dreary as the daily editorial meetings in Atlanta, bleaker than the weekly future future's meetings in D.C., as confusing as the Stories-1 rundown, and more hopeless than a fishing trip aboard the Ehime Maru, the Japanese trawler that hit a U.S. submarine near Hawaii.

"You could see the despair in their eyes," commented one unctuous spectator. "Just like in January when employees were hauled into personnel offices and told to clean out their desks while armed security officers stood watch."

"They didn't have guns, and if they did, they weren't loaded," clarified

Sid Bedingfield, executive vice president and general manager of CNN/US. "It was just pepper spray and mace, the same thing the riot police used in the streets of Quebec City during the Summit of Americas.

Reached at CNN Center, network executive Phil Kent was disgusted by the aging cable news team's performance in the first few innings.

"We're talking about Fox News, for God's sake," he said, foaming at the mouth. That's when an idea occurred to him. Kent hastily arranged a Blackberry conference call with other AOL Time Warner brass to figure out how to capitalize on the doddery start to the softball season and the soaring popularity of NBC's new cringe-worthy quiz show, *Weakest Link*.

"This is a once-in-a-lifetime shot for Steve Case and Gerald Levin," said Kent. "We're looking at a long softball season with a bunch of losers. Let's develop a reality-based half-hour program hosted by Willow Bay and Bill Hemmer that follows the softball team and each of its weakest links. Then, we lay off a different player every Friday until there's only one left."

"I wish I had thought of that," said Jamie Kellner, chief executive officer of the WB Network.

Garth Ancier, new executive vice president of programming, added, "We can lighten our payroll and do 30 minutes less news, which no one watches anyway. More time for good shows like *Spin Room*, *Talk Back Live*, *What's the Point*, and a new program in development called *Truth or Consequences with host April Oliver*."

"Brilliant," shouted CNN Vice President Keith McCallister. "But we'll need some names."

A spokesman for Washington Bureau Chief Frank Sesno refused to comment. The story doesn't end there.

CNN's softball team, resplendent in spotless new uniforms, mounted a sensational return from the dead and stormed back to upend Fox News, 9-8. They scored six runs in the last three innings to avoid the shame of regifting a lead.

There were heroes galore. Greg Robertson, who clubbed a homer in the fourth inning, hit a bases-loaded triple in the bottom of the fifth to cut Fox's advantage to 8-6. John Davis kept CNN in the game, going 4-4, with a mammoth two-run homer. Heather Shaw tied the score by knocking in two runs with a consequential at-bat. Then Howie Lutt sealed the victory with a line drive to center field, bringing home Lynn, who started the inning with a single.

"We executed our game strategy beyond reproach, and I know a thing

The 2001 CaNiNes just missed a championship repeat but had a lot to smile about.

or two about staying executions," grinned Charles Bierbauer, who received a stiff reprimand from MMSL Commissioner Dennis Tuttle after teammates recognized the well-known CNN Justice Department reporter at first base wearing Supreme Court briefs.

In the second game against ABC News, CNN had another slow start, falling behind 4-2. The team came out with less energy than the Chernobyl power station and the state of California combined. But gutsy performances by Erik Tavcar, 5-5, and Lynn, 4-7, with 2 RBI, propelled the team to victory in the nightcap, 10-4.

CNN broke the game open in the sixth inning when the first four batters (Lutt, Robertson, Alex Dermanis, and Bierbauer) got on base and scored.

There was also welcome support and defensive gems from the other players: Kyle Johnsen, Jessica Rosgaard, Beth Lewandowski, Kim Abbott, David Gracey, Lindy Royce, Angie Tarrant, and Jim Barnett.

"ABC has *Who Wants to be a Millionaire*, CBS has *Survivor* and Fox *Temptation Island*, but nobody can beat our *Ask CNN* reality segment," ballyhooed Jim Walton, CNN news group president of domestic networks, who owned up that his quote was off message and irrelevant.

The two wins put CNN in first place in its division, one of only five teams left undefeated in the league after just the first week. CNN faces challenging games this weekend at Layhill Field against last year's champions, Gazette and NewsChannel 8.

For the very latest, go to the MMSL web page or peruse the CNN dead file in BASYS for something better.

April 28, 2001

GAME 1		GAME 2	
CNN	12	GAZETTE	14
NEWSCHANNEL 8	7	CNN	12

- **CNN experiences thrill of victory and agony of defeat.**
- **MTV's _Jackass_ to run highlights of media softball games.**
- **Socialite Denise Rich and legal firebrand Roger Cossack host new show called _Beg Your Pardon._**
- **Eds: Note language in 3rd graph; correct name Headline Nudes to Headline News.**
- **DELETES reference to no high school diploma nor any journalism experience.**
- **ADDS links and tips on how to get job as network anchor.**

By Joe Baseball Jr.
Bureau Sports Writer

LAYHILL, Md. (UPI) — Three games into a season full of strategic ambiguity, things seemed to be turning around for CNN's softball team.

Shrugging off the label that its players were a bunch of manipulative Machiavellian psychopaths, CNN won its third in a row, slapping hapless NewsChannel 8, 12-7, on a fab Saturday at Layhill Park.

It was such a convincing win that the tottering local news station changed its name to NewsChannel 3 and promised never to associate itself with the news business again.

Then, in the second game, before opposing players could say the name Louise Schiavone, CNN zipped in front of Gazette with six runs in the first inning. CNN batters treated the weekly newspaper like it was target practice on the island of Vieques.

What a week!

CNN scooped every other media outlet when it let the cat out of the bag and said _Moneyline_ anchor supremo Lou Dobbs had been rehired. "He's baaack!" is the new advertising slogan conjured up by CNN's crack PR department.

Headline News plucked Andrea Thompson, the former actress on _NYPD Blue_, from Albuquerque to anchor their primetime news. "We got her before Hooters did," said a strutting Rolando Santos, executive vice president and general manager.

If that wasn't good enough, TV Guide reported that CBS and CNN had agreed in principle to a partnership that would merge the two news organizations.

"It's the crème de la crème of the broadcasting world," CNN's Eason Jordan, the head of CNN newsgathering, referenced in a company-wide memo in Internat.Insights. "Other than the softball team, we have little prestige, no stars, but lots of money in the coffers. By the way, I'll be opening up a bureau next week in Punta Arenas, Chile."

Industry insiders say Executive Vice President in Charge of Domestic Programming, Sid Bedingfield, at a recent weekend retreat with other company executives at The Homestead, discussed replacing *Crossfire* with *Everybody Loves Raymond* episodes.

"We think we can build an audience in that time slot," commented Bedingfield. "Right now, we have an average of 62 people watching between 7:30p and 8p. But if we get Fox to give us *Malcolm in the Middle* and *Ally McBeal*, it would be a dynamite lead-in to *Larry King Live*."

"What about *Wolf Blitzer Reports*," asked someone sporting a skull tattoo on his forehead.

AOL Chairman Steve Case blurted out, "Never mind that. Did you see the company stock option plan is now worth something? Maybe people will think positive thoughts and stop dwelling on the negative."

The comments came after the stock market closed and AOL Time Warner reported first-quarter earnings of $56 billion.

CNN continues to make flubs. The network expressed remorse for running a package about a phony CIA officer. "We were two minutes into it when my producer told me the CIA segment was about the Culinary Institute of America, not the Central Intelligence Agency," said anchor Daryn Kagan. "I asked Leon (Harris) to be sure, but there was confusion in the control room."

On *Inside Politics*, anchor Judy Woodruff was interviewing Senator Bob Kerrey when an OA hollered that they were running a VO of comedian Drew Carey. "At least we had the font spelled correctly. So, get off my back," said irate Executive Producer Tom Hannon with molar-grinding distaste.

And when things couldn't get worse for the network, CNN's softball team choked against the feckless ne'er-do-well Gazette, losing a heart-breaker, 14-12. After the game, opposing players rubbed salt in the wound by taunting CNN with a chorus of "Cable Nudes Network."

"Nothing more than a delusional power grab by print journalists," rebuffed Washington Bureau Chief Frank Sesno. "We're tired of feeling demeaned and beaten down. It's high time we have grandiose fantasies instead of half-baked ideas from the future's meeting like a three-part series on Jenna Bush's alcohol citation."

"What we need is some warm magazine lighting," remarked producer Jeff Milstein on his way out the door to a Wolf Trap performance.

No one was willing to point fingers at any amateurs.

"I want names," ordered CNN Vice President Keith McCallister. "Who can we blame? Was it Charles Bierbauer, Greg Robertson, John Davis, Howie Lutt, John King, David Gracey, Alex Dermanis, Darrin White, Heather Shaw, Jessica Rosgaard, Pete Hartogs, Ralph Marcus, Kyle Johnsen, Virginia Nicolaidis, Jim Barnett, Erik Tavcar or the lone bystander Arthur Hardy?"

From the top of the order to the bottom, it was like a self-destructing tape on *Mission Impossible*.

Ahead 6-0 after the first eight batters reached base, CNN allowed the Gazette to come back and tie the game 10-10 in the bottom of the fifth inning. Gazette took advantage of a porous defense and took the lead for the first time all day, and CNN fell just short of what coulda, woulda, shoulda been a sweep.

"I hadn't seen so many pores since I put powder on Catherine Crier's face three years ago," said makeup artist Skip Smith.

It was all smiles in the opening game as CNN assailed the journalists from the regional cable outfit NewsChannel 8, dispelling any notion that softball is all local.

The CNN Stars of the Game went to Tavcar, 7-7 (12-12 for the season); Robertson, 8-8; Davis, 3-4, 5 RBI, two-run homer; and Gracey, 5-6, including two triples and a two-run homer.

A special citation goes to Johnsen, Hartogs, and Marcus, who willingly sat out the second game to allow the starters to finish. "Hey, what's a few splinters? We can stay on the bench as long as Sandra Day O'Connor," they said.

The team has two weeks to recalibrate because no games are scheduled this Saturday. CNN is back in action on May 12 at Veirs Mill Park in a matchup of have-nots, WTTG and WUSA.

May 12, 2001

GAME 1		GAME 2	
CNN	19	CNN	12
WTTG	4	WUSA	4

- **CNN softball team administers lethal injection in doubleheader execution.**
- **Timothy McVeigh rings closing bell on Wall Street alongside Lou Dobbs.**
- **Andrea Koppel denies hugging Secretary of State Colin Powell, says she was performing a new Heimlich Maneuver.**
- **Eds: Also moving on financial wires.**

By Joe Baseball Jr.
Bureau Sports Writer

SILVER SPRING, Md. (UPI) — It's the buzz from Wall Street to Peachtree Street, Hollywood and Vine to Constitution Avenue and 17th Street. They're calling it the "Lou Dobbs" effect.

There's no other plausible explanation for what happened on Saturday at Veirs Mill Park, where CNN's softball team pureed its two opponents, WTTG and WUSA, 19-4 in the opener and 12-4 in the nightcap, before the largest crowd of the year, six people.

"The D.C. Bureau doesn't need lily-livered local affiliates to tell us how to play the game," screeched Washington Bureau Chief Frank Sesno. "We're not like Atlanta. Those folks down South couldn't cover a story in their own backyard if it bit 'em in the butt. WAGA-TV is always bailing their asses out. By the way, if you allow me to provide a transition line, 'Welcome back, Sir Lou!'"

The conservative commentator, author, conspiracy theorist, and former TV host made a triumphant return this week to the fledgling network after a brief hiatus trying to launch Space.com. He brings the kind of conviction CNN hasn't seen since Ralph Wenge anchored the weekends, Don Lennox produced *NewsNight*, and Eric Gershon did the two-minute week-in-review.

CNN's first-place ranking has not gone unnoticed. Even wires.cnn referenced the lopsided games in a story written and edited by Paul Varian about J.Lo and Destiny's Child among today's top entertainment stories.

"We screwed up some numbers and the dateline, but I dare you to find anything else that's exculpatory," Varian growled.

Against WTTG (3-3), CNN (5-1) used a stockpiled nerve agent to score in every inning as they played with pop and fearlessness. Thankfully, mercifully, the mercy rule was invoked in the fifth, which helped put the Fox affiliate and the home plate umpire out of their misery.

"There was no connection between my headache and my inability to read every lower third CNN banner," said the ordinarily loquacious umpire, who won $50 for correctly pronouncing the name of CNN's new Medical Correspondent, Dr. Sanjay Gupta.

Among the standout performers in the first game was Howie Lutt. He handled the bat like a control room joy stick, clubbing three home runs and getting eight RBI. John Davis hit for the cycle with four RBI, and Greg Robertson had four RBI of his own, going 3-4, including a three-run homer. Along with Erik Tavcar, who also went 3-4, the first four batters in the lineup accounted for 17 of CNN's 19 runs. Everyone played and got on base at least one time.

"I hadn't seen that many hits since the last batch of SX tapes were degaussed," said Operations Manager Mark Sweet, sporting an 'I Love Lou' button.

"It's not a recession unless I say so," uttered Dobbs during a three-camera sit-down interview with himself in the Royal Suite at the Four Seasons Hotel in Georgetown. When asked to comment about the action on the field, Dobbs looked in the mirror and replied, "Tell Kaplan to kiss my ---. I'm back on top and taking the softball team to the Promise Land with or without the Rim, the Super Desk, and the White House unit."

In a wide-ranging interview that included such topics as the banality of *The Spin Room*, the importance of interns in the back row on *Burden of Proof* and Joie Chen, Dobbs promised to forfeit part of his $44 million salary to buy new bases for the softball team as well as help teach Andrea Thompson how to read a TelePrompTer.

"I've given myself fast-track authority. That means cutting *IP* back to 30 minutes and expanding *Moneyline* to four-and-a-half hours. I also want to see more Joe Baseball stories in read-me with plenty of references to Eason, Sid, Keith, and the Chad Lad."

"Don't forget CNN's complete reinvention of newsgathering to align our activities with the varied needs of worldwide, multi-platform news business services," CNN News Group Chairman Tom Johnson added.

"Fuhgeddaboudit," seethed Executive Producer Nancy Ambrose during a meeting with company executives to discuss what to do about the proliferation of meetings at the company. "I won't make any decisions about anything until after my next meeting. In the interim, I will fill the weekend producer slot with someone from ABC. I have scheduled three meetings with Frank to talk about it."

The second game against WUSA was no talk, and all action. It was a decimation from the start, as CNN was ahead 11-0 before giving up four runs in the sixth inning. John King (no relation to Larry) was 4-4 with five RBI. Shannon Feaster-Stewart collected three hits in four at-bats.

Mandatory courtesies also go to Ralph, Charles, Willie, Angie, Jack, Heather, Lindy, and Jim for fine performances and team spunk. CNN's sweep allows it to maintain a one-game lead in the Capitalview Division against ABC.

CNN is back in action this Saturday against NBC News Channel and the National Press Club. Catch the wave. Come see what everyone is talking about. It's twice as much fun as reading bureau.wx.read-me.

June 2, 2001

GAME 1		GAME 2	
WASHINGTON POST.COM	11	CNN	20
CNN	6	U.S. NEWS	10

- CNN players implicated in Gold Club inquiry after showing bipolar traits.
- Softball team rolls over like SUV on I-95 in opener, then launches D-Day offensive in nightcap.
- DELETES animated TV series *Clifford the Big Red Dog* gets better ratings than *Moneyline*.

By Joe Baseball Jr.
Bureau Sports Writer

WHEATON, Md. (UPI) — For a fleeting second on Saturday at a soggy Wheaton Forest field, CNN's softball team played like the company it represents: helter-skelter and in need of shock therapy. Think Checkout Channel. Satellite News Network. Cable Music Channel.

It got so bad Paula Jones, who dropped her sexual harassment lawsuit against former President Bill Clinton three years ago, threatened to reveal "distinguishing characteristics" about each player.

CNN had more chances in the first game than Darryl Strawberry at a Florida parole hearing. "I couldn't tell who was more plastered, CNN or Jenna Bush, after a night at Chuy's," said a Secret Service agent who happened to be driving by.

Unable to keep to a 3-0 lead after two innings, CNN (6-2) unraveled against undefeated Washington Post.com, losing 11-6.

The funk didn't last too long as the team rebounded from just its second loss of the year to eviscerate U.S. News, 20-10, in the second game, a football score that looked closer than it was, thanks to a generous gift of six runs from CNN in the last inning.

It was an unusual day. Both games were played on the outfield grass to avoid the saturated base paths following a day of rain. Former CNN anchor Bernard Shaw took time from his gardening in Takoma Park to tend to the water-logged infield. "Call me again, anytime," chortled Shaw, who spends his days watching his Shirley Temple and Ed Sullivan video collections. "Sometimes, I turn on *The Final Point* for a laugh," he added.

The doubleheader split leaves CNN and ABC sharing first place in the Capitalview Division, with CNN holding the tiebreaker. "It's a power-sharing thing like Daschle/McCain," extrapolated Bill Schneider in his widely popular Political Play of the Week segment.

The unanswered question is, what accounted for the day and night difference between the two softball games? According to CNN's Frank Newport in Princeton, New Jersey, "Our latest Gallup poll showed the other team scored more runs than CNN."

"It's helpful to break it down like that for our viewers," said Lou Waters. "Back to you, Natalie, what's next?"

AOL Time Warner executives responded to the public indignity at the hands of Post.com. CEO Jamie Kellner immediately shuffled the CNN primetime lineup and hired the Video Professor to supplant anchor Bill Hemmer, who was reassigned to stand in the newsroom and talk to a cardboard cut-out of Joie Chen twice a day and then wave to tour groups.

"It's not as easy as it looks. It's gotten my dander up," Hemmer said.

The Cable News Network could barely muster a scoring threat in the opener. Only three times did it manage to send more than four batters to the plate in an inning. Said a disgruntled interloper, "CNN's knack for losing is not limited to viewers and laid-off Digital Interactive employees."

A smart aleck source within the company dared to say that CNN's lack of offense makes California's power problems pale in comparison. "Vermont Senator James Jeffords lights up a room with more energy than our entire team put forth against Post.com."

"I haven't seen a collapse like that since Lucent broke off merger talks with Alcatel," fumed Lou Dobbs, host of *Lou Dobbs Moneyline*.

"Let's hope the money we make from higher monthly AOL access rates will lead to new initiatives, help attain ambitious financial goals, support Space.com, pay for my future speaking trips to Amelia Island, and teach our team how to hit a softball," he grumbled. "Then maybe we can stop running those Ditropan XL commercials about the woman with the overactive bladder."

In an unrelated segue, Dobbs denied published reports he's demanding the network put an apostrophe after the 's' in his last name.

Thankfully, the first part of the day wasn't a total loss. Jack Lynn, 2-3 (reactivated from the DL after six weeks with a broken finger), David Gracey, 2-3 including a home run, Greg Robertson, 2-3, and Brad Wright, 2-3, were human wrecking balls. The rest, including Willie, Jim, Howie, Alex, Charles, Heather, Beth, Lindy, Ralph, Eric, and Virginia, mostly watched, kept score, and discussed the parliamentary crisis in Nepal.

It was a stark contrast in Game 2. CNN left its calling card in the form of a cogent attack, scoring in every inning but one against U.S. News. "Someday, maybe your company will have as many vice presidents as ours," trilled one CNN fan in silhouette.

Each batter got at least one hit as the team amassed its highest run total of the season. Brad went 4-5 with two triples. Eric Hoffman made his debut, going 4-4, and Lindy was 2-2 with an RBI. CNN scored four runs in the first inning and added six more in the fourth. That's when most of the fans (two) headed for the exits.

Credit also goes to the coaches who shrugged off the woeful opening performance and worked their magic to lower the level of vitriol and dampen the visceral feeling of betrayal. But enough about Mrs. Lee's garlic muffins. (And you didn't think I'd get that in.)

The next games for CNN aren't any easier or more significant than the doubleheader on Saturday against division rivals CBS News and Fox News at Capitalview field.

June 9, 2001

GAME 1		GAME 2	
CNN	15	CNN	16
CBS NEWS	4	FOX NEWS	4

- **CNN delivers big hurt to rival networks in doubleheader romp.**
- **Softball team holds on to first place as season passes halfway point.**
- **Eds: SUBS 3rd headline Missing intern Chandra Levy hired by Headline News.**

By Joe Baseball Jr.
Bureau Sports Writer

KENSINGTON, Md. (UPI) — *In a stunning development, top executives at AOL Time Warner summoned Joe Baseball Jr. to Atlanta for urgent talks after growing weary of his weekly softball writeups. Company officials reacted with commando-like precision, hauling him to the North Tower at CNN Center for what was described as "frank" (no relation to Washington D.C. Bureau Chief Sesno) discussions about Joe Baseball's ongoing series of excoriating wire stories, loosely disguised as mainstream journalism. Here are excerpts from that meeting:*

SID BEDINGFIELD: Come in and have a seat, Joe.

JOE BASEBALL: Thanks.

SID BEDINGFIELD: It's good to see you. Been too long.

EASON JORDAN: Do you know why you were on an AirTran flight and ordered down here for our regular Monday leadership meeting?

JOE BASEBALL: Not precisely. Does it have something to do with the softball games over the weekend or the decision by the affiliate desk to spend $2,500 on a live helicopter feed of a bear swimming in a California pool?

SID BEDINGFIELD: Joe, you know that was a legitimate news event. Our audience research shows that viewers love animal stories as well as boat shows.

JOE BASEBALL: What about McVeigh?

EASON JORDAN: Execution stories rank right up there, too. That's why we sent Jeff Flock and a support staff of 350 to Oklahoma. I put a note in Internat Insights. Now, what about the softball games?

JOE BASEBALL: Well, let me start at the beginning. CNN creamed CBS News in the opener on Saturday at Capitalview Park, 15-4. Then they stomped all over Fox News in the nightcap, 16-4. It was so ugly the umpire ended the game so everyone could hurry home and watch *Pinnacle*.

KEITH MCALLISTER: I once watched that program. It was on right after *Newsmaker Saturday*.

PHIL KENT: Keith, please. Tell me about the games, Joe.

JOE BASEBALL: Well, there's not much to say. CNN's first eight runs came from homers. CNN hit four taters: two by David Gracey, who celebrated his 24th birthday, and two by John Davis. Between them, they had 11 RBI.

SUE BUNDA: What's a tater and a rib-ee? Sounds like Mrs. Lee's daily special, which I hear so much about.

ROB YOON: Hey, anybody want a prune muffin? I also picked up a garlic-flavored one.

SID BEDINGFIELD: Rob, this is a private conversation. Please hang up. Joe, keep going.

JOE BASEBALL: Before I forget, Erik Tavcar, Willie Lora, and Ralph Marcus each went 3-4. Charles Bierbauer even had a triple.

SID BEDINGFIELD: Wow. He's remarkable! I hate to see Bierbauer go. I'll never forget the day he told me what SCOTUS and POTUS meant. He's the only person on our staff who understands and can use words with more than three syllables, albeit surreptitiously.

JOE BASEBALL: His leaving is a significant loss for CNN. He's had more scoops at first base than Major Garrett, Kelly Wallace, and John King combined.

JIM WALTON: Excuse me for interrupting. This is Jim Walton. I used to be in charge of CNN Sports Illustrated. Were there any highlights that would work for the sponsored Play of the Day segment?

JOE BASEBALL: Not really, even though CNN demolished Fox in the second game.

EASON JORDAN: Does Bill O'Reilly play for them?

JOE BASEBALL: No. Even if he did, he's not a "factor."

KEITH MCALLISTER: This is not the time or the place for your irreverent sense of humor, Joe. Give me some more names.

JOE BASEBALL: How about Lindy and her parents, Alex and her boyfriend, Heather, Jessica, Jim, Eric, and Virginia? They all showed up when they could have just stayed home and watched Jeff Greenfield.

EASON JORDAN: How about a read-out on the Fox game?

JOE BASEBALL: CNN batted around in the first inning and scored eight runs. The team looked out of this world despite not having three regular starters. Fox couldn't do anything except shout: "We have Catherine Crier and Terry Keenan. Nana nana boo boo."

SID BEDINGFIELD: Did CNN ignore their taunts?

JOE BASEBALL: No way. They yelled back, "Big deal. We have Miles O'Brien, Tim O'Brien, Pat O'Brien, and Bill Hemmer."

TON JOHNSON: Who's Hemmer?

EASON JORDAN: Tom, uh, I'll talk to you after the meeting. *(Phone rings)*

GARBLED VOICES: Floyd Abrams report… Moorer… $100 million… Buskirk … Oliver… Smith… Kaplan.

INTERCOM: Frank Sesno, call your office.

FRANK SESNO: If you'll excuse me, the Rim has dropped the ball again. I've gotta say the Atlanta job is looking better and better. Oh, I have some good news. The new electronic ankle monitors are in. We can start assigning them to package producers this week.

SID BEDINGFIELD: We've been joined on this conference call by Steve and Jerry, who are in New York. Gentlemen, Joe is here with us.

JOE BASEBALL: Whoa, this is better than AOL Instant Messaging.

STEVE CASE: Jerry and I have earmarked a billion dollars to hire a staff of speech writers for Lou Dobbs. We might have some money left over to pay for Aaron Brown's PR people. Where do things stand with the softball team, Joe?

JOE BASEBALL: CNN and ABC are tied for first place with 8-2 records, but CNN holds the tiebreaker since they beat ABC earlier in the year. Next Saturday was supposed to be an off week, but CNN will make up the two games rained out against NBC News Channel and the National Press Club.

GERALD LEVIN: It's imperative that we maintain our superiority. I can't stress enough the importance of AOL Time Warner's grand unified theory of media cosmos. Who cares if CNN is dull TV? It's a GREAT brand. We have Looney Tunes, HBO, People, Sports Illustrated, the WB, the Braves, and you can't leave out Jeanne Moos.

STEVE CASE: Sid, that was some package she did on pantyhose for men. It doesn't get any better than that.

SID BEDINGFIELD: Thank you, sir. We were proud of it.

EASON JORDAN: First-rate programming and production. Now, if we could just do something about the New York Bureau's softball team. I haven't seen garbage like that since Sonia Friedman was on our air back in the '80s.

SUE BUNDA: Where do we go from here?

KEITH MCALLISTER: I'm headed to Stone Mountain for the laser show. Aren't the carvings of Confederate leaders amazing?

SUE BUNDA: Keith, please.

PHIL KENT: But what about Joe? He always writes embarrassing stories about CNN, bringing dishonor to the entire company.

TOM JOHNSON: It's the first thing our employees read every Monday morning. He makes up quotes and exaggerates. But I will say he's got quite a following and keen insights.

EASON JORDAN: He taunts management. But I heard the people in charge of standards and practices always sign off on the softball writeups. Pilar in legal, too. They like his wry wit.

KEITH MCALLISTER: We are the laughing stock of the network, except for *Moneyline*. It's outrageous. Joe Baseball thumbs his nose at all we stand for.

JIM WALTON: What should we do with him?

SID BEDINGFIELD: The same thing we do with any employee around here who thinks they know too much. We need to promote them, give them a raise, and make them vice president.

JOE BASEBALL: I wouldn't mind becoming vice president of something. I know it's not a big deal because everybody is a vice president. I could be the official fill-in for David Bernknopf.

KEITH MCALLISTER: We must figure out how to end the wise-cracking and brash talking. There's enough blame to go around. I'm not just talking about Bob Franken's packages on the missing intern. It's high time we start cracking the whip around here.

JOE BASEBALL: If you gentlemen are through, I need to get back to work. I have another softball column to write.

(Tape ends)

June 23, 2001

GAME 1		GAME 2	
WASHINGTON TIMES	14	USA TODAY	14
CNN	3	CNN	2

- **Softball team takes gut punch and gets swept in doubleheader fiasco.**
- **IBM supercomputer Deep Blue has breakdown after CNN's performance.**

By Joe Baseball Jr.
Bureau Sports Writer

BETHESDA, Md. (UPI) — It's an early Saturday morning in June. It's been raining for two days in Montgomery County, Maryland. Humidity is at 100%. The setting is a mucky softball field at Burning Tree Park in Bethesda. The ground is saturated. Huge puddles dot the perimeter of the infield. It's the kind of mess not seen since CNN officially changed its name to the Chandra News Network.

Swarming gnats dart for the eyes. Blisters form on the players' hands after raking divots filled with water along the third base line. Welcome to Lake Lanier. It's also a good day for fishing.

Stand motionless for a nanosecond and close your eyes. Is this a hallucination? Shouldn't ordinary people be asleep on Saturday morning or watching live shots of the Gadget Man and Donna Kelly riding bikes through Centennial Park? Maybe this is reality television or, as the Washington Post put it, 'a continuance of the summer of sadism'.

It's the setting for another theatrical matinee off-Broadway with CNN and the Metropolitan Media Softball League.

(Curtain rises)

(Bleachers have been constructed on the stage to resemble a softball field. Current and former CNN employees are all around. It's reunion day, and CNN is playing a doubleheader against the Washington Times and USA Today.)

(CNN softball players enter stage left. The umpire throws out the first ball. The leadoff hitter for the Washington Times gets ready for the first pitch.)

ANDREA ARSENAUX: I'm glad to see so many of my CNN pals.

This brings back great memories like the time I anchored *Evening News* and called the people of Lebanon 'Lesbianese.' How was I supposed to know? I've never been to Pennsylvania.

(Faster than anyone can spell Kaczaraba, the Washington Times scored eight runs in the top of the first inning.)

DON FARMER: *(shaking his head)* This is bush-league. There are more women than men in the lineup! Was there a Million Man March in D.C. today? U.S. military forces in the Persian Gulf are on higher alert than this softball menagerie. If you want to talk about talent, bring back the team of Ham n' Cheese. Three cheers for *Prime News*!

DANIEL SCHORR: Don't forget, all things considered, I brought instant eminence to *Newswatch* with my thought-provoking commentaries years ago. We had quite a group: stumblin' Lou Waters, veteran Bill Zimmerman, and the phone lady, Mary Alice Williams. We did more news in two hours than the rest of the network in a month.

CHARLIE CAUDILL: Those were the days. Don Miller and Marcia Ladendorf doing the news for the TBS cut-ins, and Dallas Raines on weather. We were flying by the seat of our pants, baby, rock 'n roll, none of this musical chairs-around-the-newsroom stuff with Joie Chen.

BARRY GOLDWATER: Hey, Dan, in the early years, Coretta (Scott King), Ralph (Nader), and I did commentaries, too, in the basement at Techwood and answered the call whenever asked, unlike the calamitous effort we're witnessing today on the softball field.

(CNN gets one hit and no runs in the bottom of the first. Washington Times 8, CNN 0.)

DAVID WISE: Talk about coming through when the chips are down. I notch bigger ratings than *Take Five* will ever see with my weekly scintillating espionage stories. Back in 1989, I did a commentary about a U.S. spy at the FBI who was dating a stripper. Does that ring a bell? No one believed it at first. Ed Turner said it wasn't in the New York Times.

PETER ARNETT: *(pointing to the field)* Don't quote me on this, but I think the team uses sarin. CNN players look like they're in a fog. I don't have any hard evidence to back up my claim. I'm just reading what April Oliver gave me.

(The game is now in the third inning, and a CNN player realizes the team bats have not been taken out of the bat bag.) {Author's note: This is true.}

DAVE FARMER: Our softball team needs help, and I'm just the person who can do it. When I ran the New York and LA Bureaus, I got results like the time I saved $258 by cutting out plastic forks in the break room. I also installed the Fridge Cam to deter employees from stealing food and ordered staffers to pay for their FedEx shipments.

(CNN responds with three runs in the next four innings. Heather gets an RBI after singles by Ralph and Alex. Brad scores after a hit from Willie. Greg crosses home plate when Jim doubles. But the Washington Times scores six more runs of its own.)

(Beth, Monica, Lindy, and Kim have lost interest in the game and have cornered Charles. They want him to recount stories about when he and Frank covered the Reagan White House. The umpire stops play in the sixth inning with the score 14-3 because the game has reached the 65-minute time limit.)

(The public address announcer orders an immediate start to the second game against USA Today.)

ERIC GERSHON: I've only got two minutes, but I'll stick around and see if CNN does any better in the nightcap. What about you, Jerry?

JERRY LEVIN: I guess I'm gonna have to stay. Kinda feels like I'm a hostage in Beirut all over again. I had more fun when I was chained to a radiator.

DAVID FRENCH: Come on, Jerry. That never happened. We, and by 'we' you know who I mean, have proof you orchestrated the whole thing to get out of being the D.C. bureau chief.

(It's the top of the first inning of the second game. CNN takes a 2-0 lead on successive hits by Willie, Charles, and Greg. Fans are standing, clapping to the music of John Denver's 'Thank God, I'm a Country Boy'.)

DAVE WALKER: It's always good to go first.

LOIS HART: We did, and we made a career of it. Maybe some of that will rub off on our softball players.

DON LENNOX: I've always said it's all about what happens between the white-powdered lines. You know what I mean? It's not easy to walk and talk and produce week after week. I did, and look where it got me.

(Things get worse for CNN. A player on USA Today hits a single between first and second base. The CNN right fielder is playing so far back that by the time he runs in to pick up the ball, the baserunner has circled the bases for an inside-the-park home run on what should have been a single.) {Author's note: This is true.}

RALPH BEGLEITER: Before I started teaching in Delaware, I spent my career traveling the globe, watching democracy flourish, reporting on the Berlin Wall coming down, and learning about *Style with Elsa Klensch*.

But what I, as the one and only world affairs correspondent, see happening now on this softball field has shaken me to my core.

LYNNE RUSSELL: Worse than my acting debut on Canadian TV?

EARL CASEY: More unbelievable than my return to CNN?

DAN SILVA: As unimaginable as my advance from Knopf Publishing?

BELLA SHAW: More remarkable than when I anchored *Showbiz*?

BILL HEADLINE: CNN became the MMSL champions on my watch. Those were the glory years when we had people like Tony Collings and Kyoko Altman. Oh wait, she joined CNN after I left.

KATHLEEN SULLIVAN: Anyone interested in going to a Weight Watchers reunion?

JEANEE VON ESSEN: Who has time for that?

(USA Today scored four runs in the second inning, four in the third, two in the fourth, one in the fifth, and three in the sixth. The score is now 14-2.)

BOB FURNAD: *(screaming)* You're f---ing me, CNN. Let's get it together.

SANDY KENYON: *(gets up to leave)* Well, gang, this has been as entertaining as a Hollywood Minute. Too bad it wasn't equally as short.

MIKE KLEIN: I made up some full-screen graphics promoting next Saturday's games at Capitalview Park against the Washington Post and America's Most Wanted.

PATRICK GREENLAW: Stick around. Reid Collins will teach Mark Leff, Molly McCoy, Patrick Emory, Beverly Williams, Bob Cain, Linden Soles, and me how to read the news with authority. It should be fun.

PAM OLSON, FRANCES HARDIN, CISSY BAKER, PATRICIA OCHS, CLAIRE SHIPMAN, SUSAN ROOK, MARY TILLOTSON, CATHERINE CRIER, AND STEVE HURST: *(enter stage left) (in unison)* Count us in!

Music reaches a crescendo, and lights fade.
Curtain slowly comes down.

June 30, 2001

GAME 1		GAME 2	
CNN	27	CNN	12
WASHINGTON POST	3	AMERICA'S MOST WANTED	6

- **CNN eviscerates opponents in Milosevic-like manner as playoffs loom.**
- **Softball success overshadows management shakeup and theft of Diet Cokes from refrigerator.**
- **Players welcome distraction from round-the-clock employee goodbye parties.**

By Joe Baseball Jr.
Bureau Sports Writer

KENSINGTON, Md. (UPI) — Buoyed by the successful operation on Vice President Dick Cheney's heart, doctors at George Washington University Hospital disclosed shortly before CNN took the field that every player had received a pacemaker implant.

How else can you explain the power surge that hit the softball team on a sweltering, all-around bad-air-and-hair day at Capitalview field?

CNN (10-4) masticated, then for good measure, brought the Washington Post to its knees, 27-3, in the opener and ditto America's Most Wanted, 12-6, in the nightcap.

The weekend carnage was so brutal House Democrats put the Patient's Bill of Rights on a fast track when the Post and AMW requested immediate treatment under their insurance plan as an excuse to get off the field.

The first 17 CNN batters (that's not a typo) got on base in the first game against the Washington Post in a display of intermedia synergy that news group managers can only fantasize about. Even the little girl in the Allianz commercial, who repeatedly whines, "Promise you'll come visit," said CNN's offensive prowess made her temporarily forget about her dad.

CNN scored 14 runs against a team whose tainted motto is "If you don't get it, you don't get it." How true. There were seven singles, six doubles, and a home run. That was just the FIRST inning! Four batters got two hits apiece. It wasn't a fluke. In the third, CNN put the first 12 batters on base, scoring 10 more runs and stretching the lead to 25-0.

The softball performance was the biggest eye-opener to hit the network since CNN sanctioned conservative pundit Tucker Carlson for wearing clip-on bow ties.

All 19 people who showed up for CNN, a cherished hotbed of talent, got in the first game: Erik, Greg, John D., Howie, John K., David, Alex, Jack, Heather, Ralph, Shannon, Brad, Willie, Jim, Charles, Monica, Darrin, and first-timers Aaron and Betsy.

"We would have played Dick Uliano, Arthur Hardy, Pete Hartogs, Don Carson, Stacy Jolna, Mike Clemente, and Sasha Foo at the rate we were going," said a Human Resources manager.

Howard Kurtz, Washington Post media reporter and host of *Reliable Sources*, surmised "CNN went through its lineup faster than staffing for the weekend talk shows."

Official scorer Virginia Nicolaidis simmered, "Next time, our opponents will think twice before they confuse us with the Women's Entertainment Network."

Even Federal District Judge Thomas Penfield Jackson was apoplectic. "If ever you needed proof of a monopoly, this was it. What CNN did to the Post was deliberate, repeated, egregious and flagrant. I laughed my ass off reading the briefs."

TBS Chairman and CEO Jamie Kellner praised the team. He promised to give each player an immediate discount on the special TV offer of the two-CD set, The Best of the Kingston Trio, and if they call now, he'll throw in a videophone autographed by Bill Delaney.

In the second game, America's Most Wanted seriously needed a parole hearing. During warmups, AMW's manager said his team had much on its mind. He accused CNN's Bob Franken of hiding Washington intern Chandra Levy somewhere to aggravate the Super Desk in Atlanta.

Facilities Manager Kim Linden flipped reporters the middle finger and said he had "never heard of" Chandra Levy or Bob Franken. He refused to concede CNN even had an office building in Washington.

Franken groused, "Bite me."

Despite the pregame hype, AMW charged in front of CNN with six runs in the first inning. It was a depressing and downright distressful start to a good day. "I hadn't seen that many glitches since Nasdaq shut down its computer system," said a perplexed Lou Dobbs, anchor of *Lou Dobbs Moneyline*. "I take that back. I once watched *Street Sweep* Shakers."

CNN cut into the six-run deficit by mounting a three-run, two-out rally in the bottom of the first. John King (4-4, 5 RBI) got the big hit with a two-run triple and then scored on an errant throw. "I told the idiots in Atlanta I'm the go-to guy, not Jeff Flock. It's in my new contract," he exalted. Howie Lutt wasn't too shabby, either. He embodied consistency 4-4 (6-6 on the day.)

While CNN scored in every inning but the second, AMW struggled to make contact. Greg Robertson shut down the efficacious Manhunter's offense, and the defense did not allow another runner to cross home plate after the first inning.

When reached for comment at the Bistro Bis, CNN Washington Bureau Chief Frank Sesno waxed poetic: "It was nice to celebrate something other than another D.C. employee leaving the network."

"At the rate we're losing reporters, producers, and library staff, there's going to be no one left to play on the team except Skip in makeup," hooted one manager, protecting his identity with a paper bag over his head. "More importantly, our CNN baseball caps and umbrellas stash is running low."

The doubleheader sweep catapulted CNN to the precipice of the playoffs. ABC leads the division by two games. Four games remain in the regular season.

This Saturday, CNN is back in action with a pair of makeup games at Layhill Field against NBC News Channel and the National Press Club. Two wins next week mean punching a ticket to the playoffs. The stars are aligning for a deep run.

July 7, 2001

GAME 1		GAME 2	
CNN	16	CNN	3
NBC NEWS CHANNEL	4	NATIONAL PRESS CLUB	2

- **CNN softball team wins fourth in a row and makes playoffs for third straight year.**
- **On-field success helps lift company morale; smiles abound in bureaus from Los Angeles to Lagos.**
- **CNN and People Magazine to sell pin-up calendar featuring team players.**
- **DELETES 4th graph New CEO Walter Isaacson mandates Joe Baseball to "tone it down."**

By Joe Baseball Jr.
Bureau Sports Writer

LAYHILL, Md. (UPI) — Desperate for any signs of life, even a faint pulse, the Chandra News Network stumbled across a winning formula over the weekend. It turned up in the most unlikely of places and has nothing to do with the missing intern, cadaver dogs, polygraph tests, or love affairs with congressional lawmakers.

Leave it to the softball team to bring giddiness and optimism back to the entire network. "This calls for a celebration," said a fired-up D.C. Bureau Chief Frank Sesno, from the Bistro Bis, where CNN recently opened a satellite newsroom.

For months the company has spent millions of dollars in a management reorganization, endured crippling layoffs, hired a Hollywood actress in a naked attempt to boost ratings, rejiggered its programming lineup with rip-roaring talk shows like *Greenfield at Large*, and created a rapid response unit to monitor every movement of Representative Gary Condit.

Industry gazers say the tinkering has done little to revitalize the network, which is "in a state of deepening despondency... having lost its way."

You can tell Mark Leff he can stop writing CNN's obit. This patient doesn't need an artificial heart or Jeff Flock dangling from a helium-filled balloon to rake in viewers. The long-awaited turnaround at CNN has begun on a field of dreams that is not the *Burden of Proof* set.

The softball team (12-4) whipped the dickens out of NBC News Channel in Game 1, 16-4, on Saturday at Layhill Park and then toyed with the National Press Club in Game 2, before winning a cliffhanger, 3-2.

The doubleheader sweep guaranteed a trip to the Metropolitan Media Softball League postseason no matter what happens in the final two games of the season. Eighteen dedicated souls took part in the fun.

Finally, something to lift the spirits of the staff that has nothing to do with Abbe Lowell (white collar criminal defense attorney), Anne Marie Smith (the other woman in Gary Condit's life), Fox News Network, Billy Martin (Washington's go-to lawyer), Linda Zamsky (Chandra Levy's aunt), Charles Ramsey (D.C. Police Chief), Carolyn Condit (Gary Condit's wife), Marina Ein (Washington publicist and Condit's spokeswoman) or Robert and Susan Levy (Chandra Levy's parents).

Before the first pitch, the coach for NBC swore her team knew nothing about the former intern with the Federal Bureau of Prisons until they saw the 'Ask Bob Franken' call-in segment over the weekend. "I guess we were following other in-depth stories such as the economy, Medicare, and Social Security reform," said NBC anchor Soledad O'Brien.

As for the game, 11 different CNN players (Charles, Dave, Alex, Greg, John D., Howie, John K., Erik, Ralph, and Darrin) had at least one run batted in. The big inning was the third, when CNN scored six times with the help of four triples, one after the other— a team record.

The squad's ace-in-the-hole, Jessica Rosgaard, got the game-winner when she grounded out in the fifth, prompting the umpire, Mr. Quincy Magoo, to invoke the 12-run slaughter rule. "I guess you could say I was ahead of the curve," said Rosgaard, the young protégé of Lou Dobbs and a devotee of the smash hit "CNN.Dot.Com."

In the nightcap against the National Press Club, a long-established loser in the MMSL, CNN needed help from Brad, Jack, Jim, Willie, Lindy, and Monica to slink away with a low-scoring one-run victory.

"Talk about embarrassing," guffawed producer Jeff Milstein and part-time Ticket Master wannabe, now the newly-appointed angel of the Chandra Unit. "Now, if you'll excuse me, I have to go to my 24th staff meeting of the day to discuss the latest developments. By the way, I have an extra pair of tickets to 'Kiss Me Kate' that I can't get rid of. Front row, balcony, no less."

CNN scored single runs in the second, third, and fourth innings, which was barely enough. NPC, winners of only three games all year, hung in there with two runs of its own. Neither team scored in the last three innings. The game was so dull fans were seen reading 1996 transcripts from *Crier & Company* with 'special guest' Pat Schroeder.

"Thankfully, our defense was as avaricious as our company, and we made the most of our opportunities, but it wasn't pretty. Offensively, we were offensive," babbled team manager Virginia Nicolaidis, who came dressed to the games as Martha Washington for some unexplained reason.

"I haven't witnessed ineptitude like that since some idiot left the Red Phone off the hook for an hour," glared Senior White House Correspondent John King, now filling in on the Rim. "This newsroom job is a lot more hellacious than it looks. Much harder than playing shortstop."

He added, "So far, this morning, I've gotten 28 reminders from David Schechter on the Assignment Desk to update the rundown, plus seven requests from Senior Editor Paul Varian to write a note for wires.cnn. That's on top of making eight trips to the feed room and library looking for a missing tape that was not checked out, waiting three hours to get graphics to make a simple reveal, booking three interviews for Kelly Wallace, and going over the Middle East peace process with Andrea 14 times. I also was second-guessed by nine vice presidents in Atlanta."

{Editor's note: Human Resources confirms the total number of vice presidents at CNN Center is 579}

The final regular season games are at 10 a.m. this Saturday at Capitalview Park against a down-and-out team from CBS News and ABC News, the division leader and No. 1 seed.

July 14, 2001

GAME 1		GAME 2	
CNN	15	CNN	14
CBS NEWS	6	CBS NEWS	12

- **Regular season ends on high note with doubleheader sweep; team has third-best record in MMSL.**
- **CNN wins sixth straight, knocks off CBS and ABC this week (without Cokie and Sam).**
- **ADDS 2nd graph AOL Time Warner proclaims July CNN Softball month.**
- **DELETES 3rd graph Company promises 10 across-the-board raises, plus enhanced high-speed broadband service if team goes all the way.**

By Joe Baseball Jr.
Bureau Sports Writer

KENSINGTON, Md. (UPI) — CNN executives wrestling with what to do about their down-in-the-dumps all-news channel are reportedly prepared to make a major proclamation in the coming days. Insiders say it could be connected to Amma, the hugging Indian guru, who is replacing Greta Van Susteren on *The Point.*

"Pure fiction," said a perturbed Keith McAllister. "If you want the truth, just read Drudge. Everyone knows Amma will co-anchor a new flagship show with Aaron Brown once we renovate our brand-spanking new Manhattan studio on West 57th Street. We're going to call it *Late Night with Aaron and Amma.*"

But the big news, say sources, is the decision by the triumvirate of CNN executives Jamie Kellner, Sid Bedingfield, and Eason Jordan to revamp the entire network, not just Headline News, so it "more closely resembles the characteristics of the softball team."

"I've only been on the job a week, but from what I've heard at my dinner table, the softball team has what I'm looking for," said Walter Isaacson, the new chairman and CEO of CNN news group. "There's zeal. A winning attitude. Star power. Teamwork. Ability to execute under pressure. Solid communication. Happy faces. Willingness to go all-out. Respect for every position. John King. Even giving blood if that's what it takes."

"What a crock. That's what they said about the Wolf Blitzer show when it first started," squawked Vito Maggiolo, now relocated to the statue area outside the bureau at 820 First Street, where he intends to make all the noise he wants. "Tell Walter I've got 83 walkie-talkies and 12 police scanners cranked up. I can listen to play-by-play of the softball games AND move Team crews around while police search for dog bones in Rock Creek Park, and nobody can stop me."

No one could stop CNN on a sublime Saturday at Capitalview Park, where the team out-networked CBS News in the opener, 15-6, and swatted ABC News in the nightcap, 14-12.

Despite the sweep, No. 1 seed ABC (15-3) claimed the division title based on a better record. As a consolation prize, CNN beat ABC in both head-to-head meetings this year. In an odd twist, CNN became the first team to ever go undefeated in its division (8-0) but not win the division. Strange but true.

Ten people plus Ranger the canine helped set a CNN global mark for attendance. If this keeps up, the team might start charging admission.

In Game 1, CNN pounded the eye right off CBS's logo by scoring six runs in the first inning and adding four more in the second to take a 10-0 lead.

"The spirits were so high Frank (Sesno) asked me to stop by and take back all copies of 'FISH!' (a manager's guide to bolstering morale in the workplace and currently number three on the New York Times Business Best Seller List)," said show producer Bob Waller. "Don't quote me, but the bureau chief is thinking about coming out to watch the playoffs in two weeks, not to do the wave but to scout ABC for replacements to fill the Nancy Ambrose position."

Five CNN batters were the bee's knees. Willie Lora hit for the cycle, going 4-4 with five RBI, and was offered a three-year contract on the spot by Telemundo. John Davis went 3-3, Ralph Marcus 3-3, Jack Lynn 3-3, and David Gracey, 1-1.

"We scored a direct hit on the field and in outer space," chimed Rear Admiral Craig Quigley during a lull in a Pentagon briefing to discuss the latest interceptor test. "I saw a great many similarities. Projectiles launched. Dummies in the field. There were a few successes, but mostly misfires. Everything except mock warheads. I will acknowledge I couldn't figure out how to tie that last one into the softball theme."

CNN was so far ahead in the first game that it loaned several players to the ABC/Fox game on a different field, hoping this would help winless Fox pull off a tour de force. It didn't work.

CBS had CNN's number after the second inning, but it was too little too late. Thanks to Heather Shaw, Darrin White, Howie Lutt, Brad Wright, Alex Dermanis, Charles Bierbauer, Lindy Royce, Jessica Rosgaard, Shannon Feaster-Stewart, Virginia Nicolaidis, Betsy Korona, Beth Lewandowski and Jim Barnett.

Taking a page from the Cal Ripken Farewell Tour, several players rose to the occasion in the second game. Lutt thwacked a three-run homer to the delight of his teammates, his parents, and his girlfriend on hand to bear witness to his brute strength. His hit in the second inning established a comfortable seven-run cushion, 11-4.

Also making noteworthy plays in the field were Alex, Shannon, and Charles. They caught everything that came their way, unlike Jim, who was left with a shiner and pondering the Saturday "*Ask CNN*" question: Can you catch a pop-up with your face?

CNN collected 20 hits against ABC, 16 of them singles. Leading the brigade was tried and true tri-captain Lynn, who turned in a 4-4 performance. Alex got her first career triple to fuel an eight-run first-inning marathon. Every little bit was needed. ABC returned fire with two runs in the third, five in the fifth, and three in the seventh. They had the tying run at second with two outs before CNN slammed the door.

The brackets for the upcoming playoffs remain TBD, pending the completion of make-up games next weekend. CNN's 14 wins make this the most successful regular season in their history.

Mark your calendars, get out of bed, and come out to see the team play in two weeks.

July 28, 2001

GAME 1		GAME 2	
CNN	14	CNN	7
WASHINGTON TIMES	12	WASHINGTON POST.COM	1
GAME 3			
GAZETTE	8		
CNN	3		

- Remarkable season keeps rolling along as CNN lives to play another day.
- Only four teams remain; rain postpones final games until next Saturday.
- All eyes on CNN Washington Bureau, where softball success resurrects company reputation.

WHEATON, Md. (UPI) — Q&A with Joe Baseball Jr.

The tables were turned on sportswriter Joe Baseball Jr. during an online discussion over the weekend. Players, managers, and fans were allowed to ask Joe questions about CNN's softball team. Here are some excerpts:

Q: Before I ask you, Joe, about the softball games this past Saturday, can you give us the schedule for the next CNN goodbye party? As a follow-up, is it true they will rename the Bistro Bis… CNN's Bistro Bis?

Joe: I have nothing official for you on the name change, but it is under consideration. As for the first part of your question, there is a gathering at the Bistro Bis on Wednesday for Peter Kendall, the latest to leave the company, and three more parties next week and four the week after that. That's assuming there's still somebody on the payroll.

Q: The softball games ended too late on Saturday for your write-up to make it into Sunday's paper. You follow CNN closely, Joe. What happened against the Washington Times? I thought they were a good team. CNN lost to them earlier this year, correct?

Joe: Yes, the Moonies, as they're often called because Unification Church leader Sun Myung Moon founded the paper, have always played CNN tooth and nail, but this CNN win was extra special. They scored four runs in the first inning. Then the Times came back to tie it and take a 12-5 lead. Things looked as harrowing as the latest AOL quarterly earnings report. CNN batters couldn't have gotten a hit if Walter Isaacson had shown up and mandated it. The whole team looked like it was infected with the West Nile Virus.

Q: CNN was down by seven runs and still won?

Joe: It was unbelievable. Howie had a triple in the fifth to make it 12-8, and the score stayed that way until the top of the seventh. Jack started a six-run rally with a single. Heather followed with a solid single up the middle. Erik, likewise. After one out, John D., Howie, Dave, John K., and Alex got on base. CNN pulled ahead to stay 14-12. The Washington Times never knew what hit them. There were CNN smiles all around, like a reunion of Gary Condit's girlfriends.

Q: Was there any time between games to watch the new and improved Headline News with "more breaking news, better graphics, and an edgier feel with less repetition and more correspondents?"

Joe: No. The team had to switch fields at Wheaton Regional Park to face Washington Post.com.

Q: How did the players maintain their intensity?

Joe: CNN has a lot of depth and Type A personalities, including Willie, Charles, Greg, Darrin, Lindy, Jessica, Virginia, Ralph, Brad, Betsy, Jason, Shannon, and Jim, who, by the way, received a shiny new rake during an inspirational pre-game ceremony.

Q: Wow, did everyone get to play?

Joe: No, but they provided moral support. Marty and Amy Kramer, and Ranger came out. Ditto Jim Connor. Alex's mom, Shannon's husband, and Lindy's beau. Jeff Milstein and his son stopped by on their way to Nissan Pavilion to see Carol King in concert.

Q: Was Game 2 also a nailbiter?

Joe: Is Bill Hemmer an anchor? Does Keith McAllister want names? Will the balcony doors at the CNN bureau ever be unlocked again?

Q: Huh?

Joe: CNN beat Post.com without breaking a sweat. CNN scored in all the odd innings: three in the first, one in the third, and three in the fifth. They didn't allow a run until the sixth, and by then, the game was over, and CNN players were taking bets on whether the network would hire the "anchor" in the Discount Broker dot com ad to co-host with Aaron Brown.

Q: Isn't that a disparaging crack at CNN? I've always viewed Fox and MSNBC as laggards. Television is a business of hits and stars. It's

all about programming, production, talent, storytelling, and writing.
Reporting is the backbone of CNN.

Joe: You're a little off the ideological reservation. What's your question?

Q: Well, Joe, it's a comment and a two-part question. First, my comment: Watching the revamped IP show to figure out where Judy will pop up next is fun. Secondly, did CNN employees have to share blankets during the big ice storm in Atlanta a couple of years ago? And aren't you trying to divert attention from the third playoff game?

Joe: Yes, and yes. In Game 3 against the Gazette, CNN did so poorly that bleary-eyed players were wiping themselves off with antiseptic towelettes between innings. Where's an *Iron Chef* when you need one?

Q: So, I take it CNN lost?

Joe: Yes, 8-3. The Gazette, which won the MMSL championship last year, scored six runs in the bottom of the first and two more in the second. Neither team got a run after that. During one stretch of 21 batters, CNN only got three people on base. It was a bitter pill to swallow after two tremendous wins.

Q: Wasn't the team supposed to play on Sunday since it's a double-loss elimination tournament?

Joe: CNN was going to face the winner of Post.com/USA Today, but it rained. The games are next Saturday.

Q: Can the team go all the way like it did several years ago?

Joe: Anything is possible. A meteorite could fall from the sky in Pennsylvania and land on Frank Sesno. FN could get a rating above a point three. Lou Waters could say something other than, "What's next, Natalie." The lady on the American Express commercials could stop getting her money stolen every time she goes to the beach. CNN could throw a pep rally at the Bistro Bis. You never know.

Q: Thank you, Joe, for taking the time to answer our questions.

Joe: My pleasure.

August 4, 2001

GAME 1	GAME 2 (CHAMPIONSHIP)
CNN 6	GAZETTE 7
WASHINGTON POST.COM 5	CNN 3

- **CNN goes out a winner despite excruciating loss in championship game.**
- **Season comes to an end as team of under-achievers exceeds expectations.**
- **Runner-up trophy on display at newsroom assignment desk.**
- **Cash-strapped AOL Time Warner to put studio desks and chairs up for auction on eBay after CNN anchors are forced to stand in front of cameras.**

By Joe Baseball Jr.
Bureau Sports Writer

LAYHILL, Md. (UPI) — Harken back to April, when CNN was rife with declining ratings, politics of personal destruction, a leadership vacuum, plummeting morale, bitterness, and fleeing employees.

What a difference five months can make! The network has come a long way and not just in the newsroom!

The same can be said about CNN's softball team, which, over the weekend, did its best to impersonate Tropical Storm Barry.

For several days, the gigantic weather system gathered strength in the Gulf of Mexico, churning and threatening, looking for a place to unleash its fury. Where would it go, and how much damage would it cause?

Like the storm, the softball team petered out in the end, but not before making sure everybody took notice.

CNN came up short in its methodical march through the Metropolitan Media Softball League. It was attempting to reclaim the title it last won in 1999 and unseat the reigning champions. The season began with 20 teams, but only two were standing when CNN took the field against the Gazette at Layhill Park on Saturday.

The news network nearly missed the final dance. The players had to first do a tango with the Washington Post.com. A week ago, CNN trampled Post.com 7-1 to advance in the playoffs, but this being a double-loss elimination tournament, only one of the two teams would go on. Each team had one loss.

CNN took a 2-0 lead in the first inning when Howie Lutt doubled home two runs. Then, over a stretch of 16 batters, CNN only got three hits. Post.com wasn't much better, but they produced enough offense to lead 5-2 going into the bottom of the sixth.

The deficit would have been even greater if not for two terrific plays at home plate when CNN's defense tagged out two runners trying to score. CNN also had two inning-ending double plays.

In the bottom of the sixth, CNN dished up four hits (Erik Tavcar, Brad Wright, David Gracey, Howie) along with a run-scoring sacrifice fly from John King, and a grounder from Darrin White to take a razor-thin one-run lead, 6-5.

Post.com put the go-ahead runners on base with one out in the top of the seventh. But Howie snared a sharp grounder to the pitcher's mound and threw to John, who touched second for the force and threw on to a stretching Ralph Marcus at first to double up the runner by a step and stave off a loss.

It was a gutsy performance by the entire team: Alex Dermanis, Willie Lora, Betsy Korona, Charles Bierbauer, Jessica Rosgaard, Virginia Nicolaidis, and Jim Barnett. Then it was time for the big enchilada and who would get bragging rights.

Like a shark smelling blood and looking for an arm to chomp, the Gazette took a 7-0 lead against a capsizing CNN, which could only scratch together three hits in the first four innings.

"We were getting blown around like Judy Woodruff's hair," said one scout studying the team closely on film.

CNN made a game of it by snuffing out a Gazette rally with an electrifying double play between David and Alex. Then, in the fifth inning, CNN got six hits (all singles) to narrow the gap to 7-3 but could get no closer. The Gazette, known as the Green Machine, retired the side in order in the last two innings (five of seven times in the game) to once again claim the MMSL title in back-to-back years.

After the trophy presentations on the field, CNN players gathered at the nearby Stained Glass Pub and held a victory celebration with cold mugs of beer to watch Headline News broadcast news from its modern studio at the "speed of life."

"It's the news you need when you need it," said Teya Ryan, executive vice president and general manager of CNN Headline News, in a statement released after the game. "We have our finger on the pulse of American viewers."

Chairman and CEO of Turner Broadcasting Jamie Kellner added, "Introducing unknown personalities is another way to attract an audience. That's why we've hired Michael McManus and Phil Donahue and rejected Consumer Product Safety Commission nominee Mary Sheila Gall to attract younger viewers."

None of that has a thing to do with CNN's softball team, which, over five productive months, carried the network on its shoulders. More than 25 people played during the season, and countless other employees praised their dedication to helping restore the luster of the CNN brand.

"You've done the company proud. At least one thing works around here," said CEO Walter Isaacson.

TOP OF THE 5th

Do You Believe in Miracles?

April 8, 2002

- **Long-awaited softball season begins Saturday amid lofty expectations and low ratings.**
- **CNN's _American Morning_ revamps lineup; Jack Cafferty and new _Moneyline_ host Louis Rukeyser square off in Celebrity Boxing segment.**
- **DELETES reference to Lou Dobbs joining Arthur Andersen.**
- **Eds: SUBS 4th graph with Dobbs denounces himself in searing commentary.**

By Joe Baseball Jr.
Bureau Sports Writer

WASHINGTON (UPI) — Ah, life is good.

Taliban and al Qaeda forces are on the run. Colin Powell is in the Mideast to clobber Yasser Arafat for hanging up on Christiane Amanpour. Subway, the fast-food chain, has agreed in principle to sponsor reporter Jonathan Karl's Capitol Hill subway series. Now comes word that CNN executives have forked over enough money for this year's Metropolitan Media Softball League entry fee.

"We came this close to not making it," said a CNN spokesman, who agreed that a string of goodbye parties in the Washington Bureau put a crimp in the network's operating budget. "We were forced to decide whether to fund the softball team or the Futures Desk in Atlanta. The turnaround in the economy now means we can have both."

The latest Nielsen ratings put CNN slightly ahead of _Iron Chef_ on the Food Network but far behind _Trading Spaces_ on TLC.

"Thankfully, the Red Skelton ads will pocket some much-needed revenue this quarter, plus pay for the flow chart to explain my new management team," reasoned Teya Ryan, general manager of CNN/US. "Next week, we roll out the Queen Mum bloopers and the 'Best of Milton Berle' commercials."

Yesterday, Chief Executive Officer Walter Isaacson confirmed what many industry insiders had long predicted: "We're going to play ball." In a Q&A session with local high school students first reported by Fox in a lower third crawl, he set forth that news is a priority at CNN. "It's our middle name. If we didn't do news, we would just be the Cable Network," Isaacson said while staring into space.

In a riotous move, *NewsNight* anchor Aaron Brown will throw out the first ball at the opener on Saturday at Capitalview field in Kensington, Maryland. Brown was slightly injured last week doing The Whip. Sources say he was droning on during his nightly Page Two and a Half diatribe about cumulus clouds when he suffered a paper cut. "I'm a little light-headed, but thankfully I avoided the 15-day DL."

"I know the feeling, my friend," chimed in a cheery Bill Hemmer during a lull in the latest Israeli offensive in Nablus. "Leon and Daryn, will one of you record tonight's CBS show *Baby Bob* about the six-month-old kid?"

While much of the world is preoccupied with the Middle East conflict and AOL's plummeting stock price, there is increasing focus on the softball team's promising season.

"I'm going to shave my mustache if CNN goes undefeated," confessed American Taliban John Walker Lindh.

"Me, too," said his collaborator Yasser Essam Hamdi. "It will be a treat to follow the games. It was hard to get Direct TV in our cave at Mazar-e-Sharif."

CNN faces powerhouse ABC News (last year's division winner) in Game 1 of the doubleheader and bona fide also-ran Fox News in the nightcap as the MMSL begins its 12th year. Last season, CNN (17-6) finished second out of 18 teams. The league has added two teams: Comcast SportsNet and WJLA.

You won't need a program to recognize some of the names in the line-up: Jessica Rosgaard, Lindy Royce, Jack Lynn, Howie Lutt, Ralph Marcus, Alex Dermanis, James Knott, Willie Lora, Brad Wright, Jim Barnett, John King, John Davis, Darrin White, Evan Howell, David Gracey, Erik Tavcar, Greg Robertson and Gabriel LeMay.

"Softball is the only reason I took the D.C. job," rhapsodized an ebullient Washington Bureau Chief Kathryn Kross. "I can't wait to kick ABC's ass on Opening Day."

The first pitch is at 10 a.m.

Preview the upcoming season on the MMSL home page and then bookmark it.

Read the latest stories weekly and catch up on some of your favorite players. Check out the standings, who's hot, who's not, and be part of the allure.

April 13, 2002

GAME 1		GAME 2	
CNN	12	CNN	18
ABC NEWS	10	FOX NEWS	6

- **CNN wins doubleheader as 17 players propel season opener.**
- **Old faces wearing new uniforms put on clinic against pompous networks.**
- **Former anchor Bernard Shaw sues CNN after Paula Zahn inserts his name into copy story about Cardinal Bernard Law.**

By Joe Baseball Jr.
Bureau Sports Writer

KENSINGTON, Md. (UPI) — Forget the image consultants and the network makeover. Don't bother calling extensions 1501 or 7930. Up until this past weekend, what CNN needed was a crisis management team. Where's Marty Kramer when you need him?

It was a BAD week. The Atlanta Journal-Constitution quoted executives who said the "frumpy" network "needed new DNA." Salon.com described *Crossfire* as "too long and too incoherent." Colin Powell asked the Palestinians for forgiveness for Andrea Koppel's repeated mispronunciation of Yasser AraFAWT's name. And on Friday, AOL's stock price hit a new 52-week low.

That is all ancient history.

Enter stage left. The CNN softball team is back, sporting orange caps and spiffy gray shirts with the once-relevant tagline, The World's News Leader.

In case you missed it on CNN SI, or the Life Support Network as some call it, the softball team eviscerated, demolished, gnawed on, and otherwise beat the crap out of ABC and Fox News over the weekend, 12-10 and 18-6, respectively, but definitely not respectably.

With the score tied at eight against ABC, hot-hitting Lindy Royce led off the sixth with a single. Dependable Jack Lynn followed with a double. Rookie Laura Robinson knocked in a run with an out. Birthday boy Erik Tavcar walked as did eagle-eyed Greg Robertson. Slugger John Davis singled to score two more runs, and CNN hung on for the W.

The second game against Fox News was stopped after five innings when the umpire got the jitters and began singing Marvin Gaye's What's Goin' On. CNN conveyed a clear message to Rupert Murdoch's squad: When it comes to facelifts, Fox should concentrate on the softball field and not Greta Van Susteren.

"I'll go face-to-face with anyone at CNN," Van Susteren cursed, "except for maybe the White House unit."

Meanwhile, in Atlanta, bureau chiefs gathering for their annual jamboree at CNN Center did not waste a minute to make their first decision.

"We are going to disable every TV set throughout the network, so not one producer can watch Fox," threatened Detroit's bureau chief.

"Hey, Detroit doesn't have a bureau. I ordered it closed a year ago," Vice President Keith McAllister lashed out in a churlish company-wide Blackberry message.

"I think Fox is kind of edgy," said an energetic Frank Sesno, putting his two cents in at the start of class in an empty lecture hall at George Mason University. "Tell Sid Bedingfield if you want ratings, no more car chases. No more happy talk. No more sharks. No more Chandra. No more softball."

The day began with a thumping of last year's division winner, ABC, 12-10, in a thrilling game that was a lot closer than it needed to be.

Thanks to John Davis, who went 3-3 with 4 RBI, David Gracey's two solo home runs, and Howie Lutt's first-inning two-run blast, CNN never trailed against ABC. But CNN did its best to make it interesting by surrendering a four-run lead, committing two throwing errors to hand over five runs, and leaving the bases loaded twice with big bats due up.

"We had more opportunities than Headline News has boxes on the screen," said Jim Walton, the president of something at CNN. "The Venezuelan government looks more organized than we do. I'm headed to Caracas tomorrow with Eason."

Game 2 against Fox was funnier than watching *Hannity & Colmes*. CNN scored in every inning: four in the first, six in the second, five in the third, one in the fourth, and two in the fifth.

All 17 players for CNN saw action, and several even had time to file their income taxes. Jessica Rosgaard, John King, Alex Dermanis, Jim Barnett, Darrin White, Brad Wright, Willie Lora, Todd Huyghe, and Aaron Payne made it into the scorebook.

"At least Fox had a better after-party at the Radio & Television Correspondents' Association dinner," said dejected Fox News chief Roger Ailes. "We couldn't beat the Detroit Tigers at this rate."

CNN will attempt to keep confounding opponents and its winning streak going when it plays another doubleheader this Saturday against America's Most Wanted in Game 1 and WTTG in Game 2 at Burning Tree Park.

April 20, 2002

GAME 1		GAME 2	
AMERICA'S MOST WANTED	11	CNN	8
CNN	10	WTTG	7

- **CNN suffers galling loss in late innings but gains split.**
- **Protesters take to streets demanding explanation from softball team.**
- **Salomon Smith Barney slashes price target for AOL Time Warner from $40 to $7.50, citing slumping cable business and surplus of blue index cards for Larry King.**
- **DELETES reference to *American Morning* in turmoil; newscast changes name to *America Snoring*.**

By Joe Baseball Jr.
Bureau Sports Writer

BETHESDA, Md. (UPI) — One of journalism's cardinal rules is never to bury the lead. One of the holy commandments of softball is never to let the other team score four runs in the last inning when your team is only ahead by three.

CNN learned both the hard way on Saturday when America's Most Wanted found all the missing children in the country AND had time to hand CNN its first loss of the year in throbbing hemorrhoidal pain, 11-10, at appropriately named Burning Tree Park.

"An absolute disgrace," seethed shortstop and Senior White House Correspondent John King, who wasn't at the game. He stayed away in protest after a CNN live producer last week used a picture of Anwar Sadat during a King live shot on the Arctic National Wildlife Refuge vote.

"I told (Mike) Maltas I would talk about ANWR, not Anwar. I knew something was wrong when I heard the other reporters on the White

House lawn laughing. Do Wolf and I have to do everything around here?"

As it turned out, there were other screwups. The softball team (3-1) frittered away a seven-run lead against the Manhunters in the opener, and then CNN needed divine intervention from the Pope in Game 2 with WTTG to win 8-7 and manage a split in an emotionally draining doubleheader.

Pope John Paul II emerged from his pre-papal summit with American Cardinals at the Vatican to read a prepared statement between games. "CNN softball players must keep their vows of chastity and not blow late-inning leads."

Several players, including Howie Lutt, Lindy Royce, James Knott, Jack Lynn, and Erik Tavcar, took the news to heart and led the team to victory in the nightcap.

The day began well in Game 1. CNN, led by John Davis with the bat and newly promoted Alex Dermanis with the glove, batted around in the top of the first inning as eight players hit safely to build a 7-0 lead.

"We were having more fun than a *Talk Back Live* audience," said one of three spectators, the largest crowd this year. But shoddy fielding and cruddy hitting opened the door for a comeback by AMW. CNN was ahead 10-7, needing only three more outs for the win. It was not to be.

Host John Walsh showed up mid-game and promised to give each of his players a week off if they could find Chandra Levy and beat CNN on the same day. America's Most Wanted put its first two runners on base. CNN watched in agony as the next batter blasted a three-run homer in the woods to tie the score.

It got worse. The next hitter lined a scorcher in the gap for an inside-the-park home run. Just like that, visions of an undefeated season vanished faster than viewers (or "customers" as CNN executives in Atlanta call them) turning off *NewsNight*.

"At least my show is bringing in the key demographics and more revenue than *Headliners and Legends*," Lou Dobbs hit back.

"We gave the other team full, unfettered, unconditional access to do what they wanted, just like a U.N. inspection team," said Washington Deputy Bureau Chief Steve Redisch. He immediately ordered each CNN player to retake gas mask training. The fun was just beginning.

Before the second game, the producers of *American Morning* proudly heralded their first-ever multiple-choice Big Question of the day. Which recent events are worthy of a lead story: an Amtrak derailment, MSNBC

We are the champions again in 2002. Top row (L-R) David Gracey, Kathryn Kross, Willie Lora, John King, Howie Lutt, Noah King, Jack Lynn, Jessica Rosgaard, and Laura Robinson; Bottom row, John Davis, Jim Barnett, Darrin White, and Lindy Royce.

re-branding itself 'America's News Channel' or CNN's inability to hold a late-inning lead? "I think you'll find the results fascinating," said Anderson Cooper, who admitted during a commercial break he hadn't heard about the train accident.

Game 2 against WTTG followed the same script as the opener. Howie Lutt hit a towering three-run homer to put CNN ahead. Thanks to RBI hits by Darrin White and Ralph Marcus, it was 6-3 in the top of the seventh when déjà vu happened all over again. WTTG added four runs to take a 7-6 lead heading into the last frame.

With one out, Lindy Royce smashed a single into left field. James Knott followed with a double in the gap. Intern Kris Reyes, making her first appearance for the team, just missed getting her first base hit. Now, there were two outs. The tying run was at third, the winning run at second, and Erik Tavcar was at the plate.

"We got it in the bag, Jimmy-boy," said a determined Jack Lynn with a combination of desperation, bafflement, and defiance in his voice. And right he was. Erik lined a clean single to center to give CNN the win and keep the Cable News Network in a tie with ABC for first place after a second weekend of softball.

It has been pure cohesion, from those on the field to bench players Brad Wright, Aaron Payne, Todd Huyghe, Jim Barnett, and Sarah Shepherd.

There are no games scheduled for this Saturday. CNN will be back in action on May 4 against the undefeated Washington Times and fearmongering USA Today.

May 4, 2002

GAME 1		GAME 2	
USA TODAY	12	CNN	17
CNN	11	WASHINGTON TIMES	10

- **CNN trips over itself, loses another one-run game to fall into second place.**
- **Team rebounds in nightcap; report of CNN's demise (unlike AOL's stock price) is greatly exaggerated.**
- **Softball players receive Botox injections and displace Aaron Brown as new face of network.**
- **DELETES reference to Newshound video showing reporters bribing *American Morning* producers to air their packages.**

By Joe Baseball Jr.
Bureau Sports Writer

LAYHILL, Md. (UPI) — Reporter John King took the recently stipulated network edict of "more reporter involvement" to a new level on Saturday as he smashed two home runs over the left field fence to lead CNN and 19 other cast members to a much-needed win against the Washington Times, 17-10, at sun-drenched Layhill field.

The victory allowed CNN to save face after an embarrassing loss in the opener against USA Today, 12-11, in eight innings.

It was such a shameful defeat Headline News refused to find room on its fact-filled screen to display the score. "We haven't seen that kind of stumbling since Lou Waters was on Newswatch reading anchor intros," vented Headline News' only viewer. "Bring back compelling television like Fitness by Jake!"

The doubleheader split left CNN (4-2) one game behind ABC in the Capitalview Division. Seven teams have identical 4-2 records, and two are 5-1. CNN's two losses have both been by a measly run.

It was a day of highs and lows, comedy and tragedy, innovation and desperation, pratfalls and misjudgments, but enough about *Inside Poli-*

tics. Before the first pitch, players paused for a moment of silence to pay tribute to the late Dale Solly, WJLA's weekend anchor and softball coach.

During the second game, President George W. Bush, in Marine One, flew over the softball diamond on his way to Camp David to meet with Spanish Prime Minister Aznar.

CNN's White House unit did not fritter away a minute before issuing a statement. "We're glad John King could help spread a little happiness. It's been a sapping week."

The note went on to say, "On Monday, Major Garrett was forced out when management said he had 'no future' because he couldn't handle the pressure of 'walking and talking' during live shots. On Tuesday, the 8:30 a.m. editorial meeting was canceled, leaving every bureau except Los Angeles feeling directionless. Then we uncovered a plan by Andrea Koppel to secretly interview Israeli Prime Minister Ariel Sharon at Blair House."

As for the games, CNN scored four runs on six hits in the first inning of the opener against USA Today, only to see the lead evaporate by the sixth inning.

Down 8-4, John Davis, John King, David Gracey, Brad Wright, Alex Dermanis, Willie Lora, Laura Robinson, and James Knott set in motion a rally to tie the score and send the game into one-pitch extra innings.

Confidence was high. The New York Times was ready with a full-page ad touting CNN as the 'Comeback News Network.' Then fate intervened.

Pitcher Greg Robertson committed a cardinal sin worse than anything ever brought to light by the Catholic Archdiocese. He walked two men. Each walk came with a woman due up next in the batting order. Under league rules, baserunners get to advance two bases, and the women go to first base. As a result, USA Today got four runs and took a 12-8 lead. But CNN would not go down quietly.

In the bottom of the eighth, CNN fought back with three consecutive singles and closed the gap to 12-9. The following two batters were retired. With two outs, Willie Lora, the tying run, walked ahead of a woman, making it 12-10. James Knott lined a single to center, making it 12-11. As Willie rounded third base, he slipped, apparently tripping over a discarded CD by TLC's Lisa Lopes. He never made it home and was tagged out to end the game.

CNN Executive Teya Ryan fired off a company-wide Blackberry message: "No more excuses. The next time I come to D.C., it won't be fun. You're going to feel the burn. Are there any questions?"

Each player received the message: Darrin White, Lindy Royce, Jessica Rosgaard, Jack Lynn, Howie Lutt, Ralph Marcus, Kris Reyes, Laura Robinson, Jim Barnett, Aaron Payne, Gabriel LeMay, and Ashley Hoffman.

Against the Washington Times, CNN scored runs in every inning except the sixth and seventh, and by that time, the game was already out of reach. The team forged a 16-4 lead and cruised to victory.

The Metropolitan Media Softball League season continues this Saturday with another doubleheader. CNN plays U.S. News and NBC News Channel. Take a break from Solitaire and come out to watch the action.

May 11, 2002

GAME 1		GAME 2	
CNN	5	CNN	19
U.S. NEWS	1	NBC NEWS CHANNEL	6

- **CNN vaults into first place with badass fielding, pinpoint pitching, and hot hitting.**
- **Bond investors rate softball team AAA+, but company just above junk.**
- **Turner Group Services celebrates doubleheader sweep by posting employees' direct deposit information on the Web.**

By Joe Baseball Jr.
Bureau Sports Writer

SILVER SPRING, Md. (UPI) — CNN is on a roll and just in time. Only days after CNN executives issued a read-me mandate to all newsroom employees to find ways to "think more creatively" and "add value," the softball team stepped up to the plate and won the day.

On a cloudless spring morning at Veirs Mill Park, U.S. News and NBC News Channel grasped the shocking reality of what happens when CNN is backed into a corner. It responds like a lion at Busch Gardens.

The day was one of contrasts as CNN (6-2) toyed with its first opponent before proving superior in the opener and then made mincemeat of the opposition in the nightcap.

"We needed this," said Marylynn Ryan, managing editor, CNN/US, when informed the softball team had surged ahead of ABC (5-3) to take over the top of the Capitalview Division. "We took some heat last week for running the Fungi Cure ads and devoting nine hours of coverage to the Vanilla Coke taste testing, but that's all behind us. Jimmy Carter's trip to Cuba and CNN softball are today's Day Drivers."

CNN lived up to its charter of efficiently and accurately getting the job done on the double. It took only 38 minutes to dispose of U.S. News, one of the better teams in the Metropolitan Media Softball League, in a low-scoring defensive game, 5-1.

Gold Glove Pitcher Greg Robertson gave up just six hits. In one stretch, he retired 12 of 14 batters. Jack Lynn's RBI single in the second inning proved to be the winner. Darrin White also had three hits and two RBI.

The game was broadcast nationally on CNN/Sports Illustrated, which is scheduled to have its plug pulled permanently on Wednesday. "I hope Aaron Brown will let me guest host when he's on vacation," said depressed essayist and sports anchor Jim Huber.

A spokeswoman for corporate parent AOL Time Warner said its priority now will be on innovative programming "like *American Morning*" and not S-I, which "never turned a profit" in five years.

Hoping to cash in on the softball team's winning ways and the surging popularity of MTV's *The Osbournes*, Executive Editor Sid Bedingfield disclosed that CNN is developing a similar reality-based family program featuring anchor Leon Harris condensed to 13 half-hour episodes. "If you like softball, you'll love this," he predicted.

"I hope folks watch," added Harris.

The storyline in Game 2 against NBC News Channel was all about the number three. CNN scored three runs in the first, second, third, fifth, and sixth innings (plus four in the seventh), taking a breather in the fourth inning to eat Rice Krispies Treats made by catcher Lindy Royce. NBC also did its damage in triplets, putting three on the scoreboard in the fourth and sixth. Final score, 19-6.

"It was a sloppy mess out there," said NBC's Andrea Mitchell. "Worse than the inside of the Church of Nativity."

"We Brok-awed their backs," chanted the crowd, led by Virginia Nicolaidis, who endured several contractions while on the bench. Becky Brittain, Marty Kramer (and Ranger, Howie Lutt's parents, and Alex's boyfriend Steven were on hand to catch Virginia's baby if necessary.

There were many heroes on this day. One standout was Jessica Rosgaard, who was understandably mistaken for Barry Bonds by NBC's pitcher. Jess walked three times and came around to score twice. Alex also had a great day offensively, 2-3, and in the field. She twice scooped up grounders and made Ozzie Smith-like backhanded tosses to John King, covering the bag at second.

In the second game, each player took a bite of the apple. Ten different people scored; 10 had at least one RBI. The stars were aligned for Brad Wright, Erik Tavcar, John Davis, Kris Reyes, Ralph Marcus, Willie Lora, and Jim Barnett, all of whom took turns placing bets that Joe Baseball wouldn't make it through his write-up without a snide comment about AOL's $54 billion quarterly loss, equal to the gross national product of New Zealand.

Those who predicted he would dredge up a reference to the good ol' days at CNN were also disheartened.

The MMSL is quiet for the next two weeks, but the team resumes action on June 1 when CNN faces Post.com and National Geographic.

June 1, 2002

GAME 1	GAME 2
WASHINGTON POST.COM.........13	CNN...18
CNN...12	NATIONAL GEOGRAPHIC............6

- **CNN splits doubleheader but holds on to first place.**
- **Network promises to pull Ditech.com ads if winning ways continue.**
- **Softball team shows al Qaeda-like resilience after two-week layoff.**
- **ADDS Graphic designer fired after using picture of cashmere sweater instead of map of disputed Kashmir region.**

By Joe Baseball Jr.
Bureau Sports Writer

LAYHILL, Md. (UPI) — Forget the ominous tug-of-war between Islamabad and New Delhi. Never mind that 'NSync's Lance Bass recently became a certified cosmonaut. The world is facing other front burner and day driver issues.

On the brink of an epic crack-up after a lackluster effort in Game 1 against the Washington Post.com, CNN's softball team stared into the cra-VAHS and stormed back in Game 2 to drown National Geographic in six innings on Saturday at Layhill Park, 18-6.

"Put this on your map," gestured one unidentified player, wearing a CNN T-shirt with the word 'Synergy' written in faded lettering.

A spokesman for the Human Resources department cautioned employees to control their emotions on the field. "If this disrespectful, harassing, inappropriate continuum of softball behavior keeps up, I will mandate weekly 'Building Respect' workshops and start hitting people upside the head," he said defiantly.

The blowout victory against National Geo helped lessen the sting of losing the first game, 13-12, only CNN's third loss of the year, each by one run. CNN (7-3) has a one-game lead over division rival ABC.

"It was like ending up with half a loaf," chimed CNN's Richard Quest during a Golden Jubilee marshmallow roast inside Buckingham Palace over the weekend.

"Everybody is invited to join me for the dedication of my brand-spankin' new trillion-dollar studio on Sixth Avenue and 51st Street this month," said an enraptured Connie Chung, who was contacted for comment about the games. Instead, she used a megaphone to describe her upcoming unnamed show as a cross between Paula Zahn's *Yap Fest* and Aaron Brown's *Info Hour*. "Between you and me, that's not my quote. I read it in the New York Observer."

Immediately after the games, Frank Newport conducted a Gallup Poll about recreational softball and other worldly matters covered only by CNN. It found 85% want just 'walk and talk' packages; 15% said Michael Skakel, the Kennedy cousin soon-to-be convicted of murder, should dethrone Larry King, and 5% urged CNN to triple the number of factoids on the screen and change its name to the Clutter News Network. Newport yammered, "The survey has no margin of error."

"This was more fun than re-booting computers," said Tech Support's Tom Bentz, who showed up with his family for the late-inning action.

"The bureau is blowing through money by flying Bob Franken to Guantanamo each month and spending a king's (no relation to John) ransom relocating the make-up room," gleaned Administrative Manager Patti Kloehn. "It's nice to see a low-budget success story like the softball team."

The day started out a cluster after a hazardous chemical spill halted traffic on the Beltway and delayed the Washington Post.com. Under normal circumstances, a game is forfeited after a 10-minute grace period if one team can't field enough players. But it was pushed back an hour to allow for late arrivals. Too bad for CNN. Fourteen players made it on time and were forced to cool their heels in the hot morning sun.

That proved to be the turning point in the game. Already suffering from dehydration and with only chocolate brownies made by Lindy Royce to sustain them, CNN fell behind early but staged a comeback with three runs in the third inning to take a 5-4 lead. Monica Suber, who burst onto the scene for the first time since she was an intern, started the rally with a single. Erik Tavcar also hit safely. With two outs, John King (4-4, 2 RBI) doubled in a run. Howie Lutt brought in two more runs with a triple. Darrin White, John Davis, and Laura Robinson also answered the call.

CNN couldn't hold the lead, and Post.com took advantage of fielding snafus to move in front 13-7 with only one at-bat left. CNN scored on a Jack Lynn double. With two outs and the bases juiced, Howie struck a ball that sailed over the center field fence for a grand slam, bringing CNN within a run, 13-12. The team had one last moon shot, but Post.com's center fielder made a running catch of a line drive by David Gracey to end the game.

In the nightcap, CNN never trailed against National Geographic. The team took navigational control in the second inning by sending 17 players to the plate and scoring 11 runs courtesy of six walks. David had the biggest hit, a three-run homer. He also added a two-run shot. In addition, Alex reached safely, as did Aaron, Lindy, Brad, Jessica, Erik, Greg, Jack, John King, and Ralph. Only Jim Barnett couldn't find a way to get on base, which some in the peanut gallery viewed as a blatant attempt to get his name in the Joe Baseball column.

Halfway through the game, the umpire passed gas and said he had to leave because of a prior commitment. Jack volunteered to call balls and strikes for the last several innings. "It was no more of a challenge than staying awake through *NewsNight*," asserted Lynn.

The softball games continue this Saturday with another doubleheader against division slowpokes CBS and Fox at Capitalview Park.

June 8, 2002

GAME 1		GAME 2	
CNN	17	CNN	15
CBS NEWS	2	FOX NEWS	2

- **Softball team stays in first place after thoroughly stomping CBS and Fox News.**
- **Players never break sweat in doubleheader romp, like tanks through Ramallah.**
- **Anchor Lou Dobbs does flip-flop, declares war against Arthur Andersen, not Islamists.**
- **Eds: Al Qaeda sympathizer Jose Padilla attempts to swap out softballs with whiffle balls before exploding dirty bomb.**

By Joe Baseball Jr.
Bureau Sports Writer

KENSINGTON, Md. (UPI) — Look closely at the faces of CNN staffers in Washington this week. Notice something different? They're smiling. And for good reason. The softball team belittled CBS News and Fox News on Saturday in less time than it takes to start and finish a future's future meeting.

CNN (9-3) decapitated CBS in the opener, 17-2, and then gutted Fox News, 15-2, in the nightcap. "I saw more bones on the softball field than in Rock Creek Park," grunted Washington D.C. Police Chief Charles Ramsey, who stopped by to check out reports of an assault worse than the Los Angeles Lakers-New Jersey Nets series.

Following the shellacking, CBS' Dan Rather immediately ordered his staff to change the name of the *Evening News with Dan Rather* to *Black Eye on America*. "Kenneth, what's the frequency?" he spouted. At Fox, Greta Van Susteren was unavailable for comment after her face tightened.

Both games ended in the fifth inning with a Lennox Lewis-like pummeling after the umpire said he was getting sick to his stomach watching the massacre. What could account for CNN's total domination? Money.

Before the first pitch, CNN Executive Eason Jordan alerted the network via Blackberry about introducing financial sweeteners for all newsgatherers throughout the company. (News Standards and Practices and

Legal are exempt.) He also promised each player an autographed ball from AOL Chairman Steve Case if they won both games. "Hang on to it," said Jordan. "One day, it could be worth as much as one share of Time Warner stock. More if there's a stock split."

The softball team responded faster than it took the graphics department to find Kandahar on a map.

During the second inning against CBS, when the score was 13-1, one CNN player advocated replaying *American Morning* every four hours at noon, 4p, 8p, and midnight and then putting together the best-of highlights and running them after *Late Edition with Wolf Blitzer* the last word in Sunday talk.

With CNN up 17-1, another player, who requested anonymity, proposed eliminating White House reports and replacing them with fullscreen factoids. He also broached charging for Red Phone calls.

In Game 2 and with CNN already ahead 8-0, someone proposed eliminating workplace distractions such as questionnaires from the facilities department. "We want to know what you think of us," Manager Kim Linden pleaded.

The best suggestion of the day came from one player, who stated that CNN employees could get more work done on Mondays if the Joe Baseball write-ups went away.

With CNN already enjoying a 3-0 lead in Game 1, Brad Wright doubled. After an out, Willie Lora singled. Lindy Royce legged out a single and got an RBI. Erik Tavcar singled, as did Darrin White, to load the bases. Greg Roberston tripled. John King tripled, too. After another out, Jack Lynn singled. Alex Dermanis kept the onslaught going with a single. Brad came up to bat for a second time in the inning and singled. Laura Robinson walked. Willie hit another single. You get the drift.

D.C. Bureau Chief Kathryn Kross made her first appearance of the year. She singled, scored, and played several innings at second base like a consummate major leaguer. "I wish I could bottle up the fervor I felt and drop it like a thermobaric bomb on Atlanta," said a misty-eyed Kross.

It was more of the same in the nightcap. Lindy (3-4) and Brad (5-5) continued their hot hitting. David Gracey went 3-3 with four RBI, including a two-run homer and a bases-loaded single. Jessica Rosgaard, Ralph Marcus, and Jim Barnett also chipped in.

It was a particularly gratifying day not only because of the way CNN played but also because of who came to watch.

Virginia Nicolaidis strolled out for a look-see with four-week-old Demetri, decked out in a pin-striped softball uniform.

Jim Connor also rolled by on his bike as the celebration was coming to an end.

There are no games this weekend, but CNN is back in action with another doubleheader on June 22 against WJLA and NewsChannel 8.

June 22, 2002

GAME 1		GAME 2	
CNN	14	NEWSCHANNEL 8	7
WJLA	13	CNN	3

- **CNN withers in summer heat; barely manages to eke out doubleheader split.**
- **Softball team clings to first place with four games left.**
- **Coach blames lackadaisical effort on the "Susan Rook" factor, orders players to undergo urinalysis.**
- **DELETES Capitol Hill Producer Dana Bash intercepts classified NSA message: "Today is Monday, Tomorrow is Tuesday, and the day after that is Wednesday."**

By Joe Baseball Jr.
Bureau Sports Writer

BETHESDA, Md. (UPI) — Veteran TV anchor Connie Chung calls it one of the "worst" things ever to happen in her storied career at CNN.

"Highway robbery," said a displeased Chung after learning CNN executives in Atlanta will run the Bank of America commercial (the one where Jeffrey locks his wife out of the room while he applies for a mortgage) just one time during the debut of *Connie Chung Tonight*. "Every other CNN show gets to play it 14 times an hour," she pointed out.

A public relations spokeswoman affirmed her department's in-house TV sets "don't get cable," so she could not comment because she hadn't seen the story.

Chung did release a statement. "I'm already freakin' frustrated because my bookers lost Catherine Crier's home phone number, and Lou Dobbs got her first on his show. Then Paula Zahn landed a big get, Richard Quest, the nutty reporter in London. Adding salt to the wound, Aaron Brown got

Stephanopoulos. That left me with my fourth choice, Ann Landers."

"I can deal with it," Chung lashed out, "But what gets me is that all the hoopla at CNN should be on me this week! By the way, did you see me on *American Morning* tying Bill Hemmer's shoelaces? Instead, the softball team spoils it all by playing like a bunch of namby-pambies, and everyone is talking about that."

No specious argument there.

CNN (10-4) did not play like a first-place team on Saturday at Burning Tree Park after blowing an 11-run lead to WJLA but hanging on to win the opener, 14-13. In the second game, CNN brought nothing to the table and fell asleep at the wheel against undermanned, or in this case, underwomanned, NewsChannel 8, 7-3.

The local all-news station only had two women on its roster, and under MMSL rules, the team is assessed an automatic out every time that open position comes up in the batting order. But NewsChannel 8 wasn't phased in the slightest.

It was CNN's most vexing setback of the year. CNN's previous losses were by a total of three runs. The combined performances on this day against two sub-.500 teams left many probing if the players just need a good car chase in California, more forest fires out West, or an anthrax scare for a pick-me-up.

"We have to look at whether this is something we want our viewers to see," said Marylynn Ryan, managing editor of CNN/US. "Does the softball team have relevance anymore?" Is it worth a factoid? Are people in the D.C. Bureau's newly renovated makeup room talking about it? We need to ask Skip."

The day started as it often does in the newsroom, but the situation deteriorated like nobody's business. This time, no one could blame it on the Red Phone.

CNN took an eye-popping 12-1 lead after four innings, riding the hot bat of Darrin White, Howie Lutt, Greg Robertson, John King, and Erik Tavcar. They were a combined 16-19 with 11 RBI.

Darrin played as if charged with radioactive particles from a dirty bomb. He went 4-4 with 5 RBI, including two homers, the last one coming in the seventh inning to build what should have been a comfortable 14-7 lead.

But WJLA, exhibiting the passion of their late coach, Dale Solly, and the audacity of the South Korean World Cup soccer team, never gave up and came back, putting the tying run on second and the winning run on first with two outs. The last batter hit a lazy fly to right to end the drama.

There was nothing left in the tank for CNN in the nightcap. Even the triumphant return of D.C. Deputy Bureau Chief Steve Redisch to his old team couldn't jumpstart CNN. "I was willing to play every position, but I can't do everything for this organization." It was a point seconded by the rest of the players whose identities have become household names: Jack Lynn, Alex Dermanis, Laura Robinson, Aaron Payne, Ralph Marcus, Lindy Royce, and Jim Barnett.

The statistics tell the story against NewsChannel 8: 18 of CNN's 21 outs were fly balls, and the first four batters were 1 for 11.

One bright spot was the largest turnout of the year. The Kramer family (Amy, Marty, and Ranger), the Redisch family (Elizabeth, Lena, and Annabel), the Payne family (Paula, Nathan, and Meghan), and Alex's boyfriend Steven and Dave Adhicary were on hand.

This Saturday, CNN faces its toughest doubleheader of the year… cross-company rival AOL (11-3) and two-time defending champion Gazette (10-4) in games that could go a long way in deciding whether CNN will make Connie Chung proud.

June 29, 2002

GAME 1		GAME 2	
AOL	9	GAZETTE	7
CNN	8	CNN	5

- **Team swept out of first place after late-inning losses.**
- **Once again, CNN is forced to suffer at hands of its corporate parent.**
- **Softball players down but not out; do-or-die scenario in season finale on July 13.**
- **Eds: Note 7th graph correcting reference of AOL stinking image to sinking image.**

By Joe Baseball Jr.
Bureau Sports Writer

LAYHILL, Md. (UPI) — Let there be no confusion. There was a transfer of power on Saturday morning in the United States, but it wasn't between two guys named George and Dick. The power vacuum occurred at Layhill Park between CNN and a pair of media titans, AOL and Gazette.

By day's end, CNN (10-6) was no longer king of the softball hill, having endured its own version of a colonoscopy. According to the box score, they lost to America Online, 9-8, after giving up a three-run homer in the sixth inning. In the second game, CNN threw away opportunities in a gut-wrenching 7-5 setback at the hands of two-time defending champions Gazette.

"Our players were wound tighter than a Timex watch," said one angry fan, who peppered his comments with some choice vulgarities like splashes of Tabasco on a plate of red beans and rice.

It was CNN's third straight loss. Four of its six have been by one run. The twin killings on Saturday dropped the inconsistent CaNiNes a game behind ABC with two to play, including one against CBS and a season-ender versus ABC. If CNN wins both, they will claim the division title and automatically qualify for the playoffs. A loss to either team sends them packing. CNN beat them both at the beginning of the season.

The showdown with AOL in Game 1 did not go as the CNN players had expected in the first-ever meeting between the two teams.

Unlike the corporate world, where AOL plays loose with the numbers and tries to write off every expense, the softball team came prepared to play hardball. The company Steve Case built showed not a care in the world as they openly laughed during the pre-game warmups about losing $54 billion in the first quarter.

"We've made bigger boo-boos in the outfield," joked AOL Chief Executive Richard Parsons. "Notwithstanding the worthless stock price, the good news is our players aren't in a slump. Wait until you see what our net worth is next month. It's all about high-speed connections. CNN's problem is not breaking news but a broken news format."

CNN hoped to take advantage of AOL's degraded image and woebegone ways. In an unfortunate case of bad timing, Lou Dobbs showed up as the teams took the field to say Lehman Brothers was raising its third-quarter earnings estimate for AOL from five cents a share to six cents. These days, you can't even purchase a postcard stamp for that price.

"I think AOL is a buy based on my calculations of cash flow before taxes, depreciation, and amortization," said Dobbs, host of *Lou Dobbs Moneyline*, a program that takes in more revenue per viewer than any other television show, a remarkable statistic when one considers only eight people watched last week. "I want each of them to know I'm a big fan of WorldCom, ImClone, Xerox, Tyco, Adelphia, and Arthur Andersen."

That was all the encouragement AOL needed to hear. Their third batter of the game smashed a solo home run to stake them to an early lead. But CNN ignored AOL like it always does and scored two runs of its own in the second inning with the help of Darrin White, Brad Wright, Lindy Royce, and Jim Barnett.

AOL then went in front 3-2. CNN barreled ahead thanks partly to Erik Tavcar, David Gracey, John Davis, John King, and Howie Lutt, who helped push across six runs in the fifth inning to take an 8-6 lead. With time running out, the pendulum swung one last time in favor of AOL. Their clean-up hitter blasted a pitch just over the center field fence for a three-run homer. That was the ball game.

"You'll always be a subsidiary," berated AOL founder Steve Case in a prepared statement after his team walked off the field. "CNN will never understand synergy. Mark my words."

Media mogul Ted Turner, the largest individual shareholder of AOL, lambasted the online provider with his salvo. At a luncheon of cable executives in Atlanta, he said, "That company in Virginia is just a bunch of tech geeks. Don't forget I ousted Jerry Levin as chief executive so he could pursue moral and social issues. I might take charge again of CNN and get rid of everyone at AOL if that helps."

Producers for *Connie Chung Tonight* were asked to comment, but a young person answering the phone in New York said frantically, "Can you call back? The fire alarm has gone off again, and Connie's going ballistic."

The second game against Gazette was every bit as painful for CNN. With the score tied at five, Alex Dermanis got caught off first base. She tried to scramble back to the bag, but her left knee buckled. Her boyfriend and several players assisted her off the field as the Royce family applauded Alex's effort. Hospital x-rays proved to be negative, which did little to allay concerns.

Even with the help of Ralph Marcus, Jessica Rosgaard, Laura Robinson, and the rest of the gang that couldn't hit a cabbage ball if their lives depended on it, CNN went down to defeat after a defensive lapse handed Gazette two gift runs in the sixth inning. Unlike AOL, which showed no remorse and only concern for its growth prospects and balance sheet, several Gazette players exhibited class by going out of their way at the end of the game to check on Alex as she iced her knee under the shade of a tree.

So, the season has come down to this… a must-win situation for CNN, the once proud company with three distinctive letters personifying the best-known brand in news. Put July 13 on the calendar, Blackberry, or PowerPoint.

Come one, come all. Beat CBS and ABC and help push the creative envelope that executives in Atlanta have demanded.

July 13, 2002

GAME 1		GAME 2	
CNN	18	CNN	13
CBS NEWS	6	ABC NEWS	10

- **CNN captures MMSL division title, next stop the playoffs.**
- **Softball team sweep makes waste of broadcast networks.**
- **Tears, cheers, and beers as regular season ends with flourish.**
- **DELETES reference to John Walker Lindh vowing to form his own team with al Qaeda and Taliban.**

By Joe Baseball Jr.
Bureau Sports Writer

KENSINGTON, Md. (UPI) — More over feng shui. You've got company. Look no further than CNN's softball team, where energy flow, balance, and luck have found a foothold.

There is no better feeling as a journalist than being an eyewitness to a compelling and historic event. On that rare occasion when the storyline and the reporter intersect, it has the makings of something extraordinary.

That's precisely what happened Saturday at Capitalview field as CNN's squad played as one and embarrassed CBS News, 18-6, teaching the smug commercial network a valuable lesson that if you're going to have a motto like 'Wake Up to What's Happening," you better not screw up.

CNN then knocked the stuffing out of ABC News in a come-from-behind game for the ages, a rollicking 13-10 victory en route to winning the Capitalview Division. Talk about corporate responsibility. No fuzzy math here, as President George Bush would say.

The scores don't even begin to tell the enticing, anxiety-ridden story. Wait until you hear the tale about the Dirty Dozen, the 12 players proudly wearing the CNN logo. They persevered when it counted in two tension-filled games. It was more nerve-wracking than trying to watch Headline News. It was more distracting than receiving 325 Outlook emails daily about updated rundowns and more distressing than tracking a dwindling 401K portfolio.

Look who's laughing now. Everyone is talking about CNN's Dream Team.

Check out the partial transcript of The Whip (copyright) from Saturday night as anchor Aaron Brown hosted a special edition of *NewsNight*.

"Kelli Arena, a headline, please."

"More devastating than an anthrax attack. CNN's softball team today causes widespread mayhem and butchery."

"Kelli, thank you. To Arizona and Ed Lavandera, a headline from you."

"Aaron, we missed the Elizabeth Smart news conference and the police detailing an arrest in the kidnapping case, but we do have a reaction about the CNN softball games."

"Ed, thank you. We'll be back to you. Now a headline from Nic Robertson in Bagram."

"U.S. troops celebrate CNN softball victories. Also, Osama bin Laden is captured."

"Thanks, Nic. I didn't know about OBL. Hopefully, we'll have time to get into that in our Segment Seven after our interview with the new HIV-positive Sesame Street Muppet."

Saturday was a remarkable day on many levels. CNN (12-6) needed a sweep to have any mathematical probability of making it to the postseason. In a moving pre-game ceremony, the daughters of Dale Solly presented Jim Barnett with a sportsmanship and camaraderie award named in honor of the late WJLA anchor. A befuddled Barnett was injured during a group hug.

CBS, winners of only five games all year, played like a bunch of Martha Stewart fanatics in the opener. CNN held a shaky 9-6 lead thanks largely to Jack Lynn's first-inning two-run homer and a two-run single in his next at-bat, plus a solo home run from John Davis.

CNN took command in the fifth inning when EVERY hitter got on base. Jessica Rosgaard pumped up the team by staring down the opposing pitcher. She was one of five batters issued a walk and scored. Three players got two hits in the inning as the club exploded for nine runs. The carnage ended, thankfully. One game down, one to go.

ABC took the field in a rematch of the season opener, which CNN won. That was then. This is now. ABC jumped in front 7-1 after two innings. John King, whose diving catches at shortstop snuffed out several rallies, smashed a three-run homer to cut the six-run lead in half. But ABC got those three runs right back to take a 10-4 advantage.

CNN squandered a bases-loaded gift in the fourth by hitting into an inning-ending double play. Many of those on hand, including Jessica's mom, Darrin White's wife, and the King and Barnett family ensemble, started packing their picnic blankets and heading for the exits. But wait. This was just a tease, an appetizer. The main course was coming, and CNN was ready to feast in the fifth.

Darrin (7-7 on the day) continued his blistering assault with a leadoff single. One out later, the double Johns (Davis and King) got on base. Dependable Howie Lutt brought in a run on a sacrifice fly to make it interesting at 10-6, but there were now two outs.

The bottom of the batting order had something to prove. Lindy Royce hit a single, one of her four against ABC. She adamantly denied putting steroids in her Rice Krispies Treats. Fresh from his award ceremony, Jim Barnett stopped weeping long enough to single and load the bases. Willie Lora, hungry after two weeks of hospital food while helping his father sail through surgery, socked a back-breaking grand slam to put CNN in the lead. Laura Robinson kept the rally going with a rocket through the infield. Kathryn Kross stuck it to her former employer with a solid base hit and several bone-bruising catches in the outfield. Darrin followed with another hit before the inning ended. It was now 11-10, CNN's advantage, and a whole new ballgame.

Stretching the lead to 13-10, CNN needed only three more outs in the seventh inning to seal an automatic invitation to the playoffs and the team's second straight undefeated year in the Capitalview Division. And they would have to do it with DEE-FENCE.

ABC sent up its three, four, and five hitters. Jack scooped out a mitt full of dirt and the ball and made a perfect throw to first base for the first out.

ABC's next batter hit a moon shot that sailed well over 350 feet from home plate that a streaking David Gracey nabbed in the webbing of his glove as he pirouetted around trees in center field for out number two. You had to see it to believe it. The giant sucking sound was the air escaping from the Mickey Mouse blimp.

But it wasn't quite over. ABC kept things interesting by getting the next two batters on base and the tying run at bat, but a pop-up ended the game. Signed. Sealed. Delivered.

Will the merrymaking continue? Tune in next week as CNN joins the elite nine in a playoff tournament at the fabulous fields of Cabin John Regional Park. Grab your pom-poms. If you live in New York, Atlanta, Los Angeles, or any other CNN bureau city, make your reservations now.

July 20, 2002

GAME 1		GAME 2	
CNN	12	CNN	17
WASHINGTON POST.COM	10	AOL	4
GAME 3		GAME 4 (CHAMPIONSHIP)	
CNN	8	CNN	12
USA TODAY	4	AOL	8

- **CNN! Champions of the Metropolitan Media Softball League for 2002.**
- **Team wins all four playoff games, including two against AOL.**
- **Softball team king of the mountain, top of the heap, numero uno! How sweet it is!**
- **DELETES reference to *American Morning* sidekick Jack Cafferty ordered to stop chronic grousing and say something nice about softball team each day for a week.**
- **Eds: Add 7th graph with AOL stock price tumbles to 49 cents.**

By Joe Baseball Jr.
Bureau Sports Writer

ROCKVILLE, Md. (UPI) — The waiter at Ledo's Pizza near Cabin John Regional Park had a premonition Saturday. He knew who the MMSL champions would be before anyone else. He saw the confidence on the faces of CNN players who stopped by after the first day of the playoffs.

"Take care of business, and come back to see us tomorrow," he said.

CNN did that and more on a magical, memorable, and muggy Sunday afternoon at Shirley Povich Stadium. You read that right. It happened in a stadium setting, with billboards lining the warning track—no overgrown, gnat-infested, pebble-strewn, worn-out soccer surface fields here.

CNN played with intestinal fortitude and doggedness worthy of a deserving champion.

The CaNiNes walked away with the big trophy (plus a division trophy, individual trophies, and T-shirts imprinted with the word 'Champions') after soundly defeating America Online by a score of 12-8. It was emblazoned on the electronic scoreboard.

This was AOL's second loss in two days to CNN and further signaled that the Internet behemoth has more problems than being a pitiful company with no future and net worth. When it comes to softball, AOL has nothing to offer. "They're wussies," said the two umpires as they collapsed with laughter on the infield grass.

On Saturday morning, the first day of the playoffs, CNN started its march to the finals with a workman-like effort against Washington Post.com, 12-10. Then, the team administered a complete pasting of AOL, 17-4, in Game 2. The day of marathon back-to-back-to-back games ended in three-part harmony in the early afternoon as CNN did twice as well as USA Today, 8-4.

Everyone was a hero. Not a weak link in the bunch.

The three straight victories left CNN atop the winner's division on Saturday, awaiting the outcome of the loser's bracket. That was settled on Sunday morning when AOL beat both the Gazette, aiming for an unprecedented three-peat, and USA Today to knock those teams out of the double-loss elimination tournament.

The table was set. Judgment Day. CNN, a No. 6 seed with a regular season record of 12-6, versus AOL, a No. 2 seed, which finished 15-3. On paper, the odds makers gave the edge to the Dulles-based company in its second year in the MMSL. CNN, champions in 1999 and runner-up in the title game last year, had history, experience, and much more heart.

It took less than an hour for AOL to implode on the softball field, slightly more time than the giant media empire needed to lose most of its dwindling stock market value.

As the Washington Post reported in its Sunday edition, it has been a remarkable arc for AOL. In a little over a decade, the company has gone from just another Internet service provider to a chest-beating leviathan with a sky-high stock price and then back to a flash-in-the-pan business that's at the point of joining the Junior League next year instead of the Metropolitan Media Softball League.

"Let's face it, we haven't had a good week," said outgoing Chief Operating Officer Robert Pittman, who was caught panhandling outside the DuPont Circle Metro station. "Things just haven't worked out the way we thought they would. Brother, can you spare a dime?"

CNN wasn't in a charitable mood over the weekend despite the fact the CaNiNes did gift the first three runs of the game in the first inning against AOL. CNN also considered extending *Late Edition with Wolf Blitzer* an extra three hours, but a spokesperson for the last word in Sunday talk said the show had run out of things to rehash. "We were so immersed in our Blackberries and reports we were getting about the softball games, we forgot about Condoleezza Rice in the Green Room," foamed Executive Producer Bob Kovach.

AOL retired the first five CNN batters. It was an ugly start if you were a fan of the CaNiNes. "We came out more blah than every Connie Chung show open," whispered one unidentified player. CNN escaped serious damage in the second inning when, with the bases loaded, shortstop John King grabbed a slow grounder, tagged a runner, and fired to first to complete a double play and keep the score at 3-1.

Red-faced executives at AOL immediately seized the stadium's public address system and encouraged the standing-room-only crowd to dance to the Village People's Y.M.C.A. song to rattle CNN. The move backfired. Between innings, 62 people immediately switched Internet providers.

In the top of the fourth, CNN took a 5-3 lead, a lead it would never relinquish (I love that cliché). Erik Tavcar, John Davis, John King, and Birthday Boy Howie Lutt hit safely. After an RBI out by David Gracey, Laura Robinson singled in a run, and then Jack Lynn doubled.

All the pre-game talk about a company needing genetic engineering fell by the wayside. DNA matter from AOL was now spread across the manicured grass from first to third.

The message was clear. AOL's promise of energy, youth and vision had merely been wishful thinking. If an aging media species primed for crossbreeding to adapt to 21st-century trends existed, it was AOL, not *Larry King Live* or *Inside Politics*.

"We went on a retreat this past weekend," babbled an IP producer, speaking on condition of anonymity. "We decided we're going to follow the softball blueprint from here on out. You can't lose."

The next inning, CNN saw to that.

Kathryn Kross led off with a solid single up the middle. After a fielder's choice by Lindy Royce, Darrin White, Erik Tavcar, John Davis, John King, Howie Lutt, David Gracey, Laura Robinson, Greg Robertson, and Jack Lynn worked their supernatural powers as they've done all year both at bat and in the field.

With Willie Lora, Ralph Marcus, Jessica Rosgaard, Aaron Payne, and Jim Barnett igniting the troops and sharing fresh supplies of steroids in the dugout, CNN grew the lead to 12-3. AOL was getting the message this game was moving toward high-speed internet access. But they were too consumed with trying to dial up help and getting a busy signal.

Like a cat with a mouse, CNN toyed with the upstarts from northern Virginia over the next two innings. AOL crawled back to 12-8 in the seventh. That's as close as they got. Jack recorded the first out of the inning, catching a line drive. Then came a force at second for the next out. In a game full of symbolism and irony, the CaNiNes highest-ranking teammate in management, Washington Bureau Chief Kathryn Kross, reached up and reeled in a fly ball in the webbing of her glove for the last out in center field and yelled, "Who's got mail now?" Let the celebration begin.

If any of this doesn't ring true, ask some of those who came out to witness AOL's train derailment caused by the Little Engine That Could. There was Rebecca Ratliff from National Geographic, Abbi Tatton, Amy Kramer and Ranger, Becky Brittain, Charles Bierbauer, Steve and the entire Redisch family, Jim Barnett's family and Katy the Corgi, John Kings' kids, Lindy Royce's parents and sister, Greg Robertson's son Kevin, Barbara Starr, Gary Krakower, Evan Glass, John Davis's brother and photographer Michelle Poley, who chronicled the deciding game with her Nikon and took hundreds of action-packed photos.

After the victory speeches and the celebration on the field, CNN players cruised to Ledo's Pizza, where the prognosticating waiter once again greeted the team with pizza and beer.

The CaNiNes' win was all the buzz on local FM alternative rock radio station DC101.

AOL may have thought it could become the international e-mail gateway when it started decades ago, but there's more to life than hubris. They discovered that being a catalyzer may be intoxicating but also fleeting. If you're going to walk with a swagger and talk the talk, you must be able to back it up with character, purpose, dedication, and teamwork.

In this dog-eat-dog world of three-letter media companies, AOL has become a dinosaur, a pop-up ad, a trivia question, and something to tell your kids to look up on Google's search engine.

If you've assimilated anything about softball this season as a reader and fan, put your money on CNN. You can never go wrong with a winner.

CNN's players are champions!

Check out the championship trophy and team photo in the newsroom.

If you want to be part of the action next year, start planning to get off the weekend shift now.

TOP OF THE 6th

Clash of the Titans

April 20, 2003

- **CNN softball team poised to unleash WMD.**
- **Returning champions ready for start of season.**
- **Dr. Sanjay Gupta and Devil Docs to throw out first ball, then perform brain surgery at third base.**
- **DELETE all references to Aaron Brown.**

By Joe Baseball Jr.
Bureau Sports Writer

WASHINGTON (UPI) — The battle for Baghdad is over. The fight for softball supremacy is about to begin.

Much has happened since July, when CNN defeated AOL to complete a spellbinding season.

TV critics have battered CNN's reputation. Editorial writers are taking potshots whenever possible, and competitors are laughing behind the backs of a demoralized staff. And that's just because of *NewsNight*.

So, what does CNN's softball team do for an encore after going 16-6 and undefeated in division play in 2002, winning its last six games, including four in the playoffs, and earning the championship trophy?

Rinse, repeat, of course. But it won't be easy. The team will need more luck than the Fedayeen insurgents. Is foreign correspondent Ryan Chilcote still embedded with the 1st Airborne Division?

CNN will have to rely on its mix of experience and youth. Only two teams have won back-to-back titles since the Metropolitan Media Softball League began in 1991.

"It's open season," said CNN's news chief, Eason Jordan, in a memo from his bunker in Conyers, Georgia. "I told Uday (Hussein) to tell his father that if the remnants of the Iraqi Republican Guard want the full effect of shock and awe, they should look at our softball lineup."

Ten hardcore CNN players ignored Saturday morning's chilly and damp conditions to get in a few practice swings. Perhaps they merely wanted a team shirt and cap. They postponed dying Easter eggs long enough to scrimmage against archrival ABC, among them Howie Lutt, Lindy Royce, Willie Lora, Ralph Marcus, Darrin White, Laura Robinson, and Jim Barnett, along with rookies Darryl Diamond, Josh Braun, Stephanie Kotuby, and Stephen Bach.

It will be the only practice this preseason marred by lousy weekend weather, the Iraq war, and a 24/7 work schedule so complicated that Newsroom Manager Pam Kelley needed four Excel spreadsheets to handle the live producer shifts.

"We want all our players to be chirpier," sang out domestic executive Teya Ryan in an edict officially changing CNN's name to the Chirpy News Network. "If we can't have happy people on our staff, I'll have to re-hire Allan Dodds Frank. All three of them. We'll do anything to keep the good times rolling."

"I'm thinking of a new interactive, variety program anchored by that dude from Travelocity," advertised CNN President Jim Walton. It will be part *Larry Sanders*, part *Talk Back Live*," said Walton, who promised to give the softball team his total commitment after he figures out what to do with curmudgeon commentator Jack Cafferty. "I like sports."

CNN's softball team is prepared to carry the network on its back again to attract viewers. "I don't know what SARS stands for, but I do know what the letters C-N-N mean to this company," whispered Richard Griffiths, a marquee attraction on the Row.

"We've got some folks ready to make a difference," said Guest Bookings' Gail Chalef, whose Rolodex contains the phone numbers of every guest who appeared on *CNN & Co*. "I came this close (indicating with her thumb and index finger) to getting the teacher of the year. At the last minute, Connie Chung booked her to spite us. I did snag Jeffrey Toobin for *IP*."

Former CNN Chairman Walter Isaacson took time out from his frantic schedule running a ski lodge to wish the team well. "I've wised up a lot since I left the newsroom. Did you know the Aspen Institute is not in Aspen, Colorado?"

CNN faces National Geographic in the season opener and WTTG in the nightcap. The games will take place at Burning Tree Park in Bethesda.

"Bookmark it. Put it on your 'favorites,'" implored News Systems Manager Joe Murphy, who denied he's number 56 on the Pentagon's Most Wanted Iraqi list.

"Personally, I like reading about the field conditions," yakked Facilities Manager Kim Linden, proudly displaying his new hard hat with a CNN logo. "I hope the softball team can cause as much leveling as we have done already on the 10th and 11th floors."

May 3, 2003

GAME 1		GAME 2	
CNN	17	CNN	18
DISCOVERY	3	WASHINGTON POST	5

- CNN opens season with impressive victories.
- Defending champs whipped up by fury of Midwest tornadoes; players literally cut path, not swath, of devastation.
- Softball team displays more cohesiveness and unity than *American Morning.*
- ADDS 3rd graph Company considers turning early show into comedy/variety series.
- DELETES 5th graph CNNI anchors ordered to wear surgical masks when reading copy to avoid spreading SARS.
- Eds: Note repeated improper use of the word 'literally' throughout copy.

By Joe Baseball Jr.
Bureau Sports Writer

ASPEN HILL, Md. (UPI) — President George W. Bush did not declare victory aboard the aircraft carrier USS Abraham Lincoln last week. But CNN's softball team certainly did on Saturday after it literally steamrolled over its two opponents in the opening weekend of the Metropolitan Media Softball League.

Don't organize a victory parade at least not yet. Like the sluggish economy, it's a long way to Tipperary.

In the first game, CNN literally devoured the newest MMSL team, Discovery Channel, 17-8, and then had plenty of time to watch an hourlong documentary on South American piranhas.

The Discovery players responded by participating in a group self-flagellation. "We saw the Iraqis doing it so many times on CNN, it looked like fun," cracked a team spokesman whose head was bloodied from repeated blows by his own bat.

Chief Editor Paul Varian literally climbed the newsroom wall after hearing CNN anchors repeatedly misuse the word 'literally' in copy.

The carnage continued in the nightcap as CNN reenacted a Turkish earthquake and crushed the Washington Post, 18-5, in a game called after five innings.

In an eleventh-hour maneuver to keep the score low, the Post's coach repeatedly chanted the name of Deep Throat, claiming it was broadcast legend Bruce Morton, in the misguided hope the breaking news would cause the entire CNN team to walk off the field and file for radio.

"There'll be no quid pro quo while I'm around," executive Sid Bedingfield spat. He dismissed the newspaper's ploy, but in a show of good faith he immediately ordered a limit to the number of times Miles O'Brien could talk about Kyra Phillips' call sign.

"It's long overdue," said Dr. Sanjay Gupta, who demanded good friend Daryn Kagan introduce him as Devil Doc before each medical segment. Kagan was on assignment getting Kuwaiti knick-knacks appraised and unavailable for comment.

CNN's twin wins at Aspen Hill put the team in a tie with ABC News atop the Capitalview Division. The squad has won eight straight games dating back to last season. D.C. Bureau Chief Kathryn Kross promised to literally replace the cake and ice cream at next month's birthday celebration with Veuve Clicquot and caviar if the winning ways continue.

The 35 runs in the doubleheader against Discovery and the Washington Post are the most scored in back-to-back games in CNN's history. All 17 players on the roster got on base at least once.

"Talk about your Day Driver; this will spike our ratings," added a delighted Phil Kent, company executive, ahead of an internal probe headed by News Standards and Practices and McKinsey & Company to look into what is so super about the Superdesk.

The softball team took a 4-0 lead in the first inning of Game 1. John Davis, John King, Willie Lora, and Laura Robinson all drove in runs. A testy public relations spokeswoman at Discovery accused the news network, along with Fox and MSNBC, of being part of the Axis of Evil. "Nothing but a bunch of evil-doers," she wailed.

The score was 7-5 in favor of CNN after three innings. It would have been closer if not for the team's unrivaled defense. Center fielder Erik Tavcar threw one runner out at home. Two batters later, he made a Willie Mays-like catch over his shoulder and whipped a relay throw to King, who threw out a Discovery runner who fortuitously stumbled over third base and fell flat on his face.

"It was literally the most embarrassing thing I've seen all week except for when the control room punched in color bars in every box during The Whip," Executive Producer David Bohrman confided. "The funny thing is nobody noticed, not even Aaron until he was through his Page Two soliloquy."

After the game, opposing players spoke candidly about their introduction to the MMSL and their first taste of losing.

"Our performance was more disgusting than those CNN ads for Finishing Touch, the sleek precision hair removal system," said one despondent Discovery player. "But I do like the eyebrow attachment that comes with it."

CNN's offense was propelled by leadoff hitter Darrin White, who went 4-5 (7-8 on the day). John Davis was 3-4 (6 RBI), including a two-run homer and a bases-loaded double. Howie Lutt (3-3) obliged with a two-run homer and a bases-loaded double. Laura and Ralph Marcus also performed great, both going 3-4.

"It was nice to see everyone involved much like our Iraqi coverage," articulated Teya Ryan, general manager of CNN/US. "Let's face it, our team's batting average last year looked like blood-alcohol readings. So, anything is an improvement.

Newcomers Stephen Bach and Silvio Carrillo announced their presence and left their calling cards.

"I think our friends at Discovery literally 'discovered' (uses fingers to indicate quotation marks) we can do more than just good journalism and clean out the 11th-floor refrigerator," blabbed CNN Vice President Keith McAllister.

The first game effort was by no means a fluke. Against the Washington Post, CNN scored in every inning, hitting three home runs, including solo jobs by Greg Robertson and Brad Wright (3-3) in the second frame. An inning later, the route was on.

CNN batted around and scored eight times on nine singles and a double. Darryl Diamond (3-3), Josh Braun and Stephanie Kotuby reached base. Darrin got two hits in the inning and dependable Lindy Royce joined in on the fun with a single.

"Tell Kyra, this is what a laugher looks like," said one kibitzer.

With the team safely ahead 18-1, Jim Barnett was dragged in to pitch the last inning. He did his best to keep the Post in the game by immediately giving up four runs.

The umpire, already late for his corneal transplant surgical appointment, called an end to the route so CNN players could make a beeline to the Stained Glass Pub for beer and pizza. "I hadn't seen that much carnage since they dropped the MOAB on the Mansour neighborhood in Baghdad," said the man in blue, who moonlights as a Saddam Hussein double. He then lowered his veil and walked away.

CNN's next big test is on Saturday when it plays a make-up triple-header against division rivals ABC News, CBS News, and NBC News Channel at Capitalview field.

May 31, 2003

GAME 1		GAME 2	
CNN	19	CNN	19
NATIONAL GEOGRAPHIC	9	WTTG	7

- **CNN sweeps another doubleheader to remain atop Capitalview Division.**
- **Discredited former journalist Jayson Blair writes he's never seen a softball team with so much talent.**
- **D.C. Bureau to build batting cage on 11th floor as part of newsroom renovations.**
- **ADD 2nd graph Bush advisers livid that softball games and Eric Rudolph's arrest dominated agenda at Sharm el-Sheikh.**
- **DELETE 14th graph Bureau chiefs hold annual retreat in Atlanta to discuss true meaning of Super Day Drivers and editorial value of 11 a.m. conference call.**

By Joe Baseball Jr.
Bureau Sports Writer

BETHESDA, Md. (UPI) — A clear storyline has emerged in a softball season that's been more challenging to follow than *Live from the Headlines*. The CNN CaNiNes, winners of four straight games, are out to prove the 2002 championship was no fluke.

This year's squad has depth. It has spunk. And it will be featured tomorrow on Judy Woodruff's Page Turners on *Inside Politics*.

CNN showed no rust on Saturday after four weeks of rain postponements. Despite threatening skies, the team submerged National Geographic, 19-9, in the opener at Burning Tree Park and decided it was so much fun it would do it again against WTTG, 19-7, in the nightcap.

The two wins bump CNN's unbeaten streak to 10 games dating back to last year. Only four of the 20 teams in the MMSL have perfect records.

"It may be the day for the Queen's coronation, but I think CNN can be crowned softball champs," shouted an effusive Richard Quest, who used rope to tie himself to the gates of Buckingham Palace.

"Anything's possible," said grandiose anchor Aaron Brown during a break while filming PSAs for United Health Care. He hinted that his show is eyeing a nightly segment called 'Mea Culpa,' featuring ordinary people sharing extraordinary acts of contrition. "The first show is going to feature just me."

CNN has averaged 18 runs a game this season and scored in every inning except for three. The team would have scored in those, except it held an impromptu and politically incorrect powwow on the pitcher's mound to help develop an upbeat *Saturday Night Live* format for the new Paula Zahn show.

"We're calling it, *Live from New York, It's the Paula Zahn Show*," crowed Jim Miller, the media veteran recently hired to relaunch the evening news broadcast for the 14th time in the past three years. Miller says his immediate goal is to increase the audience in the 7p-9p slot by at least six viewers each night and bring back 7a package recuts.

"If you enjoy people stories like mountain climbers who cut off their limbs and high school girls who wrap pig intestines around each other's necks, you're gonna love what we have to offer," said the former television executive, news producer, screenwriter, political veteran, and author. "Don't forget, I was also a consultant for *Extreme Makeover: Home Edition*, which is what this broadcast needs," Miller added.

That's undoubtedly one thing CNN's softball team didn't require over the weekend. It bolted to a 14-0 lead against lowly National Geographic despite an appearance at shortstop by someone who looked a lot like Jacques Cousteau.

Leading the way was Howie Lutt, who went 4-4 with four RBI. Darrin White (3-3) was up to the challenge. His day included a mesmerizing baserunning shot in the arm when he rounded third base and looked to be out by a country mile, but he completely faked out the catcher by holding so still she didn't see him. John Davis clubbed a two-run homer. Ralph Marcus and Stephen Bach also got into the fun, going 3-4.

National Geographic charged back with nine runs to close within five,

14-9, but CNN put the game out of reach by sinking the Explorers with five additional runs in the last two innings.

Game 2 was not quite a carbon copy. WTTG scampered ahead with four runs in the first inning, but CNN stormed back with five in the bottom and took the lead. CNN added five more runs in the second, all coming with two outs on five consecutive hits.

The head of the FCC immediately exhorted the agency to ease media ownership restrictions and allow the local Fox affiliate to hire air traffic specialist Rally Caparas and Jack Cafferty.

Considerable input came from Jocelyn Hatch, making her first appearance for CNN. She went 3-4 and led off two innings with singles. "I'd like to see golfer Vijay Singh come out here with a bat and compete with our women," she gasped. Greg Robertson pitched a terrific game and was a singular offensive juggernaut, 4-4 with five RBI. Six of the seven runs by WTTG were unearned. For those not familiar with the terminology, it means the pitching was great, but the defense screwed up.

There was nothing shabby about the other players, including Laura Robinson, who had all three putouts at second base in the second inning. Jack Lynn made the defensive play of the day by loping in to catch a sinking line drive on one knee in left field and then, in one continuous motion, firing a one-hop throw to first to complete a double play.

Everyone got at least one hit, including Darryl Diamond, Erika Dimmler, Lindy Royce, Aaron Payne, and Josh Braun, who was rewarded for his hustle with a throw to the back of the head while rounding first. He stayed in the game, but the ball was taken to nearby Suburban Hospital for observation.

Jim Barnett did not play. However, he did see action on the field, riding a power mower for an hour with Carolyn Hong from WTTG before the games started.

Following the last out and a brief dust-up over which company had fewer lapses in journalistic integrity, Fox or CNN, a dozen players from both teams headed over to Ledo's for pizza and beer. WTTG showed great sportsmanship by having the restaurant manager serve a complimentary pitcher of water with lemon slices to CNN's table.

Weather permitting, CNN is back on the diamond this Saturday at Layhill Field against stepparent AOL and Washington Post.com. If you want homemade cookies by Lindy or autographs from any CNN softball players, join us for the fun.

June 28, 2003

- **CNN softball team consults Marge Schott and Eleanor Roosevelt before sweeping tripleheader.**
- **Network is undefeated despite weeks of canceled games and rejiggered schedule.**
- **Eds: Joe Baseball Jr. is on vacation. He will be back in this space in two weeks.**

By Jayson Blair
Bureau Sports Intern

KENSINGTON, Md. (UPI) — After another rain-soaked couple of weeks reminiscent of a Paula Zahn sabbatical, the CNN softball team took the field at Capitalview Park and came out swinging against division rival ABC News.

The first inning set the tone, as the CaNiNes scored seven times to run roughshod over ABC 21-6. The team went on to beat NBC News Channel and CBS News to improve its first-place position with a 7-0 record.

The offensive outburst in the opener included home runs by Greg Robertson and John Davis and an over-the-fence jog-around shot by Howie Lutt. The hitting was solid throughout the lineup, with John King going 4-5 and leadoff hitter Darrin White furnishing three hits.

The veteran squad, with just two of the eight starting men under 40 (and one of those just barely so), showed no signs of rust after a saturated sit-around spring.

"Let's just say our men are experienced," said catcher Lindy Royce.

The game also featured a strange play at first base. An ABC baserunner, apparently out to lunch on a double-play grounder, tried to return to the base and became entangled with first baseman Brad Wright. How do you describe that one?

"Just got to tell it like it is," said CNN intern Jayson Blair. "A woman was falling all over Brad Wright."

"You sure it happened that way? It doesn't seem very plausible," chimed in Joe Baseball Jr. from Maine, where he's hunting for caribou.

Sure did, Joe, just like that.

"Well, I don't know," said Joe. "Those quotes ring hollow. And what's with the Paula Zahn reference in the lead? You think a scolding at the expense of others is the way to get readers?"

"No, Joe, I just thought…" replied Blair.

"And look at all the numbers you've dropped into the first few graphs… sheesh. Scores, innings, runs, and even players' ages, for cryin' out loud. Ever hear of perspective… maybe backing into a story?"

"Well, Joe, it's just that…"

"Never mind, kid, get on with it."

CNN had its hands full for the second game with NBC News Channel. The teams were never separated by more than a run after the top of the first. The lead changed hands four times before CNN took command for good in the bottom of the sixth.

There was some excellent defense, including an astounding catch by Stephanie Kotuby in right center field. But the orange hats' bats were quiet as the team tried to figure out NBC's pitcher. Maybe some segment producers from New York could help.

"Jayson, that's a dig at our colleagues," spluttered Joe Baseball. "You and your fabricated quotes. I've heard enough. Go on and tell 'em how the second game ended."

It was pretty stupefying stuff. Down by a run late in the game, with two outs and Darrin on first, John D. smashed a triple. That tied it up. John K. followed with a double to put CNN ahead. NBC went down quietly in the seventh.

The day wasn't over. CNN had one more to go against CBS News.

The CaNiNes came out slugging in the third game, scoring four runs in the first. Scrappy CBS kept battling with timely hitting and aggressive baserunning and tied it up 9-9 late in the contest. However, CNN had some gas left in the tank and added five runs in the final two frames to close it out 14-10.

"That's it?" snickered Joe Baseball.

"Yes, what now, Joe?" asked Jayson Blair.

"Aren't you forgetting something?"

After a marathon five playoff games, the 2003 CaNiNes came up short and finished third.

"Oh right, ya mean the part where I rattle off all the names and close it up?" said Blair.

"Yes, and it's not rattling. I resent that."

"Sorry, Joe, ok, here you go."

"Teya, Eason, Keith, Walter, Rick, Furnad."

"No, not those names, you idiot!" howled Joe Baseball. "The players. Didn't you learn anything faking it at the Washington Post?"

"Got it. Laura, Erika, Darryl, Ralph, and Jack were also a huge help. There are no games next week because it's July 4th weekend."

"Is that how you're gonna button this thing up? Ever heard of ending with a flourish, leaving 'em wanting more?" asked an incredulous Joe Baseball.

"I don't know, Joe. What would you suggest?"

"Maine is nice this time of year. I'll be back next week."

July 12, 2003

GAME 1		GAME 2	
CNN	18	CNN	14
NBC NEWS CHANNEL	16	CBS NEWS	2

GAME 3	
CNN	15
ABC NEWS	3

- **CNN improves to 10-0, clinches division title/playoff berth with another tripleheader sweep.**
- **Undefeated team walks all over Big Three Networks as Brokaw, Rather, and Jennings stew.**
- **CIA accuses reporter David Ensor of being a mole**
- **DELETE 3rd graph Softball success has CNN execs fuming; Anderson Cooper spends entire hour recapping the games before his show is canceled.**
- **ADD graph Frank Sesno to host *Talk Back Live Prime Time*.**

By Joe Baseball Jr.
Bureau Sports Writer

KENSINGTON, Md. (UPI) — If you don't like stories with happy endings, divert your eyes and watch *NewsNight with Aaron Brown* for the latest on Hurricane Claudette. You've come to the right place if you're looking for something uplifting to start your day.

CNN (10-0) is headed to the Big Dance and post-season play. For the second time in three weeks at gnat-infested Capitalview field, the CaNiNes swept a tripleheader, beating NBC, CBS, and ABC. The losses sent shock waves through the parent companies of General Electric, Viacom, and Disney, where grumbling hit 5.8 on the Richter scale. Fox News Channel was not impressed.

"B-F-D," decreed Greta Van Susteren. "No one watches CNN anymore except for late-night comedians and Teya Ryan."

The latest demographic research shows she may be right. The average Fox viewer is between the ages of 15 and 83. CNN gets everyone else.

"So, what," ranted company executive Phil Kent. "More viewers die while watching us than any other cable news network."

{Editor's note: The Fox News Network no longer has a softball team, only the local Fox affiliate.}

Before the games started, both teams were out raking standing water in the base baths, spreading kitty litter to absorb the moisture, and even using plastic cups to scoop out the puddles.

CNN outlasted NBC in a slugfest, 18-16, in the opener and then was obligated to demolish CBS News in the second game, 14-2, ditto ABC News in the third game, 15-3. The last two games ended under the mercy rule. It's the fifth time opposing teams have crumbled this season before all the innings were played.

The CaNiNes are division champions for the second straight year, so the team and each player will receive a trophy. CNN could lose its last three games, and it wouldn't matter.

"This will require a complete redesign of our trophy case," said a very pleased Washington Bureau Chief Kathryn Kross. "Our bureau continues to lead the way for the entire network. Need I remind everyone that we turn more packages in a day than LA, Chicago, Miami, Dallas, and Boston do in a year?"

CNN has not lost a division game in three YEARS, which coincidentally is the last time Carl Rochelle's hair was its natural color. Their remarkable tear has reached a mind-numbing 16 games, dating back to June 2002. Only two of the 20 teams in the Metropolitan Media Softball League have an unblemished season. The Gazette is also 10-0 and will face CNN next Saturday in a colossal showdown.

Despite missing four regular Medicare-eligible starters, CNN's youthful colts came out possessed against NBC News Channel. Faster than you can say Maria Hinojosa and sing the complete lyrics to American Pie, it was bye-bye NBC as CNN scored the first 11 runs of the game.

Before the third inning was even over, every player had reached base at least once: Darrin, Erik, John Davis, Howie, Brad, Darryl, Laura, Willie, Jim, Stephanie, and Lindy. It was a love-in with high fives and smiles—time to break out the chocolate chip cookies.

Not quite. The Peacocks ground away to close within one run, 17-16, at the end of six innings as the CaNiNes looked more cluttered than the daily editorial rundown. In the top of the seventh, CNN added an insurance run. NBC came up for one last try. They got two runners on and the winning run at the plate with one out. But the next two batters tapped soft grounders back to pitcher Jim Barnett to end the threat.

Hitting heroes included Tavcar, who went 4-5 with a homer, two doubles, a triple, and five RBI. John D. contributed three RBI, going 4-5 with two triples.

The game's most memorable play occurred off the field in the first inning. Silvio Carrillo was hit in the nose when a foul pop-up deflected off the dugout fence. Pedro, Silvio's canine companion, became so distraught the Pet Psychic was called in for counseling. "I was impressed," brooded Human Resources Manager Tim Traylor, who appointed the dog to fill in for Jennifer Gibson as intern coordinator.

Game 2 against CBS was not a nail-biter. It couldn't even hold a candle to an Andrea Koppel script about enriched uranium. It was more like listening to the musings of Jeff Greenfield around a campfire while making S'mores. "That's right, Judy. The 2004 election is the over-arching, epochal story of our lifetime, which we haven't seen since the Cold War," he said. "How about those CaNiNes?"

The fresh legs of Ralph, Stephen, Jocelyn, and Silvio, along with sideline assistance from scorekeepers Josh and Virginia and her parents, plus baseball-clad Demetri, completely hypnotized the opposition.

"We didn't need *48 hours* to paste CBS... more like *60 Minutes*," said company chief Jim Walton. "CNN was all over them from the start before I could read a relevant line of the ticker. Rolex watches for everyone!"

Stephen set the pace with two triples, but each batter got on base. CNN scored in every inning but one. Nine players had at least two hits. Howie pitched with devastating accuracy, and except for the occasional exuberance from Erik in the outfield when he attempted to throw out runners at first base from 300 feet away, there was little cause for concern.

Game 3 against ABC was more of the same. In the first inning, CNN batted around and scored eight times. By the time Howie hit a three-run walk-off home run, ABC recruiters were looking to hire CNN players in exchange for Barbara Walters.

For those aficionados who want more numbers and less color, the first five batters in the lineup tell the story about what kind of day it was: Darrin (7-10), Erik (9-12), John D. (9-13), Howie (7-11), and Brad/Ralph (9-10). CNN was retired in order only once.

As if there wasn't enough good karma, CNN players have raised $170, surpassing their goal of helping the MMSL build a better website.

Don't sit at home next Saturday. If one-year-old Demetri can wear a diaper and come out, you can, too.

July 19, 2003

GAME 1

WASHINGTON POST.COM.........12

CNN...10

GAME 3

GAZETTE 14

CNN...9

GAME 2

CNN...12

USA TODAY 5

- **CNN hits brick wall as win streak ends with deflating losses.**
- **CaNiNes manage one win but blow huge leads in tripleheader.**
- **Softball team to begin playoffs as No. 2 seed.**
- **ADD 4th graph D.C. managers immediately suspend free café mocha latte samples.**
- **Note nature EP Jim Miller orders nude paintball coverage to hoist Paula Zahn ratings as show tries out new name: "Hunting for Bambi."**

By Joe Baseball Jr.
Bureau Sports Writer

ROCKVILLE, Md. (UPI) — If there are weapons of mass destruction somewhere in this world, one thing is obvious: CNN's softball team didn't have any over the weekend.

That's the conclusion of a classified U.N. report made public after the CaNiNes imploded not once but twice, ending any hopes of finishing the season undefeated.

Looking flatter than a Lance Armstrong tire, CNN (11-2) lost its first game of the year, falling to Washington Post.com, 12-10, in the opener. CNN awakened in the second game by flattening USA Today 13-5. Game 3 was for bragging rights and the best record in the MMSL. It wasn't CNN's day as the Gazette overcame a seven-run deficit to pull out a victory, 14-9. Before these two defeats, the CaNiNes' last loss was coincidentally against the Gazette, a stretch of 16 games dating back to June 2002, the last time the LA Bureau turned a package. The two teams have finished 1-2 every year since 1999. It could happen again next weekend when the playoffs get underway.

At the start, CNN had everything going its way against Washington Post.com. Trailing 9-3, a Post.com player literally walked his team right out of a rally. The batter reached first base on a fielder's choice. Then inexplicably, he started walking back to his house, hoping to catch the edgy Gimme a Minute segment on *American Morning*, featuring the ubiquitous Donna Brazile and Jonah Goldberg.

CNN appealed to the umpire, who immediately called the runner out for leaving the field. To help soften the embarrassment, the umpire fined CNN $100 for airing the stupidest segment on TV called What the …

It was all downhill after that to borrow a cliché (which itself is a cliché). Post.com took advantage of several crucial fielding goofs and capitalized in a big way. CNN gave up five runs in the fifth inning and four in the sixth to fall behind 12-10. The CaNiNes had the bottom of the seventh, but a rally fizzled with the tying runs on base.

In a break with tradition, this column will not name names. "The softball team is eating into our revenues, and I'm left with no choice but to start firing people or send them to Monrovia," said annoyed news manager Keith McAllister.

In Game 2, USA Today played like it was hit with a rocket-propelled grenade as CNN stunned its opponent into early submission. Laura Robinson started the third inning with a single. Erika Dimmler did the same thing. Then Darrin White singled. So did Erik Tavcar. After John Davis made an out and John King hit into a force play, David Gracey tripled, Willie Lora (3-3) singled, as did Stephanie Kotuby, Greg Robertson (10-10 on the day), Darryl Diamond, and Laura again.

When it was over, 12 batters rung up eight runs. The women led the offensive charge by going 4-5 in just one inning.

"It was more exhilarating than watching CNN replay the story about my rescue after being captured by Iraqi forces," shouted 19-year-old Army Private Jessica Lynch on the eve of her release from Walter Reed Hospital. "Thank you, Special Ops, Navy SEALs, Army Rangers, Marines and CNN."

Would the victory in the penultimate game provide enough impetus to get CNN past the Gazette? A quirk in the schedule gave the Gazette the edge on paper. This would be the CaNiNes third game of the day but the Gazette's first. It didn't matter as CNN took a seven-run lead, 9-2, after three innings.

The Green Machine was not undefeated for a reason. Feeding off Cooperstown-like defensive plays, they started wearing out the leather on the ball and tacked on 12 runs just as CNN hit the worst batting slump in its history. Of the last 14 batters, only two got singles. Eight players went down in order. Game over.

As it turned out, the Gazette was later beaten by USA Today, the same team CNN torpedoed hours earlier.

Stephen Bach, Josh Braun, Aaron Payne, and Jim Barnett could only watch from the bench.

It was not the scripted end to the regular season that the players or the dozen fans expected. The turnout was record-breaking and probably would have been greater if not for Joe Baseball's cut-and-paste nonsensical street directions to Cabin John Regional Park.

Those who did manage to get there included Steve Redisch and eldest daughter Lena, Kathryn Kross, Marty Kramer, Sital Patel, Noah and Hannah King, Kerith McFadden, Nancy Groves, Rebecca Ratliff, and Marci Starzec, who dropped in from New York.

Three canines were also in attendance: Ranger, Katie, and Mulder, who, despite the heat, found plenty to bark about.

This is how the double-loss elimination, 10-team playoff weekend, is shaping up. As a No. 2 seed, CNN will play the winner of the game between the Associated Press/U.S. News. That winner moves on to play the winner of USA Today/Washington Times. The loser drops into the loser's bracket. Any team that loses twice is out. The survivors meet on Sunday for the championship. Will CNN repeat as champions?

Now is the time to plan to come out to Wheaton Regional Park next weekend for more drama than you'll ever get watching *Late Edition with Wolf Blitzer*. In lieu of ice cream and cake to mark monthly birthdays, the D.C. Bureau is contemplating giving every employee who comes out an unscheduled day off.

July 26, 2003

- **Late-inning heroics on Saturday propel CNN, but CaNiNes run out of gas on Sunday.**
- **Softball team finishes in third place as goal to repeat as champions quashed.**
- **CNN and AOL reach brink of bench-clearing brawl after 'You've Got Mail' taunt.**
- **ADD 4th graph Cash-strapped CNN to follow AOL business template; network plans to sell individual reporters; FN offers to trade Allan Chernoff for Bob Franken plus an OA to be named later.**

By Joe Baseball Jr.
Bureau Sports Writer

WHEATON, Md. (UPI) — Stephen Case, the mastermind behind America Online's record-breaking acquisition of Time Warner, left behind more than a debt-ridden company.

The ex-chairman also departed with a legacy that included mass defections of AOL's narrowband subscriber base, a stock not worth the price of 12 rolls of toilet paper on sale at Price Club, and a 24-hour cable news operation in a perpetual state of angst.

But give credit where credit is due. Neither Case nor his successor, CEO Richard Parsons, messed with CNN's softball team, and for that, players were thankful. But before getting to the dessert part of the menu, let's begin with the appetizers.

CNN started the double-loss elimination 10-team tournament early on Saturday morning with an efficient and workmanlike victory over the Associated Press, 9-4, in Game 1. CNN's next opponent was USA Today, (spoiler alert) the eventual champion.

The Gannetoids, as they're called, were not impressed with the Ca-NiNes or last week's 10-minute stirring and teary tribute to Leon Harris' 20 years at the network. "Who is Leon Harris?" they kept asking. USA Today hammered CNN, 10-6, in Game 2 and promised to devote in-depth analysis about their softball victory with two lines of copy.

Up next is Game 3 and the main attraction: AOL against CNN, squaring off in another gargantuan battle, with the winner moving on in the Metropolitan Media Softball League playoffs and the loser logging off for the year. CNN defeated AOL in the title game last year. This match-up had a grudge written all over it.

It was scoreless after three innings, a pitching duel, and almost as remarkable as watching Aaron Brown read tomorrow's newspapers. In the fourth inning, with most of the CNN Library staff on hand instead of pulling tape for editors, AOL went out in front with three runs. CNN responded with two. That's how it remained until the seventh inning when AOL picked up what they thought was an insurance run to make it 4-2, setting the stage for something witnesses say they will never consign to oblivion.

No one will ever forget where they were when JFK was shot, when Elvis died, and when Jeanne Moos last did a serious package. Now, they can add this to the list: the downfall of AOL, the company that couldn't cut the mustard in the boardroom or on the softball field, the day CNN said, "It's time for you to reboot."

John Davis led off the bottom of the seventh with a single. John King walked. With one out, Howie Lutt stepped to the plate. On the first pitch, Lutt sent the ball over the 276-foot sign in left field for a three-run walk-off home run that sent the CaNiNes into such a delirious state someone called for medical backup. As the team rushed to home plate to celebrate the shot heard 'round Wheaton Regional Park, King let out a primal scream, expressing the sentiment everyone at CNN was thinking: "You've Got Mail!"

AOL players did not take the remark kindly, or maybe it was more about the slogan, which is the only thing people will frankly remember about the ridiculed company 10 years from now. AOL accused King of following the quip with a word commonly used to describe a female dog. The two teams interrupted the time-honored traditional end-of-the-game handshake and high fives with some down-home testosterone-laden jawboning. No punches were thrown, but AOL did accuse CNN of changing its on-air appearance more times than Greta Van Susteren.

Aggrieved executives immediately ordered AOL to be spun off from the Time Warner side of the company, saying everything about the Internet provider was stained.

CNN was left for an hour to contemplate what life would be like without AOL, and as it so happens, that was also the same amount of time it took to decide CNN's next opponent. It was now mid-afternoon under a broiling sun.

CNN had no problem in Game 4 against the Washington Times. It wasn't even close. Ahead 12-4, the CaNiNes coach played everyone who showed up: Darrin, Greg, John D., John K., Howie, Erik, Stephanie, Darryl, Ralph, Erika, Laura, Brad, Stephen, Josh, Jack, Jocelyn, and Jim. Even bystanders volunteered to pile on, including Kerith McFadden, Nancy Groves, KD Fabian, John D.'s brother Patrick, Carolyn Hong, Virginia Nicolaidis and Demetri, Abigail the dog, Jayme Swain, Melissa Cartwright, Rebecca Ratliff, Skip Nocciolo, plus half of ABC's team, which stayed around to get a good laugh.

The day ended with CNN victorious in three out of its four games.

Only three teams were left as the sun rose on Sunday morning, with CNN facing off against Washington Post.com. The winner would go on to play USA Today for all the marbles.

Lindy Royce was back from vacation to provide a much-needed sugar rush and a fresh pair of legs. What CNN needed more was a timely hit from the heart of the lineup, which went 3-12. The CaNiNes fell behind Post.com 5-0 but got on track with a six-run fourth inning. After the lead changed hands twice, CNN found itself down by a run going into the last inning, 8-7. There were no more heroics in its bag of tricks, and CNN (14-4) left the tying run at second base and, with it, any thought of repeating as champions. They came oh-so-close.

The CNN players didn't leave empty-handed. They each received a division championship T-shirt. In addition, the team was awarded a division trophy and one for a third-place overall finish.

Then it was on to the Stained Glass Pub for some festive cheer and to lift a glass and down a few for the only team to finish in the top four each of the past five years.

CNN vs. AOL Dust-Up

The 2003 CNN-AOL playoff showdown, a high-stakes clash between rival units of the same conglomerate, did not go unnoticed by the Metropolitan Media Softball League or the general public. This was no ordinary game, as journalists took the spotlight and became the story.

It all started with a dramatic three-run walk-off home run by CNN's Howie Lutt in the final inning.

White House correspondent John King was rounding second base as the ball sailed over the fence. He shouted, "You've got mail!" and then reportedly added a choice expletive for good measure. That part remains open to interpretation. In any case, AOL's shortstop took vigorous exception and responded in kind. Meanwhile, AOL's center fielder stepped in, leading to a shoving match during the traditional postgame handshake line.

Darrin White and Howie Lutt celebrate CNN defeating AOL in the playoffs.

The Washington Post got wind of the incident and followed up with a story in the Style section, a fitting placement for what happened.

"If [the AOL player] took it the wrong way, I'm sorry," King later said, admitting he was a little pumped playing against a corporate rival. "I'm a boy playing softball, not consulting with my PR advisers before I speak."

AOL spokesman Andrew Weinstein said CNN and America Online are "two very competitive organizations and both clearly like to win. Apologies were exchanged after the game."

None of it sat well with the Commish, who threatened suspensions if it ever happened again. He said if anyone had been hurt, it could have led to job losses over behavior at a recreation activity representing the company.

In a stern memo sent to every team, the Commish wrote: "The MMSL is not a frat house league, a beer hall league, or the weeknight county men's league. Don't say or do something irrevocably stupid on softball Saturdays." He implored players to keep "your yaps shut."

TOP OF THE 7th

Rebuilding

April 19, 2004

- **CNN ready to start softball season after tumultuous year of turnovers, backstabbing, fumbling, and obfuscating.**
- **CaNiNes hope to improve upon last year's third-place finish.**
- **Metropolitan Media Softball League expands to 22 teams.**
- **Bob Woodward admits his book *Plan of Attack* not half as compelling as 9 a.m. CNN editorial conference call.**
- **ADD 2ND graph Howard Stern prankster verified through Caller ID as former Executive Producer Jim Miller; Blue Ribbon panel launches internal fishing expedition headed by Keith McAllister.**
- **Note language in 6th graph.**

By Joe Baseball Jr.
Bureau Sports Writer

WASHINGTON (UPI) — There's only so much buildup a sports fan can stand in a lifetime. Well, wait no longer. The 14th MMSL season is about to begin. Get ready for an eight-week, 16-game odyssey that promises not to disappoint.

Even Jordan's King Abdullah will be on hand at the CNN Washington D.C. Bureau on Tuesday to sign team posters and offer batting tips.

The first pitch will be thrown out by Tyler Crotty, the yawning, squirming, wiggling little boy from Orlando who delighted viewers with his antics while standing behind President Bush last month. Catching the ball will be anchor Daryn Kagan, who hopes her appearance will resurrect her career and perhaps even get her in Bill Schneider's Play of the Week segment or, even better, a cameo in The Whip on *NewsNight*.

"I think Tyler and I will make a dynamite on-air team," said an enthralled Kagan. "(Jim) Walton predicts viewers will stop watching Fox in droves."

CNN will dive right into the thick of it when it faces ABC News in the opener on Saturday at Capitalview Park in Kensington at 10 a.m. The nightcap features CNN against NBC News Channel.

Seeing something different about this year's squad won't take long. It will be as apparent as the shirts on the players' backs. Thanks to the kindness of the Marketing Department in Atlanta, CNN will take the field sporting new-look caps and a two-tone uniform in heather gray and blue sleeves with a specially designed logo that might just scare the pants off opposing teams.

"Outrageous," boomed Lou Dobbs, a raving trade protectionist. The television performer-turned-economist threatened to conduct an immediate postmortem into who made the new uniforms and whether it violated NAFTA free trade regulations. "We have 350 corporations exporting America. We import beef, and illegal aliens are running around pretending to be softball players."

It's a war out there.

And Fallujah is not the only place feeling under siege. CNN lost half of its starting lineup after last season, and despite some promising free-agent acquisitions over the winter, the club is scrambling to find enough players to field a team. The front office has proposed using the money lost in the D.C. Bureau's broken vending machine to help pay for a few ringers.

CNN finished with a 14-4 record in 2003, good enough for third place in the MMSL. The team won the championship trophy in 1999 and again in 2002 and had a second-place finish in 2001. It hasn't lost a divisional game in two years. As prominent historian Robert Dallek once pontificated, "We all know history repeats itself. But it would be historic if CNN won again. On a personal note, is it 'an' historic or 'a' historic?"

The lineup will include some familiar names to those who regularly read this column: Lindy Royce, Willie Lora, Laura Robinson, Stephanie Kotuby, Greg Robertson, Stephen Bach, Josh Braun, Jessica Rosgaard, Jim Barnett, and Brad Wright—not seen but rumored to be playing David Gracey, Erik Tavcar, John King and John Davis. Rookies Bill McGraw and Aaron Lewis look good and might make up for the loss of Darrin, Howie, Darryl, and Ralph.

Scouts predict it will be a transitional year as CNN looks to rediscover its charmed identity.

The MMSL welcomes new members: The Journal, Atlantic Video, WUSA-TV, and Dow Jones. Check out the website for more information about the league and your favorite team. It's chock full of features and pictures with links to weather forecasts and traffic reports, plus a real-time ticker. You can even order an MMSL T-shirt.

"The new uniforms are not a fashion must. They're a fashion statement for the classes, not the masses," the team said in a press release.

May 1, 2004

GAME 1		GAME 2	
AP	10	CNN	10
CNN	9	WASHINGTON TIMES	5

- **CNN loses opener in frightful effort but bounces back to win nightcap.**
- **Company executives torture players with Abu Ghraib interrogation methods.**
- **Paralysis and jitters grip team in Game 1; fledgling start forgotten by Game 2.**
- **SUBS 1st graph Jordan's royal family threatens to call off wedding between Prince Ali and Rym Brahimi if erratic softball performance continues.**

By Joe Baseball Jr.
Bureau Sports Writer

LAYHILL, Md. (UPI) — The new-look CNN softball team lived up to its billing on a sultry Saturday at Layhill Park.

With five of its starters from last year no longer employed by the company, several other players missing because of injuries and weekend commitments, and the 2004 squad decked out in fancy schmancy uniforms, not some sleepy throwback, the CaNiNes displayed a multiple personality disorder to begin the season.

The ill-equipped Associated Press, a longtime bottom-dweller in the Metropolitan Media Softball League, took full advantage and scratched out a 10-9 upset win. CNN left the tying run at second base in the last inning. It was the first opening game loss for CNN in six years.

"They played like they were in some sort of noxious cloud of anthrax," noted one scout.

It didn't take long for CNN to get back on track. "Our guys have a lot of experience shuffling rundowns at the last minute, so I ordered "(Steve) Redisch to roll up his sleeves and kick some butt in the control room like the good ol' days," said CNN Washington Bureau Chief David Bohrman, who floated the idea of a second round of "getting-to-know-you" lunches at La Colline followed by mandatory naps.

The batting order was reconfigured between games of the doubleheader. It was a good move. Like the 17-year cicadas, CNN crawled out of the ground to launch an all-out assault on the Washington Times, swarming them, 10-5, to gain a split. How good was it? Officials at NORAD told Homeland Security Secretary Tom Ridge they mistook some of CNN's line drives for surface-to-air missiles.

The frolicking pandas at the Smithsonian's National Zoo had more success over the weekend than CNN did against the AP. The first, third, and fifth hitters in the lineup were a collective one for 10. To put that into perspective, the number six batter, (2B) Laura Robinson, alone had twice as many hits. CNN scored only two runs in the last four innings.

CNN Senior Vice Presidents Sue Bunda and Jack Womack issued a curt statement: "We didn't accumulate all those frequent flier miles to D.C. for the Hell of it. We're holding the entire Washington Bureau accountable, and that means making every player stand on a box with electrodes attached to their DataWatch keycards."

The team could have tied the score in the sixth inning against the Associated Press. With a runner on third and just one out, the third base coach held the runner on a deep fly to center field. "That was a must-have play," grumbled media critic Howard Kurtz, adding, "CNN was more conservative than Fox News on a good day." The Pentagon immediately approved the transfer of one of Saddam Hussein's former generals to skipper the team.

Kim Linden took time from x-raying the exterior of the CNN building and showed up with diagnostic equipment before the start of the second game. "We determined there were more cracks on the softball team than between the 10th and 11th floor," said the relieved facilities manager.

"CNN looked like a total wreck," interposed Jim Connor, the lone fan who biked a dozen miles from Bethesda for what he described as a car accident that had already happened. "Pimp My Ride is more entertaining."

The only production in Game 1 came from EH (Extra Hitter) Willie Lora and SS John Davis, who each went 3-3 and accounted for more than half the team's runs. Ever the alarmist, Lou Dobbs immediately proclaimed a jihad and demanded company president Princell Hair suspend CNN's relationship with the Associated Press. "We don't want any more of their crummy write-thrus."

"Our wires.cnn does a better job than AP," boasted CNN executive Phil Kent shortly after releasing first-quarter earnings of $76.28, double

CNN's 2004 team, bottom row (L-R), Jessica Rosgaard, Lindy Royce, Stephanie Kotuby, and Erika Dimmler; (middle) Greg Robertson, Brad Wright, Jim Barnett, and Chris Kenny; back row, Willie Lora, Juan Cabral, John Davis, and Stephen Bach.

from the same period a year ago. "Thanks to rigorous fact-checking and streamlining from the Super Desk to the Row to the Rim, we've determined how to re-energize our softball operating structure."

News of the opening loss sent Time Warner stock plummeting eight cents. Two hundred shares traded hands.

The Washington Times picked the wrong place and time to face CNN, which was smarting from a comment made by Supreme Court Justice Clarence Thomas, who chastised the network for "cartoon-like" courtroom sketches in last week's Bob Franken package.

After falling behind 3-0, the CaNiNes drew upon a mix of snakehead tenacity and a powerful surge not unlike Thoroughbred winner Smarty Jones at the Kentucky Derby. CNN scored in four of the first five innings. Defensively, the all-news cable network recorded two double plays, snagged line drives, and even had time to order a Tritek Shaver from Bell & Howell. (CF) Greg Robertson clubbed a three-run homer in the second inning to put the team ahead to stay, 6-4.

Credit also goes to (LF) Chris Kenny, (1B) Bill McGraw, (c) Lindy Royce, (3B) Stephen Bach, (P) Jim Barnett, (SRF) Stephanie Kotuby, (RF) Aaron Lewis, (RF) Aaron Payne, (CF) Brad Wright and (LF) Juan Cabral. Team photographer Skip Nocciolo captured the highlights with his disposable camera from CVS.

Another doubleheader, a pair of make-up games from an April rain-out, is scheduled for this Saturday at Capitalview field. CNN squares off against antagonist ABC News in Game 1 and NBC News Channel in Game 2. Start celebrating Mother's Day early.

May 8, 2004

GAME 1		GAME 2	
ABC NEWS	16	CNN	10
CNN	11	NBC	9

- **Another split, another day of what-ifs.**
- **Softball team gets pep talk from Donald Rumsfeld after blowing opener against ABC.**
- **Deep divisions emerge as CNN seeks support from radical cleric Moqtada al-Sadr.**

By Joe Baseball Jr.
Bureau Sports Writer

KENSINGTON, Md. (UPI) — It's way too soon to write CNN's obit.

On the other hand, don't make plans to watch the softball team in July when the playoffs begin. It's been that kind of year so far. Two double-headers, two splits.

"Watching was painful," groaned one producer. "I would have preferred logging an aviation subcommittee hearing."

CNN went belly-up against ABC News in Game 1 at mushy Capitalview field. At times, the team looked just as discombobulated as *AC360*. "Stop picking on our show," begged anchor Anderson Cooper, sulking from his dispiriting effort on *Celebrity Jeopardy*, airing all this week at 7:30p. Check your local listings. "I beat Aaron Brown and Tucker Carlson, so cut me some slack, Jack."

Leading 8-6, the CaNiNes gave up eight runs in the fifth inning and committed at least four errors as ABC batted around. It was the most runs allowed by CNN in one inning in three years. It was also their first loss against a division team since the turn of the millennium.

"We had the kind of mental miscalculations you only customarily see by the Rim," said one player, who refused to give his name but conceded he was the senior White House correspondent. "I prefer to remain inconspicuous."

That's only half the story. CNN had to play NBC in the nightcap. The team staged a comeback to make current and former cynical employees smile with pride. Trailing 7-4, CNN took a lead it would never let go of in the second inning and clung on for a well-earned win, 10-9.

The victory evened the team's record at 2-2. "Maybe the next time Stone Phillips decides to do a lame feature on spiritual leaders, they'll tell my story and not Tim Russert's," mumbled David Bohrman.

The day started on an ominous note. Overnight rains left field conditions looking like the aftermath of the Great Flood of 1927 in the Mississippi River Valley. The games were delayed for over an hour as ground crews (aka players) worked feverishly with shovels, brooms, and 10 bags of kitty litter to dry the infield.

"We're talking slick and occasionally treacherous conditions, and I'm just referring to the CNN newsroom," decried one malcontent writer, who has been stuck on weekends for three years.

Chief News Executive Eason Jordan showed up before the game and offered to pay for hitting instructions and kidney transplants if it would help beat ABC. "There's not that much left here to crow about since Teya (Ryan), Walter (Isaacson), and Jeff Flock left the network," fussed Jordan. "Don't forget about Art Harris," said Art Harris.

It was evident from the start that this would not be just another regular contest. Respected adversary ABC hadn't beaten CNN in the past four head-to-head matchups, and vengeance was in the air. Ever since the departure of Jonathan Karl, Jack Date, Kate Snow, Tony Wilson, Amy Kramer, and Kathryn Kross last year, ABC had predicted it would siphon away another dozen employees from the D.C. Bureau. "We'll give you back Pierre Thomas if you send us the guy who does the Gallup polls," an ABC exec said.

Then there was this little matter. There was no umpire at game time. CNN's only fan, Jim Connor, refused to get off his bike to help, but he did offer to make figure eights in the infield dirt between innings. ABC had no extra players, and CNN only had one to spare. The CaNiNes Josh Braun volunteered to stand behind home plate. "I've been calling all the shots for the Wolf Blitzer show, so I had no problem calling balls and strikes," he said. The paid umpire appeared in the second inning.

CNN gave up five runs to ABC in the first two innings. The "most trusted name in news" closed the gap to 5-4 against the "network more Americans watch" and seemed on the cusp of seizing control. That's when the game, strictly speaking, turned to crap. A dog off-leash wandered into left field during the third inning. How shall we put it? The canine did its thing, which shifted the momentum. It was an odoriferous omen.

With two runners on base, Brad Wright hit a deep fly to where the dog had just finished its business. The ball deflected off the center fielder's glove right into the glove of the left fielder, who then wheeled around and fired a throw to second to double up a CNN runner, who said he was on his way to Petco to pick up a pooper-scooper.

In the fifth inning, CNN's Aaron Lewis, wearing bedroom slippers instead of cleats, tripped in the mud pit rounding third and ate dirt while trying to scramble back to the bag before being tagged for the third out. In the sixth, CNN left the bases full but failed to cut into the five-run deficit. In the seventh, with the top of the order due up and two outs, a CNN runner got caught off base to squelch a last-gasp rally.

The only rays of sunshine for CNN were provided by Aaron (4-4) and Willie Lora (3-4), recently knighted by his home country, the Dominican Republic. CNN's harem of female players thankfully dodged participation in the Million Mom March and instead helped carry the team. Stephanie Kotuby, Lindy Royce, and Laura Robinson were on fire. They collected eight hits, a third of the entire team's production, in a losing effort. "Those girls put out for us, if you know what I mean," chuckled one player.

A disgusted John King pointed a finger at his teammates and said they were "more incompetent than the producers who put together live shots." He departed quickly to see a pee-wee softball game "the way it was meant to be played." CNN players could only lick their wounds and clean dog doo off their shoes. They were ordered to take the field against NBC even before the coach had assigned positions or decided on a batting lineup.

Chris Kenny came up limping after he pulled a hamstring sprinting to the outfield between innings. Espanol's Juan "JC" Cabral arrived to fill his shoes. Josh (2-3), who began the day as the umpire, started Game 2 in right field and ended up as the designated hitter. It was a confusing day. But all that mattered was what happened between the chalk lines.

Backed by a stingy defense and excellent play from David Gracey and Bill McGraw, Jim Barnett pitched just well enough against NBC to keep CNN in the game. But again, Laura, Stephanie, and Lindy ruled the roost. Laura hit a single with two outs in the second inning to knock in two runs. Stephanie also collected two hits. Lindy bagged a foul popup and covered home base on a force out.

It was a high-scoring affair, with CNN holding a 9-7 advantage after just two innings. With the crowd shouting, "DEE-fense," the game became a chess match. CNN scored only once more on David's solo home run in the bottom of the fourth, ultimately providing the winning margin. In the top of the sixth, NBC had two runners on with one out. Jim fielded a sharp grounder and tossed to David at short, who touched second and fired on to Bill at first for an inning-ending double play.

In the last inning, NBC's leadoff batter got on base with a double as the tying run. The next player hit a shallow fly ball caught by a sliding Aaron, who made a mind-blowing throw to second to double up the runner and salvage the game. A lazy fly ball to center field for out number three helped put this one in the books for CNN.

Next Saturday, the road gets no easier for the CaNiNes, who face Washington Post.com and undefeated and corporate troublemakers AOL in a grudge match. Fans may hold dear the walk-off home run last year that resulted in a rugby scrum of sorts with players on each team shoving one another after AOL claimed CNN taunted them with mocking war cries of "Who's got mail now, bitch." Howard Kurtz wrote about the flare-up in his media column and said it was the highlight of his career, except for when he had the exclusive about Susan Rook allegedly showing up wasted on *Talk Back Live*.

Mark your calendar to come out on May 15. Bring your dogs, your Blackberry, and a picnic. Get ready to rumble.

May 15, 2004

GAME 1		GAME 2	
AOL	17	CNN	10
CNN	11	WASHINGTON POST.COM	8

- **Third time is not a charm; CNN splits doubleheader, moves into four-way tie.**
- **CaNiNes lose grudge match to vindictive AOL but comes up big against Post.com.**
- **Geneva Conventions revised; players ordered to wear leashes and bags on their heads.**
- **Eds: Note subject matter 6th graph Bob Franken to compete in Italian sausage race event in Milwaukee.**

By Joe Baseball Jr.
Bureau Sports Writer

LAYHILL, Md. (UPI) — CNN's softball team is a lot like its parent network: rudderless and bumbling but tenacious while also a curiosity and a paradox. Some of that was on display this past weekend.

In the opener, CNN coughed up a seven-run lead against undefeated AOL — not once but twice and shot itself in the foot to lose by six, 17-11. General Mark Kimmit said at his daily briefing, "It was like the entire team was exposed to a toxic agent halfway through the game."

There was no shortage of frayed nerves in the nightcap as CNN pulled away from Washington Post.com, 10-8, to gain a split. The victory moved CNN into a four-way tie for first place with ABC, NBC, and CBS. Each team is 3-3.

It was a day when CNN, the true Seabiscuit of its era, could have called it quits and gone home to watch Bob Novak jump out of a jet fighter after the frustrating loss to AOL. The CaNiNes took care of business against Post.com despite the Haiti-like conditions at Layhill Field.

CNN players seemed oblivious to all the pre-game hype surrounding the contest against AOL. The softball commissioner had warned both sides to cool it. "We didn't know much about their team," mentioned one scout. "But we knew the media behemoth was responsible for forever destroying the link between the words stock and option."

Security was tight. John Dunaway, feeling the lingering gastric effects of last week's cicada lunch, stood near the first base coaching box, grim-faced with an AK-47 and several rocket-propelled grenades by his side. "I think some bee-otch put live bugs in my jambalaya," said CNN's security czar. "I'll look at the surveillance tape and find the culprit and then cut off his head."

CNN legitimately led 8-1 after two innings in the AOL game. Greg Robertson hit a three-run homer in the fourth inning, putting the Ca-NiNes in front 11-4. "Up to that point, it was a 'pearl' of a game," news executive Eason Jordan said without elaborating.

Teams play seven innings in the Metropolitan Media Softball League, which is too bad because CNN gave up 13 runs in the last three frames. CNN only got one runner on base after the fourth inning, and he was erased on a double play. Eleven batters came up, and 10 were retired.

It was so bad that the Project for Excellence in Journalism with dispatch teamed up with General Antonio Taguba and distributed a 500-page report detailing CNN's current sad state of affairs. They ordered Kelli Arena to stop hosting Saturday morning coffee klatches for fear it was corrupting "impressionable young minds."

"To quote Walter Cronkite, if we lose them, we've lost the war," said 37-year-old Princell Hair, CNN's executive vice president and general manager, who wasn't veritably born when the CBS anchor made his famous declaration about the Vietnam War. "Without our kids, who's going to cut SOTS in Tapes.Alert?"

The Radio-TV News Directors Association joined the chorus of protests over the network's poor play. After the embarrassing loss to AOL, it recommended that CNN immediately fire all of its camera people and hire aides to Secretary of State Colin Powell. "We, in the front office, were just so impressed with how they handled the *Meet the Press* incident in Amman over the weekend, recklessly pushing the camera aside during a live interview," said CEO Richard Parsons in a statement released through the office of News Standards and Practices.

By all accounts, AOL got the retribution it wanted for last year's inglorious loss when the CaNiNes hit a walk-off home run to kick the dial-up service offline for the rest of the summer. Some at CNN pointed to a silver lining in Saturday's six-run flagellation. "After we beat AOL in the playoffs, we got them to stop artificially inflating revenues and profits," huffed a reinvented Lou Dobbs, who threatened to move his entire staff to Topeka, Kansas. "Who cares about Aaron (sic) Brown versus the Board of Education? We're talking desecration of the First Amendment and the high-handed seizure of jobs."

The possibility of CNN losing its first doubleheader in four years was hanging out there like an anchor without a TelePrompTer. But the team found stability when it counted.

In Game 2, with the score tied 7-7 after two innings, CNN invoked its payroll business paradigm and got tightfisted with the Washington Post. com. It allowed only one run in the last five innings.

With two outs in the top of the seventh, Sir Willie Lora doubled. Then John Davis singled in the go-ahead run. After Brad Wright singled, Stephen Bach added an insurance run with a base hit. Brad was 3-3 on the day and closed out a terrific career for the network as he heads to his native Vermont this month.

The heart of CNN's lineup showed its true character as batters two through six accounted for all 10 RBI in the nightcap. They were a collective 14 for 19. Not to be overlooked were offerings from Chris Kenny, Stephanie Kotuby, JC Cabral, Lindy Royce, Erika Dimmler, and Jim Barnett. Jessica Rosgaard waited in the wings and came prepared to safeguard the network from financial ruin but was equally happy to eat Lindy's cookies. John's brother Patrick also showed up. Skip Nocciolo once again snubbed his wife's "honey do" list and digitally documented CNN's third straight split.

Players will be on hand to inscribe team photos next Saturday before CNN plays unbeaten Gazette and last year's MMSL champions USA Today at Veirs Mill. Make your plans today to come out for YOUR team. Bring a friend. Tell your neighbor.

June 19, 2004

GAME 1	GAME 2	GAME 3
CNN..........................18	CBS NEWS 15	CBS NEWS 9
NBC............................. 1	CNN 3	CNN........................5

- **Softball season resumes with familiar results after weeks of rain postponements.**
- **Team seeks group counseling as CNN loses two of three games to fall below .500.**
- **Uphill obstacles remain on road to mediocrity.**
- **DELETE 4th graph Clinton's memoir includes footnote that he once spent two weeks in deep depression after not reading Joe Baseball's column.**

By Joe Baseball Jr.
Bureau Sports Writer

KENSINGTON, Md. (UPI) — If things don't turn around posthaste for CNN, the softball team's shipwreck of a season will end up like the Titanic, a heap of rusted, twisted parts covered with barnacles and nothing more than a media curiosity. It's an analogy not lost on company brass, who count on the softball team to lift the spirits of the network.

"When I became the head of CNN," said Princell Hair in the June issue of 'The Message from Princell' newsletter, "I kept hearing two things over and over again: the softball team in D.C. was the crown jewel of the network and the food in the Green Room was for guests only."

"We can protect the edibles from moochers, thieves, and curiosity-seekers, but I'm not sure we can do anything about raising the softball team from its deep-sea depths of despair."

CNN looked nothing like a relic in the opener on Saturday at Capitalview field as it blasted NBC 18-12. The opponents tried pulling out all the stops, such as having Andrea Mitchell and Alan Greenspan renew their wedding vows on the pitcher's mound between innings. The CaNiNes would not allow themselves to be distracted. But then reality set in like a case of viral meningitis. CBS, dismantled CNN in back-to-back games, 15-3 and then 9-5.

The win and the two losses leave CNN with an overall 4-5 record, tied for second place with NBC, one game behind division leaders ABC and CBS, who are 5-4.

In light of the unsightly results, CNN said it would cancel this week's mandatory Building Respect in the Workplace seminar, which was supposed to address creating a model work environment.

"People are mad as Hell. It was as if Nancy Ambrose, Teya Ryan, Rick Kaplan, and Keith McAllister all returned to the newsroom," said one of the workshop organizers. "I haven't heard so much cursing in the newsroom since they said interns would no longer be allowed to fill in for field producers or write scripts for general assignment reporters."

The five-week layoff affected all 22 MMSL teams; CNN was no exception. Weddings, vacations, long days covering breaking news, and a backlog of people sorting through scores of tapes on the attention shelf decimated CNN's lineup.

Only nine people showed up this past weekend, barely enough to field a team. Some blamed the thin turnout on bad timing, but others cited lingering humiliation over media coverage about the box of Depends found in Larry King's garbage.

It didn't seem to matter in Game 1. CNN manhandled NBC by scoring in practically every inning. The CaNiNes used a makeshift defense that put a woman at first base and the starting pitcher at shortstop.

"They created more confusion than the FAA and NORAD trying to track a USAir jet," Joint Chiefs Chairman Richard Myers said in a stakeout during relentless prodding from revered journalist extraordinaire Fran Lewine. "She gets me to say things my wife can't even get out of me," confirmed Myers.

CNN rocketed to a 9-2 lead by the second inning and then building it to 12-3. Aaron Lewis, sporting new cleats, was the epitome of a leadoff hitter. He was followed by Willie Lora, Juan Cabral, Greg Robertson, Laura Robinson, Jim Barnett, Lindy Royce, Stephanie Kotuby, and Bill Tipper, making his first appearance.

NBC closed the gap to 12-9, but a bases-loaded triple by Greg in the sixth inning sent NBC packing, and CNN glided to a surprisingly easy win. The 9/11 Commission said the softball team had more command and control than anything it had ever seen since al Qaeda infiltrated the Saudi royal family.

CNN could not replicate the mystical magnetism of Game 1 in the nightcap. There was no rabbit to pull out of the hat against CBS, a team so understaffed it was forced to borrow a player from ABC on the adjoining field to avoid a forfeit. "When I'm officially named to overhaul the network's struggling prime time lineup, there will be no more excuses for the softball team or Anderson, Paula, and Aaron," whined former Today producer Jonathan Wald. "I'm laying bare that Damon Cruz will be our permanent handyman and set builder effective today."

The only good thing that can be said about Game 2 is that CNN unequivocally led 2-0 after a half-inning. The pitching was terrible, the fielding abominable, the hitting nonexistent, and the base-running hysterical. "Other than that, I heard CNN played well," said John King, baring his teeth as he stood in line at Verizon Wireless waiting to buy a new cell phone.

The CaNiNes scraped together only nine singles against CBS and no extra-base hits. At one point, the network that Paley cultivated into a communications empire retired seven CNN batters in a row. The umpire started feeling the entire experience was a waste of time in the fifth inning when it became apparent CNN had no more lifelines. He equated the team's performance to President Bill Clinton's dalliance with 'that woman' as "morally indefensible." The final score was 15-3, but it felt worse than that.

CNN had 10 minutes to devise a winning strategy because it would have to face CBS again in a home and away matchup. Thinking that the earlier game was an aberration, the CaNiNes kept the same lineup, and for a short time, it worked until the bottom of the third.

That's when things went to pieces like a gigantic bag of jelly beans in the breakroom. Trailing 6-4 and the top of the batting order due up, CNN was all set to churn out a big inning. The bases were loaded with one out. Stephanie hit a deep fly ball to right field, which was caught by a CBS player who threw a rocket to home base to get a sliding Bill attempting to score — end of the rally.

There was no more ecstasy to come, only agony. Down by four runs, 9-5 in the fifth inning, Jim Barnett hit a drive down the third base line, but 10 steps out of the batter's box, Barnett pulled a hamstring and was forced to leave the game for a pinch runner. Lights dim. When the inning was over, CNN had no substitutes on the bench, and the game ended with a bag over Barnett's head and his limbs attached to electrodes.

So now it's crunch time. The road to another division win or a wild-card playoff is filled with potholes. CNN's back is against the wall. The schedule for next Saturday is not final, but CNN can't afford to lose many more games.

The Metropolitan Media Softball League plans to turn the remaining seven games into triple-headers and possibly even a quadruple-header to recover the season. There's talk of perhaps instituting one-pitch sudden death rules.

Come out and support your team and see what you're missing. The first three who attend the next games will receive a choice between a CaNiNes shirt or cap while supplies last.

June 26, 2004

GAME 1	GAME 2	GAME 3
USA TODAY 21	CNN... 12	CNN......................9
CNN..........................9	COMCAST SPORTSNET 10	ABC NEWS........6

- **CNN back in the hunt after winning two of three; early mortification turns to exhilaration.**
- **Softball players get mad and even all on same day.**
- **Iraqis are not only group enjoying transfer of power.**
- **ADD 2nd graph Prime Minister Allawi infused by CNN team and Christiane Amanpour, decides to move up handover ceremony.**

By Joe Baseball Jr.
Bureau Sports Writer

KENSINGTON, Md. (UPI) — If there ever was a time to use the "F-word" on a softball field, this past Saturday at Capitalview Park was the place. Not Dick Cheney's F-word. These "F" words: feisty, flashy, and fantastic.

Facing the great void and an early exit from postseason play, CNN found its mojo when the chips were down and walked away with two victories and a loss. The team was within striking distance of first place and positioned to make the playoffs. It's been a rocky road littered with IEDs, but the CaNiNes showed more gumption than a swarm of al Qae-da fighters hunkered down in a Fallujah safehouse.

Starting the day with a record of 4-5, CNN could ill afford to lose more games if it harbored any thoughts of going to the playoffs.

In the opener, USA Today smothered CNN by a score of 21-9, snowballing the network's losing streak to three. In Game 2, it took a late-inning rally to defeat shorthanded Comcast SportsNet, 12-10. Against ABC News in the nightcap, the CaNiNes played their best game of the year and won 9-6, setting aside the contest, which was not without high drama. First things first.

In Game 1, USA Today, last year's champions, came out like they were on a crusade against television journalists.

"They had something to prove other than bragging about its staff of fraudulent writers," CNN Washington Bureau Chief David Bohrman pointed out in one of his famous Herograms.

CNN fell behind 7-0 after two innings. Former star reporter and now dishonored correspondent Jack Kelley, best known for his attempts to deceive editors at his newspaper, insisted USA Today had twice as many runs. "I haven't seen so much blatant fabrication and fraudulent behavior since we exposed Aaron Brown pre-tapes his teases."

D.C. Deputy Bureau Chief Steve Redisch, on hand with two-year-old daughter Annabel, saw a teachable moment after watching USA Today take an insurmountable lead. "You can't get ahead in life by playing with losers," he told her between innings. "I said to her, 'The good news is we are only down by seven runs.'"

Inside Politics' Paul Steinhauser also showed up to view the road kill. He said the contest was over, then headed off to make muffins with Democratic strategist Donna Brazile, author of *Cooking with Grease*.

CNN was in no mood to compete and was desperate for a lift. Human Resources reacted by handing out free samples of Cialis. The players evened the score and edged ahead 9-8 against the McNews team.

"I haven't seen a group of people so turned on since Sports Illustrated came out with its list of the Top Ten Sexiest Newscasters at CNN," said coy cover girl Paula Zahn, who dismissed as a mere technicality, her second-place finish to Rally Caparas, the dude from Travelocity. "I don't look good with my hair in a ponytail."

It was a strange game. The umpire called a CNN runner out at home plate, though he was never touched. In an off-the-record conversation, not for attribution, a USA Today player called the Red Phone and told the entire bureau the batter was safe. Not long after that, the umpire, declared legally blind by the CNN Medical Unit, blew another call at first base.

He wasn't the only one beating up on CNN. The CaNiNes were doing it to themselves.

In the next inning, Erik Tavcar caught a fly ball in left field and rifled an Andy Roddick-like 155-mile-per-hour throw to John Davis at shortstop. It would have been a great play, except John was facing the infield, and the ball drilled him squarely in the middle of the back with a thud. You could see the imprint of where the ball was manufactured on his skin.

USA Today ignored CNN's comeback bid. They proceeded to tack on 13 runs to go ahead 21-9 and end the game using the mercy rule, the second time for CNN in two weeks.

CNN switched fields to face the Comcast Sports Nuts, as they are affectionately called. CNN played the role of a gracious host and agreed to let them borrow an extra woman from another team to avoid a forfeit. Just a week ago, CNN could have accepted two wins against CBS because they didn't have enough women to play, but instead, the CaNiNes allowed them to get another person, only to end up losing both games. It just about happened again.

If the opener was *Lost in Space*, Game 2 was *The Twilight Zone*. It wasn't until the third inning that CNN realized Comcast was on the field with eight men and two women, violating MMSL rules, which only permit seven men when just two women play. They immediately had to remove a player, but Comcast had pieced together a 5-2 lead by then.

"It's bad enough they are overcharging us for cable service," grimaced an unapologetic Lou Dobbs. "This reeks of an unfair competitive advantage." Eventually, Comcast did get a third woman, and both teams played at full strength.

It took a five-run rally and every player to give CNN a hard-fought 12-10 win. Neither team was ever ahead by more than three runs. Willie Lora led off the bottom of the sixth with a single. James Knott, making his first appearance, also singled, much to the delight of his wife, Chrissy. Lindy Royce got on base with a fielder's choice. Stephanie Kotuby clouted a double to drive in a run. Chris Kenny did the same thing. After an out by Juan Cabral, Eric had an RBI single. John hit a single. Greg Robertson walked. Laura Robinson also walked before Aaron Lewis ended the inning. Bill Tipper and Josh Braun coached the bases.

Then came Game 3 against division rival ABC, a rivalry that's become much like Ali/Frazier of the early 1970s. CNN's first four batters got base hits, and all four scored to stake the CaNiNes to an early 4-0 lead.

With the game tied at five, CNN got five consecutive hits in the bottom of the sixth, including RBI singles from Greg, Aaron, James, and Lindy. ABC kept hacking away. CNN found itself staring at a 9-6 lead with the bases juiced and their best player at bat with two outs and a full count. Greg saved the game and perhaps the season when he tossed a called third strike to end the suspense.

The regular season is now down to two games on July 10. CNN is tied for second place with ABC and NBC, all three teams at 6-6. Taking into account its two gift wins over CNN, CBS is in first place with a 7-5 record.

It's do-or-die time for the CaNiNes.

July 9, 2004

GAME 1		GAME 2		GAME 3	
CNN	11	GAZETTE	10	CNN	6
WRC	9	CNN	5	WTTG	5

- **CNN wins two of last three games but misses playoffs as regular season ends.**
- **Network honors team by canceling *Paula Zahn Now* and replacing with old *Crossfire* shows.**
- **On-air shakeup: Elsa Klensch returns to join Richard Quest and Ahmed Chalabi as hosts of comedy hour.**
- **ADD 1st graph Aaron Brown is new face for Ditech.com.**
- **DELETE reference CNN staged Senate gallery press fight to jolt Anderson Cooper ratings.**

By Joe Baseball Jr.
Bureau Sports Writer

WHEATON, Md. (UPI) — Oh, so close. But so far away. Despite an optimistic preseason assessment by the CIA backed up in a just-released report by the Senate Intelligence Committee, CNN finished the regular season right about where it started in April, stuck between neutral and overdrive, in no man's land, profoundly flawed and exaggerated but on the verge of reconstituting itself.

The result was a respectable 8-7 record. It wasn't good enough, as the team with heart, character, and a whole lot of 'je ne sais quoi' missed the cutoff for the final wild card slot by the smallest of margins, only the second time in the last six years that the team has not qualified for the playoffs—a modern fairy tale with a disenchanted ending.

Coming up short was just the latest in a string of setbacks for CNN. First, in a brazen act of midnight madness, the Washington Bureau removed the vending machine from the 10th floor—no more sandwiches with February expiration dates. "Gone, forever," a clearly frustrated Facilities Manager Kim Linden yelled. But in an act of conciliation, he promised to cram an edit suite in the three-foot cavity between the Chex Mix and Skittles. "We were thinking about putting the edit room on the sixth floor, but we need some place for unused file cabinets."

Next came the insult. Assignment Desk Manager Matt Speiser was fed up because the softball results were not published in the Monday edition of his New York Daily News. Without explanation, he told employees they would have to get their daily newspapers on P2 in the garage.

The final straw came in a memo from Phil Kent, the chairman of Turner Broadcasting. "We honor the CNN softball team and are ready to usher in the annual summer hours program for all employees except those overworked nincompoops in D.C. In recognition, we will give you $25 gift cards for hotels, restaurants, and theatres in Prince George's County. But hurry, supplies are limited."

Except for John Edwards, who was tapped as John Kerry's running mate, it wasn't a good week for anyone, including Marion Jones, Lance Armstrong, George Tenet, or CNN softball players. With all its grace and elan, the team was at the vortex of a perplexing season.

The CaNiNes faced a daunting task on a summery Saturday at the manicured fields of Wheaton Regional Park. In front of the largest turnout of the year (8 people), they squared off against the MMSL's three best playoff-bound teams: WRC, Gazette, and WTTG, which collectively had lost only six times all year. CNN was hardly intimidated. Everyone knows the games are not played on paper. They are decided between the first and third base lines. The CaNiNes went out, did the network proud, and came within a scooch of pulling off a July surprise.

The storylines for each game were engrossing, and the plots were thicker than Carl Rochelle's eyebrows.

In Game 1, CNN gifted WRC, the once-proud but now tattered TV affiliate, an early six-run lead but stormed back for a rousing come-from-behind victory, 11-9. The second game against the Gazette started in a similar enervated way, with the CaNiNes immediately digging themselves in a deep hole, this time 5-0, and then fighting to make it close, only to fall short, 10-5. Game 3 with WTTG was evenly matched, but CNN squeaked by 6-5 with an awe-inspiring performance.

The day began early. It was 9:15 a.m. when the first pitch was thrown. The starting lineup for the CaNiNes featured some new faces in new positions. Unable to resist the joy of squatting for an hour behind players wielding wooden bats, Jocelyn Christensen dragged herself and her husband Steven out to take part and get a souvenir jersey. Like a well-oiled troubadour, Steve Redisch arrived on the big stage ready for action and provided instant dividends by keeping the scorebook, coaching the bases, and playing two positions. Before anyone could say, "Put it in News-Desk," CNN was behind by a half dozen runs.

That's when CNN turned on the after-burners. It was a thing of beauty to watch Aaron stretching for throws at first, Stephanie snagging line drives on the fly, David making ballet-like moves at short to start double plays, Bill diving head first á la Brooks Robinson at third, Laura consistently stepping on the bag at second to snuff out rallies, Chris covering more ground in left field than the First Marine Expeditionary Unit, Lindy showing the steely patience of a nimble batter, John giving it his all for his former employer, Erik displaying his gazelle-like speed and Jim pitching balls reasonably close to the plate.

By the end of the third inning, it was all knotted at eight. CNN kept pecking away and took the lead into the last inning. With the tying runs on base, CNN induced a WRC batter to hit into a bang-bang game-ending double play. CNN 11, WRC 9.

Now CNN was warmed up and ready to rumble, but Christmas came early for the Gazette, the CaNiNes' next opponent. From the get-go, CNN booted grounders and fly balls. It was like combining the Keystone Cops with CNN security and a touch of Helen Keller. Former Enron Chairman Kenneth Lay sent a sympathy telegram to note the team's dramatic slide. Even a previously unknown Islamist group transmitted a statement through Al Jazeera saying CNN's tortuous performance had them blindfolding each other.

CNN left the bases loaded twice, once in the first inning and again in the seventh, muffing repeated chances to make the contest more competitive. When the last out was recorded in a 10-5 final, CNN was on the short end of what was beginning to look like a long day.

The crowd started the wave, anything to pep up the team's spirits. Virginia Nicolaidis and her son Demetri, John's brother Patrick, former CNNer Rebecca Ratliff, Jessica Rosgaard and her mother Betty, and Juan's daughter Nicole did not leave disillusioned.

In Game 3, CNN trailed early 3-0 against WTTG, the Fox-owned local TV affiliate. The CaNiNes went ahead in the third inning with six singles and a walk, and they clung to a precarious one-run lead for the remainder of the game. With the tying run on base in the seventh, Steve squeezed the last out on a popup to push CNN above .500. The big question remained: would it be enough?

The CaNiNes, who won four of their last six games, tied with three other teams, all sharing identical 8-7 records: Discovery Channel, America's Most Wanted, and Dow Jones. Using a system of tiebreakers, Discovery was awarded the 10th and final playoff spot by virtue of an arcane run differential rule. Put simply, Discovery scored more times during the year and gave up fewer runs than CNN. It was time to fold up the circus tent and store the cleats.

This column pays homage to Saturday's Fab Fourteen, who gave it their all. Each deserves a shoutout because they epitomize the vanguard of CNN's best. If you see them in the hallway, tell them job well done.

John Davis, Stephanie Kotuby, Chris Kenny, Bill Tipper, Lindy Royce, Erik Tavcar, Juan Cabral, Steve Redisch, Laura Robinson, David Gracey, Aaron Payne, Jocelyn Christensen, Steve Christensen, and Jim Barnett.

The first practice for 2005 is just 250 days away.

In Heart and Spirit, CNN's Cap'n Jack Passes Away

November 2004

Jack Lynn, 43, was a highly respected senior producer, first baseman, assistant coach, and man of men. He loved a cold Budweiser, a good ball game, traveling for recreation, and living life. Big, strong, and bull-hearted, he was an Irishman and journalist to his core.

"He was a go-get-'em kind of guy, and nothing held him down," said good friend and CNN teammate John Davis. "With Jack, there's a lot of stories and emotions involved. I shed a tear for him."

The Cap'n leaves behind a wife, a loving family, a newsroom, and a softball team of deeply saddened friends. He worked in live production and had first-hand dealings with the many newsmakers who appeared live on the network. He treated people the same and with respect, no matter who they were or their status—whether congressman or summer intern.

"Everything he did was with a sense of humor, which was uniquely Jack," said friend and former teammate Brad Wright. "It was very droll, very dry, or could just be slapstick. But it was out loud funny. He had a disarming way about him."

Wright often traveled with Jack on excursions such as skiing in the Rockies or touring the Major League Baseball stadiums. Jack loved the Outer Banks, watching birds, and reading about history, especially Irish history. He had very few boundaries.

"He didn't live a sheepish life," said CNN coach Jim Barnett.

"We were tailgating at a Redskins game a few years ago, celebrating the last year at RFK Stadium," Wright said. "It was Christmastime, and we made a nativity scene out of Budweiser cans. Oh my gosh, it was hysterical. We had Mary and Joseph Bud, the three Wise Buds, and the

King of Buds. We even used a cloth to give the king his cape. We used a tire for the nativity scene. We were always laughing about that."

But there were few things Cap'n Jack loved more than softball Saturdays in the MMSL. He was instrumental in the start and rise of the CNN team in the mid-1990s, playing integral roles in recruiting players, helping with the lineups, and being a worry wart.

"Softball was everything to Jack," Davis said.

The Cap'n got his nickname because of his low-key involvement in managing the team with Barnett. A CNN player once likened the two as the Joe Torre and Don Zimmer of the media league.

"These were two guys who were very collaborative," Wright said. "They enjoyed bouncing stuff off each other so that an issue of putting somebody here or there could make a difference in a ballgame. They made sure every possibility [for success] was discussed."

No question Barnett and Jack were a perfect coaching tandem. Barnett's easygoing and sensitive leadership was the perfect counterpoint to Cap'n Jack's fieriness.

"He had a sense of who could play and who could not play," Davis added. Jack would do quick surveillance of a new hire in the bureau for softball potential. "As soon as the season ended, he was talking about next year."

Barnett points out that Jack played an enormous role in CNN's two league championships.

"Jack was always the voice of reason," he said. "I always turned to him as my sounding board during the games. We talked strategy like the batting order and, especially, substitutions. He was the best co-pilot one could ever ask for."

TOP OF THE 8th

Second to None

Dedicated to Capt'n Jack Lynn, who'll always be remembered as the heart and soul of the CNN CaNiNes.

April 16, 2005

- **CNN ready for softball opener; fresh faces and wily veterans pledge to revive network.**
- **Michael Jackson to throw out first ball wearing signature white glove; Nancy Grace to sing The Star-Spangled Banner**
- **Executive VP/GM Princell Hair to oversee concession stand.**
- **Network keeps lower third crawl but adds laugh track.**
- **NOTE GRAPHIC CONTENT 5th graph anchors Daryn Kagan and Rick Sanchez agree to shoot each other with tasers.**

By Joe Baseball Jr.
Bureau Sports Writer

VATICAN CITY (UPI) — In a historic confluence of events, namely a long-awaited reorganization of the CNN Washington Bureau and a security breach at the Sistine Chapel, something of biblical proportions happened that could have a ripple effect on the upcoming softball season.

Vatican watchers say Dallas-based reporter Ed Lavandera was spied sneaking in under the robe of one of the sequestered Cardinals minutes before the church doors were shut, signaling the start of the conclave to elect a new pope, according to unnamed sources in the all-new investigative CNN America Bureau unit.

"Despicable, outrageous, and irreverent," shouted National Correspondent Bob Franken, who broke an oath of secrecy and confessed he was ruminating joining the College of Cardinals dressed as disgraced St. Louis Cardinal Mark McGwire. "I thought if I wore a disguise, it would get me on the Paula Zahn show or an attaboy on the 9 o'clock editorial conference call."

In a somewhat related development, CNN executives say they've devised a way to bankroll the CaNiNes and get newly anointed Chief National Correspondent John King more playing time on the softball team.

Starting Monday, the company will use Concur to write off papal coverage costs as personal expenses. Bookkeepers have ordered the D.C. Bureau to construct a chimney pipe from which black smoke will billow when House Majority Leader Tom DeLay resigns. Better still, the District of Columbia will be alerted with white smoke every time the softball team wins.

"From the looks of the lineup, it might be June before that happens," said Jim Walton, president of CNN news group. "I've asked Phil (Kent) to come up with five operating principles so we can spend another half million on those classy acrylic cubes we handed out to every employee."

"We don't discuss sports or newsgathering ideas, but I would be happy to opine about character-driven stories and the new Chimney Cam," yearned a euphoric Jon Klein, president of CNN/US, no relation to Supervising Producer Mike Klein. When asked to justify allowing CNN reporters to impersonate religious leaders, he posited, "We play by the rules at CNN, fair and balanced on the softball field and in our newsroom, unlike the rhapsodical FNC."

Network distractions during the off-season are nothing new at CNN. The number of viewers since last summer has dropped precipitously into the hundreds for *Anderson Cooper 360*, which program insiders say is actively thinking through changing the show's name to *Anderson Cooper 180*. More people read this softball column, according to the latest Nielsen ratings. News junkies now depend on Headline News and the Airport Channel for value-added information on demand.

"Broken borders tick me off," grumbled anchor Lou Dobbs. "We've even outsourced America's pastime. The last time Tony Collings did a package was when he was Rome bureau chief. Do I have to fix everything around here?" A question with no obvious answer.

CNN is eager to recapture its glory years when the CaNiNes were the 1999 and 2002 Metropolitan Media Softball League winners. If championships do come in three-year cycles, 2005 could be preordained. But it will be challenging, especially since male players now have to use wood bats under new MMSL rules. In addition, the league has added two more teams, Townhall.com and The Examiner. There are now 24 clubs.

On Saturday, CNN plays a divisional doubleheader against the NBC News Channel (minus Tom Brokaw) in Game 1 and ABC News (minus Peter Jennings) in Game 2.

"CNN is hurting financially just as much as the commercial networks," one Wall Street smarty-pants conjectured. "They lost security reporter Mike Brooks, Tucker Carlson, Eason Jordan, and The Whip all in the past six months."

On top of that, the company is no longer handing out stock options like candy to employees. Said a spokesman for Smith Barney, "Our best estimate is it will take 42 years for the current stock options to be worth anything."

This year's goal is to improve its 8-7 record and make the playoffs. The team lost in a tiebreaker last July with the Discovery Channel. Company executives hope a successful season will get viewers to watch CNN for an additional seven seconds.

"Anything is possible, especially since *Dolans Unscripted*, hosted by the husband/wife radio personalities Ken and Daria, is airing on Saturday mornings," said one anonymous Atlanta sales rep. "That program is sure to draw advertisers and drive our numbers through the roof."

Spectators will need a scorecard to identify this year's roster. New faces include but are not limited to Arthur Hardy, Tom Bentz, Steve Dolce, Matt Guastaferro, Liz Flynn, Worth Kinlaw, Brett Tyler, Virginia Moubray, and Juan Carlos Lopez.

Among the returning veterans are Stephanie Kotuby, Lindy Royce, Jessica Rosgaard, Jim Barnett, co-captain Bill Tipper, Steve Redisch, Willie Lora, Greg Roberston, Chris Kenny, and John Davis.

"I don't know any of these people," certified Cynthia Barrett, the titular head of Human Resources in Washington. "I've checked with Atlanta, and they have no one on the payroll named Joe Baseball. But I'm happy to say I have discounts for King's Dominion."

Keeping the names straight is a full-time job, not just for the softball team. Over the weekend, a booker for *Late Edition with Wolf Blitzer* received a reprimand for conducting a pre-interview with singer Michael Bolton instead of Ambassador John Bolton.

"Finding the right chemistry is paramount," said someone from the D.C. Bureau's Fun Squad, a loose group of social misfits determined to curb swearing in the control room and on the softball field.

Anyone caught violating the ban will be forced to wear an ankle monitor and watch back-to-back segments of Inside the Blog and Inside the Edge with Carlos Watson.

John Dunaway, head of CNN security, has wired the bureau to monitor all phone conversations. "I'm willing to give away my Nats tickets for any information leading to the return of those non-linear monitors and the person who stole my yogurt out of the ninth-floor fridge."

Come out on Saturday and be part of something special.

May 7, 2005

GAME 1	GAME 2
NBC NEWS CHANNEL................... 7	CNN...3
CNN.. 3	ABC NEWS.................................... 0

- **CNN softball season begins with doubleheader split.**
- **Team looks like parent network in home opener, unhinged and suffering from multiple personality disorder.**
- **CNN battles back in nightcap like Giacomo at the Kentucky Derby to record first shutout in club history.**
- **Jennifer Wilbanks, the so-called "runaway bride" who faked her own kidnapping last month, vows to watch Headline News while in prison.**

By Joe Baseball Jr.
Bureau Sports Writer

KENSINGTON, Md. (UPI) — Network executives and managers were all smiles Monday morning at CNN Center in Atlanta, and for good reason.

CNN/US President Jon Klein, accompanied by the Dallas Cowboys Cheerleaders, told a town hall audience in opening remarks that the state of the company has never been better.

"Not only did we make $8.3 trillion in the first quarter by running those Miracle Hair Removal ads, we now own the cheerleader story," communicated Klein. "We're right where we want to be, especially among the 25-to-54-year-old soccer moms."

He used his appearance in front of executives to point to the CNN softball team as an exemplary business prototype. "Time Warner lost the employee data tapes last week, but the CaNiNes proved this past weekend they have an identity and know how to succeed."

D.C. Bureau Chief David Bohrman hopes to capitalize on all the attention by rotating beat reporters in and out of the White House every three hours. "This way, we give viewers a little taste, and they don't get tired of the same faces. I hope to get Ed Henry, Kimberly Osias, Barbara Starr, Bob Franken, David Ensor, Kathleen Koch, Jamie McIntyre, Jeanne Meserve, Kelli Arena, and Joe Johns all on with Kyra and Miles."

The softball team served up a BTK-like performance over the weekend in the twice-delayed season opener. CNN put a stranglehold on ABC News, 3-0, to earn a split after a nauseous opening loss against NBC News Channel, 7-3.

CNN News Group President Jim Walton hopped out of his chair at warp speed to pronounce, "Tomorrow on *Anderson Cooper 360*, we're going to put Rick Sanchez in a barrel with a DVD camera and push him over Niagara Falls. It's going to be great for CNN and our 148 viewers."

"Yes!" cried out Susan Grant, Chris Cramer, Jack Womack, Sue Bunda, and Sid Bedingfield in joyful unison during a brief lull in the State of the Company event, which was streamed live worldwide.

All CNN business operations came to a grinding halt during the presentation except at *American Morning*, where Mr. Personality Jack Cafferty kept viewers fixated on their screens with his question of the day: "Does power washing the D.C. parking garage make a difference?"

Phil Kent, CEO at TBS, electrified the audience by letting slip he had successfully taken the FISH philosophy training workshop and now knows how to complete the new electronic timesheet system. "It's neat," he said.

Time Warner's CEO Richard Parsons kept things at a feverish pitch when he let slip that he was turning over day-to-day operations of the company, including the softball team, to Nancy Grace. The former prosecutor was too frazzled to comment.

Ken Jautz, Executive Vice President of CNN Business News Operations, said Grace is not your traditional journalist and added, "nor is anyone else who works on our prime time shows."

None of this mattered to the CNN softball team. A baker's dozen showed up bright and early on a beautiful, crisp, and breezy spring Saturday at Capitalview Park.

The CaNiNes came out locked and loaded against NBC, and their optimism lasted one hitter. A leadoff single by CNN's Matt Guastaferro was wiped out in the next at-bat when he was doubled up after straying too far off the bag. Matt promised to make amends by doing every CNN/USA Today poll graphic for the next two months or until *Inside Politics* is taken off the air or *Wolf Blitzer Reports* is expanded to three hours, whichever comes first.

A spokesperson for Judy Woodruff said the anchor would have no comment, but Frank Sesno did return a call to say he would be happy to fill in for Judy or Wolf or do anything else, including serving pancakes at the next Fun Squad-sponsored breakfast.

The first inning of Game 1 wasn't total rubbish. John Davis, who no longer works for the company but is allowed to play under the grandfather clause, hit an inside-the-park home run to give CNN a 1-0 lead.

But NBC clamped down and went ahead with a four-run rally. Ex-CNNer David Shuster, now a reporter for *Hardball*, hit a two-run homer and grabbed hold of an over-the-shoulder line drive with the bases loaded to wrap up the victory.

CNN's scanty offensive prowess was provided by Stephanie Kotuby, who knocked in two runs. Lindy Royce turned in praiseworthy defense behind the plate, as did Aaron Lewis at first base. "We were as ho-hum as an Aaron Brown show open," said one player, who blamed the lack of output on using wood bats.

"I want names!" demanded Keith McAllister in a surlily-worded statement. "Me, too," added Teya Ryan. "Count me in," cursed Rick Kaplan. "Ditto!" whispered Walter Isaacson. "Don't forget about me," begged Princell Hair. "I don't care," said Eason Jordan. Gerald Levin, Jamie Kellner, and Tom Johnson could not be reached for comment. "Does anyone remember me?" piped in Nancy Ambrose.

CNN had back-to-back hits just twice. NBC retired the last six batters, and they walked away with an easy 7-3 victory. Few Metropolitan Media Softball League teams will win when scoring just three runs. CNN proved that anything can happen in softball.

Three runs were precisely the number CNN scored in the nightcap against ABC, and it was more than enough. For the first time since CNN entered the MMSL more than 10 years ago, the CaNiNes pitched a shutout. ABC players were flummoxed all day.

It was a total team effort in Game 2 from Chris Kenny, Greg Robertson, James Knott, Bill Tipper, Jessica Rosgaard, Virginia Moubray, Jim Barnett, Steve Tovarek, and everyone else. An overflow crowd of three (Chrissy Knott, Virginia Nicolaidis, and Demetri) turned out.

CNN's opening doubleheader split was reminiscent of last season's start. The team finished just out of the playoffs with an 8-7 record.

There was one notable difference this year. Players donned new duds: royal blue CNN caps and white T-shirts with an embroidered CNN logo and blue globe.

"They should be de rigueur for all employees," said internationally renowned style journalist Elsa Klensch from her summer villa in Milan.

May 14, 2005

GAME 1		GAME 2	
DISCOVERY	14	CNN	7
CNN	6	TEAM VIDEO	2

- **Inconsistency continues as CaNiNes split another doubleheader.**
- **CNN issues ultimatum: Softball team must be consistent or cease and desist.**
- **News executives issue restrictions on Joe Baseball after column provokes ideological acrimony, rhetorical stridency, partisan low blows, and bile.**

By Joe Baseball Jr.
Bureau Sports Writer

SILVER SPRING, Md. (UPI) — Over the weekend, the Discovery Channel aired a two-hour prime-time special called *Alien Planet*, a computer animation about oddball creatures that aimlessly wander the world.

A preview was shown at Veirs Mill Park on Saturday morning in the form of CNN's softball team in action against the science nerds from Discovery.

It was like watching *Night of the Living Dead* and *The Exorcist* simultaneously. Frightening and difficult to stomach. More chilling than a filibuster. Worse than trying to find hard news on CNN during prime time.

The CNN players mastered the concept that it's not easy to win when their pitchers walk half a dozen batters in the first two innings. Before anyone could utter the phrase, "Bill Hemmer, CNN, the White House," the CaNiNes were well on their way to another loss, 14-7, against the Explorers. It felt more like 140-7.

There was redemption in the nightcap as CNN throttled Team Video, 6-2, a team comprised of former CNNers who could only watch and daydream about the good ol' days.

Immediately after the game, Team Video's Mark Sweet and Darrin White logged on to CNN's Changing Channels and applied for two job postings in the Washington Bureau.

One network manager sent word the plan to roll out broadband on the

Web this year may be temporarily shelved to devote more resources to starting a minor league club for softball players and a clothing allowance for reporter Rick Sanchez, who lost several shirts while being chased live by bloodhounds.

The doubleheader split leaves CNN (2-2) tied for second with CBS and two games behind a resurgent NBC News Channel (4-0) in the Capitalview Division. It's little consolation that both of CNN's losses have come against two of the five undefeated teams left in the league.

Game 1 was so embarrassing that international correspondent Richard Quest promised to drop his fake British accent and join Carolyn O'Neil, former host of *On the Menu*, as anchors of a daily cooking show on *Wolf Blitzer Reports* in June.

WBR Executive Producer Sam Feist said, "David (Bohrman) and I are cooking up some to-die for programming this summer. Wolf makes crème brulee and a Caesar salad with homemade croutons in our pilot. We use the freshest ingredients."

"Once we get the go-ahead from the bean counters in Atlanta, we'll feature rotating beat reporters as sous chefs," said an elated Bohrman. "No more marshmallow fluff."

"It's all about synergy," said an excited frank (sic) Frank Sesno.

"CNN will use the kitchen areas in the D.C. Bureau as I intended," beamed Kathryn Kross, former Washington bureau chief. "I'm sorry I couldn't keep my promise to build a trophy case for the softball team, but I was busy spending money on the space-age newsroom. What a layout!"

The CaNiNes started the doubleheader under sun-splashed skies using three rookies who had never played in the MMSL, and it showed. Two of the three (Brett Tyler and Worth Kinlaw) left the game after getting injured simply running to first base. The third (Tom Bentz, no relation to Kathy Benz) was rotated out after the rest of the team threatened to issue an SOS to the IT department.

"I should have been playing at the Staccato Lounge instead of putting up with this bull (sense)," cursed the usually reserved Bentz, the lead performer of the Geriatrics. He could not find harmony on the pitcher's mound or the strike zone, as he walked five batters, maybe more in the first inning, and all scored. One rubbernecker said, "I thought we were at one of those walkathon fundraisers."

Discovery was equally generous. CNN players were on the receiving end of nine walks in the first four innings. But they couldn't get the big hit when they needed it. The CaNiNes managed just 12 singles and no extra-base hits.

A four-run lead for CNN became a four-run deficit by the time the first inning ended.

CNN got on the scoreboard first with an RBI single from Willie Lora, a bases-loaded walk to Steve Redisch that drove in two runs, and a hit by Aaron Lewis. In just that one inning, CNN scored as many runs as it did all of last week.

The women kept the game close but to no avail. Virginia Moubray, Jessica Rosgaard, Stephanie Kotuby, and Lindy Royce put their talents to the test and showed everyone in attendance how to play the game. They combined to reach safely eight of 11 times. "Keep it up," said Ana Marie Cox, editor of Wonkette.com, in an online chat for softball fanatics.

In Game 2, Team Video scored a first-inning run on a double, but CNN went ahead 3-1 in the home half, a lead they would never give up. Willie, James Knott, and Bill McGraw were each credited with an RBI. In a statistical quirk, the same three players drove in three more runs in the third to double the score and effectively send Team Video back to the editing room.

A dauntless defense was led by Chris Kenny in left, Bill Tipper at third, Steve Tovarek at short, and Jim Barnett on the mound. There were some great Web Gems in the field, with players diving for flies and sharply hit grounders. Even ridiculed Jayson Blair, formerly of the New York Times and now a humbled penitent, extolled the effort, saying, "I can't find the words to describe it, but I can make up some of it."

CNN has allowed just two runs in its two wins. But in its two losses, the CaNiNes have given up 21 runs—a tale of two teams.

The largest crowd of the year turned out despite the distraction of a Bruce Springsteen concert later on. Seven people, including Chrissy Knott, the entire Steve Redisch family (Elizabeth, Lena, and Annabel), and the Paul Miller family (Tricia Maher-Miller and Hannah plus Biscuit the dog), did not leave with any regrets.

On Saturday, CNN is back in action against corporate rival AOL and WJLA-NewsChannel 8.

June 4, 2005

GAME 1		GAME 2	
CNN	7	CNN	14
COMCAST SPORTS	0	NATIONAL PRESS CLUB	4

- **CaNiNes move into first-place tie with doubleheader sweep.**
- **Soggy fields and three-week layoff make for unusual games on grass.**
- **Al Jazeera to join MMSL and play part of season in Doha.**
- **Amnesty International says CNN is "gulag of our times," not Guantanamo.**
- **Note nature 3rd graph Rick Sanchez straps camera to head, swims from Miami to Aruba in search of missing co-ed.**
- **ADD 16th graph Network to rename *American Morning* the *O'Brien Hour with Miles and Soledad*.**

By Joe Baseball Jr.
Bureau Sports Writer

WHEATON, Md. (UPI) — It's been an emotional time at CNN recently, and there's no let-up in sight.

The network and *Larry King Live* celebrated impressive milestone anniversaries. Atlanta employees were treated to a Hall and Oates concert. Washington staffers enjoyed a catered party in a moving farewell to Judy Woodruff and Crossfire, one in her prime, the other way past it. The identity of Deep Throat was made public, ending 30 years of speculation. Ted Turner called Michael Jackson a pervert, sending the pop icon to the emergency room with back spasms. It's been quite a week.

Could things at Cable News Network get any better?

Indubitably.

Anderson Cooper 360 and *Paula Zahn Now* are getting a prime-time facelift from new executive producers, who promise to go beyond the headlines, break news, and do more stories about social security. One idea under consideration is to keep the show names but let Wolf Blitzer anchor both hours starting in July.

If successful, network honchos say the strategy of using Wolf all day and all night could spread to *American Morning*, *Moneyline*, and *NewsNight*.

The remaining anchors can just fight over the weekend cut-ins.

In two short hours on Saturday morning, CNN's softball team experienced what the network hasn't felt in several years: being in first place in something.

The CaNiNes squashed the National Press Club at Wheaton Forest Park, 14-4, to complete a weekend sweep and move its record to 4-2 during this rain-plagued season. CNN is now tied for first with NBC News Channel.

In the opener, Comcast Sports, formerly Comcast SportsNet, was at DEFCON 2 even before the first pitch. They didn't have enough players to field a team, resulting in an automatic 7-0 forfeit.

Ironically, it was a game CNN came close to losing after the umpire consulted the rule book and accidentally dropped his copy of the Koran in the mud, prompting a bench-clearing melee. Order was restored after Human Resources pledged to donate complimentary copies of the New Yorker cartoons to the ump's favorite charity.

There was high drama just getting the fields in playable condition. For a while, it looked like the MMSL was headed to its fourth consecutive weekend of cancellations. Two days of rain had turned the infield into a swamp, forcing all teams to play on the outfield grass.

It was an odd site. The pitcher's mound and home plate were marked with kitty litter. The left and right field lines featured miniature red cones, the kind you see on a highway when an 18-wheeler breaks down. Players could choose between wooden bats or canoe paddles in a one-time exemption.

With one win already in the first game against Comcast, CNN players were foaming at the mouth to face the National Press Club in the second game. The CaNiNes didn't leave anyone waiting because no one showed up to watch.

In the first frame, Greg Robertson (3-4, 3 RBI) scorched a two-out double and came home to score on a John Davis (4-4, 5 RBI) single, a lead CNN would never give back. Robertson scored as many runs as the entire NPC team and pitched without walking a batter.

In the second, leadoff hitter Worth Kinlaw doubled into right field and missed touching first base by at least 30 feet. Fortunately, NPC players were too busy discussing their next speaker's luncheon to notice Kinlaw had run straight from home to second base. Said the batter, "I'm not going to touch the stinkin' first base bag. That's too far to run at my age."

CNN CaNiNes-July 2005

All smiles in 2005 team photo despite losing in championship game.

Liz Flynn brought Kinlaw home with a timely double, and the romp was on. Bill Tipper made it 3-0 with an RBI single.

Protecting a 3-1 lead, CNN broke it open in the fourth. Virginia Moubray got it started with her first career hit that electrified her teammates. Matt Guastaferro followed with a single, as did Aaron Lewis. After Robertson got on base with a fielder's choice, Davis blasted a bases-clearing triple to make it 7-1.

The NPC could have scored throughout the game, but they stranded 10 runners, including with the bases loaded in the fourth. Countless rallies were cut short thanks to great defensive plays by Lindy Royce behind the plate, Chris Kenny in left, Guastaferro in center, Tipper at third, and Lewis at first. Tom Bentz went two for three as both the designated hitter and the official scorer.

When it was over, CNN had notched its most satisfying win of the year. The CaNiNes scored in every inning, but one, and six different players had RBI.

The blitzkrieg continues next week when corporate pretender AOL comes to town to play CNN, followed by a game against WJLA/ NewsChannel 8. For those unable to make it, tune in to XM Radio channel 175 to hear all the action.

June 11, 2005

GAME 1		GAME 2	
CNN	7	CNN	17
AOL	3	WJLA/NEWSCHANNEL 8	5

- **CNN sweeps again! Team in first place! CaNiNes sizzle!**
- **Addled executives implement "Summer Saturdays," allowing all M-F employees to take Saturdays off.**

By Joe Baseball Jr.
Bureau Sports Writer

LAYHILL, Md. (UPI) — Once again, the fortunes of the ham-fisted Cable News Network hung in the balance this weekend. And, as usual, it was left to CNN's softball team, not Bob Costas, not W. Mark Felt, not even Ali Velshi, to bring a glimmer of respect and optimism to the rest of the company.

The CaNiNes did not dash the hopes of their legion of followers.

On a wickedly tropical Saturday morning at Layhill Park, CNN's vaunted offense shut down AOL, 7-3, in Game 1 and roasted the identity-challenged WJLA/NewsChannel 8 team by a score of 17-5 in Game 2.

The victories give the CaNiNes a five-game winning streak and sole possession of first place halfway through the season.

The timing couldn't have been better.

Bloggers have had a field day detailing every misstep of CNN's struggle to develop a durable and sustainable style of presenting the news. In a remarkable turnaround, CNN management has mandated producers of the noon show delete any references to Michael Jackson or Natalee Holloway in Aruba.

Nevertheless, a 'feel good' story about softball is garnering its fair share of attention and might end the network's identity crisis.

In the opener, CNN spotted AOL two runs in the first inning but matched it with two of their own. It was even until the fourth when CNN retook the lead with four hits and four runs as the team coasted to a well-deserved 7-3 victory.

"I can't begin to tell you how proud I am of our softball success," said Jon Klein, CNN/US President, during a visit to the D.C. Bureau. "I saw all those trophies in the Washington newsroom and thought they were for newsgathering. This kind of collaboration will separate us from the pack in a television landscape littered with mindless diversions. That's why I've tasked our D.C. folks to take full advantage."

Executive Producer and wunderkind Sam Feist speedily conferred a new initiative. "I had hoped to keep it a secret, but Mediabistro and Drudge have already leaked it. As part of our rollout of *The Situation Room*, we will blindfold Rick Sanchez, put him behind home plate without a glove at Turner Field, and watch him catch 94-mile-per-hour fastballs from Atlanta Braves pitcher John Smoltz."

Jim Walton, president of CNN news group, issued a company statement: "We recently canvassed a select group of newsroom employees who voted to place Rick in a pit of poisonous snakes on live TV. I sincerely hope to have enough laughable Sanchez stories to fill up the summer doldrums between hurricane coverage, replays of prime-time packages, and highlights of our softball team."

CNN's dramatic come-from-behind win against AOL was felt all the way to the Dulles-based company's headquarters, where the bad news continues to come down in buckets. Industry insiders say Time Warner is sizing up a spin-off of its America Online division, leaving some to postulate that the only value left with AOL is its trademark "You've Got Mail" phrase.

At the company's annual meeting in New York, Chairman Richard Parsons roared, "If it gets to the point where we have to sell the slogan through Christie's Auction House, we'll do what we have to do in the interest of our shareholders. We've already granted a five-cent quarterly cash dividend on each share of common stock."

The optimism came to a screeching halt in Game 2. The 78ers (Channel 7 and Channel 8 combined) tried to psych out CNN before the first pitch by blasting Eye of the Tiger on a CD player. "The least they could have done is drip water and play Christina Aguilera music like they do at Gitmo," said one Afghan detainee.

The players for the CaNiNes barely noticed as they sat in the steamy shade, eating Lindy Royce's melted chocolate chip cookies and placing bets on the Belmont Stakes. All players were hooked up to margarita IVs.

The glow from the first game didn't last long. After CNN plated three runs, the 78ers responded with five runs in the bottom of the first, courtesy of at least three errors. The official scorebook registered twice that many.

The weather was becoming the story on the dusty field at Layhill.

"It was Code Orange out there," sputtered former CNN meteorologist Flip Spiceland, who last year received a lifetime achievement award for his ability to predict it would get hot in the summer and cold in the winter. "I've never seen anything like those brave players willing to risk heat stroke and take one for the team. I wish I were back at Techwood working with Dallas Raines and Al Sunshine."

CNN bats came alive in the nightcap as the team collected 20 hits and a staggering 10 walks.

The CaNiNes scored two runs in the second, three in the third, one in the fourth, seven in the fifth, and one in the sixth while shutting down WJLA. Not even former CNN anchor Leon Harris could protect the local ABC affiliate. It was a TKO that would have made Mike Tyson proud.

CNN's defense was chintzy when it mattered. Take away the first inning in both games, and the CaNiNes only gave up one paltry run all day. In the team's six wins this year, opponents have averaged just 2.3 runs a game.

Designated hitter Sir Willie Lora was red-hot, 6-6, plus a walk and four RBI. He missed hitting for the cycle when he tripped approaching third base and got a 9.9 from the judges after tumbling to the ground. Erik Tavcar, fully healed from an ankle injury, made his season debut and went 5-7 with five runs scored.

Juan Cabral dug out every throw at first base all day long. He was 3-3 in Game 1 and 2-3 in Game 2. The supporting cast included Stephanie Kotuby, who not only turned in sterling play at second base but also got a single and three walks; dependable Bill Tipper and Steve Tovarek shared duties at third; John Davis at short and speedy Matt Guastaferro in left caught everything that came their way. All received Gold Gloves.

After a hitless first game, James Knott drank from the Fountain of Youth to go 3-5 with three RBI. That pleased the sparse crowd of one, his wife Chrissy. Liz Flynn had a single against AOL and proceeded to get on base three times against WJLA. Lindy Royce showed patience, getting a base hit and two walks. She also kept pitcher Jim Barnett in the zone and throwing strikes.

Jessica Rosgaard heeded her horoscope for the day and displayed *Moneyline* precision skills to keep track of all the numbers in the scorebook and the batting order; it was no small endeavor.

Following the last out, the team drove to the Stained Glass Pub to discuss CNN Digital's groundbreaking broadband service and the network's updated employee identification system.

The season's most important games take place next Saturday when CNN faces division rivals CBS News and NBC News Channel.

June 18, 2005

GAME 1		GAME 2	
CNN	13	CNN	10
CBS NEWS	8	NBC NEWS CHANNEL	7

- **CNN spanks broadcast networks to hike winning streak to seven.**
- **Marines launch offensive in Iraq while CaNiNes conduct Operation Clean Sweep.**
- **News network to emulate softball team to shed bumbling image.**
- **Focus now on finding characters and storytelling while keeping viewers awake.**

By Joe Baseball Jr.
Bureau Sports Writer

KENSINGTON, Md. (UPI) — The CaNiNes had the Midas touch on Saturday as every move the softball team made turned to gold.

CNN thoroughly demolished CBS News in the opener, 13-8, in a game where the final score didn't reflect the utter dismantling of the once proud network made famous by Edward R. Murrow. Halfway through the contest, a muddled CBS offered CNN a choice of a half dozen Evening News correspondents plus interim anchor Bob Schieffer if it would part with Bruce Morton, Rick Sanchez, and four spare producers from *AC 360*, *Paula Zahn Now* and *NewsNight*.

Executives at CNN Center immediately agreed to unload the unnamed producers. Sue Bunda, executive vice president of content development and strategy for CNN worldwide and the holder of the longest title in broadcasting, said, "Those prime-time shows in Manhattan have so many producers with redundant responsibilities, we knew no one would notice. To show our good faith, we also sold them the copyright to The Whip."

While the first game at Capitalview Park against CBS was a laugher like Lucy and Ethel working the conveyor belt at the chocolate factory in *I Love Lucy*, the nightcap against NBC was *Law & Order*. It took two separate comebacks, an intern, luck, and well-timed plays by unexpected batters to bring home the victory, 10-7. CNN's win against NBC avenges an opening weekend loss.

The second half of the Metropolitan Media Softball League season began just like the first half ended, with CNN players sweeping a doubleheader and making a defiant statement. The CaNiNes are for real. CNN (8-2) has won seven straight and is tied for the best record in the league.

CNN's success even left Jennifer Wilbanks looking more wild-eyed than her usual deer-in-the-headlights stare. "My eyes popped out of their sockets," said the runaway bride shortly after coming clean about a $30 million deal with *Dateline*. "Now that I see how NBC's softball team plays, I wish I had given my first interview to media celebrity and legal commentator Nancy Grace instead of Katie Couric."

It was the kind of day when everything clicked.

How else could anyone explain a CNN foul ball caught 20 feet from home plate that drove in two runs? Or the CaNiNes unveiling their 10th different starting lineup? Or the team being two outs from an insufferable loss but rallying for four runs in the last inning?

"It shows what can happen when you put your mind to it," professed Ayman al-Zawahiri, Osama bin Laden's top lieutenant, on a videotape mailed to the D.C. Bureau.

It's unclear whether al-Zawahiri's comment was directly related to softball or another planned terrorist attack, according to Senior Editor for Arab Affairs Octavia Nasr. "As I understand it, the tape had been in the D.C. mailroom for quite some time, and Carlton, the mail guy, just got around to sorting the packages lying around since Christmas and running it through x-ray."

Despite crystal blue skies, cool temperatures, and absolutely 'oh-my goodness' playing conditions, CNN came out flatter than a Daryn Kagan toss to Miles O'Brien. In the opening inning against CBS News, the CaNiNes sent three batters to the plate (Chris Kenny, Matt Guastaferro, and John Davis), and not one reached first base. It didn't get much better in the second inning.

CNN, up 1-0, loaded the bases after singles by Erik Tavcar, Liz Flynn, Aaron Lewis, and Bill Tipper. Then Virginia Moubray bowled over everybody by hitting a three-foot dribbler in front of home plate. The CBS pitcher grabbed the ball, dashed toward home, touched the plate to get the force out, and fired to first base to double up Virginia, who testified she had stopped halfway down the line to check on next week's *Larry King Live* guests. CNN missed breaking the game open.

I hadn't seen such long faces since the network moved *On the Story* from Saturdays to Sundays," recounted one rabid fan. But the CaNiNes hunkered down, and their patience paid off.

James Knott blistered a double to open the third inning. Chris, Matt, John, Erik, and Howie Lutt making a triumphant return to his old haunts, hit RBI singles to give CNN some breathing room and a four-run advantage.

The lead was widened to 10 runs in the sixth with help from Juan Cabral, Jessica Rosgaard, Brett Tyler, Dave Robinson, and intern Jacqueline Wilde. CNN allowed CBS to cut the lead in half during their last at-bat, but the game was over for all practical purposes. It was a dominant performance.

The only player who didn't see action was first-timer Richard Jenrette. He said sheepishly he wasn't in the best shape, but he was all smiles. His D.C. graphics department was selected over Atlanta to do all the graphics for *The Situation Room*.

Among the spectators were fan favorites Chrissy Knott, the Virginia Nicolaidis family, and Brett's wife Ana and daughter Madeleine. They were all treated to a memorable pre-Father's Day contest.

Former CBS Executive and now CNN President Jon Klein was upbeat after the opening game despite watching his new network fritter away countless hours last week covering the Michael Jackson verdict. "Just like our softball players, I know what it's like to miss opportunities. We were too absorbed in Wacko Jacko when we should have been doing highbrow journalism."

In Game 2 against NBC, CNN took a 4-1 lead in the most unusual way. The bases were loaded with one out and Howie batting. Fearing a line drive, the outfielders were playing deep. Howie took a Herculean swing and lofted a fly ball halfway between home and third. A combination of the wind and backspin carried the ball toward foul territory. NBC's pitcher raced from the mound to catch the drifting ball but ended up in the bushes. The runners on second and third tagged up and scored.

The second game also saw its fair share of defensive plays. NBC had runners on first and second, with one out in the second inning. The batter hit a scorching grounder to John D at short, who threw to Bill at third for the force out, who in turn hurled a throw to Liz at second to complete the double play and end the rally. A web gem if there ever was one.

There was no quit in NBC. They tied the game and went ahead by a run, 7-6. But CNN never gave up its appetite for winning. After a ground out by James, the compelling story took center stage. Jessica, representing the tying run, stared down the opposing pitcher and drew a walk. Chris followed with a hit to move Jess to second. Matt showed patience and received a walk to load the bases with the tying run just 65 feet away. John, too, got a free pass to force in Jess to even the score at seven. Erik drove in a run with a single to give CNN the lead. Howie added insurance with a walk that forced in two more runs.

There were just fumes left in NBC's gas tank. They put a runner on base in the bottom of the seventh, but CNN quelled any thought of giving up the lead.

The fun continues this Saturday as CNN faces Dow Jones and Washington Post. Instead of reading all about it, come out and watch the action.

June 25, 2005

GAME 1		GAME 2	
CNN	12	CNN	4
DOW JONES	0	WASHINGTON POST	3

- CNN can do no wrong as team sweeps another doubleheader.
- Tremendous player turnout forces company to rethink hiring strategy.
- Network to drop *Capital Gang* and fill void with televised softball games.
- Bush advisors in snit as CNN preempts Ft. Bragg speech for coverage of sex trafficking, mad cow, sharks, Aruba, oil prices, Ten Commandments, Western wildfires, file sharing, BTK, and anything Rick Sanchez does.
- DELETES outdated information about Maria Hinojosa.
- Eds: RECASTS lede Female correspondents for *On the Story* threaten lawsuit after executives broaden scope of show; male reporters contend they have unique insights, too.

By Joe Baseball Jr.
Bureau Sports Writer

ASPEN HILL, Md. (UPI) — This is the season for fireworks and independence. CNN's softball team provided both at Aspen Hill Park in a pair of galvanizing games. They quickly sold off Dow Jones, 12-0, in the opener and scooted past the Washington Post, 4-3, in the nightcap.

CNN is tied for the No. 1 seed. Not bad for a club that didn't even make the playoffs in 2004. The team is blessed with a favorable schedule and a posse of committed participants who only want to achieve greatness. "It's a lot like holding a G8 Summit and a Live Aid concert each week," said Bob Geldof and Kofi Annan in a joint statement.

The CaNiNes (10-2), winners of nine in a row, haven't lost since mid-May and have an imposing three-game lead in the Capitalview Division with just four games remaining. Not only has the team swept four straight doubleheaders, but the ball club is also credited with returning all the luster to the tarnished CNN brand. Now, when opponents bring up tailwind, it refers to the airflow created by the softball team's winning ways, not the embarrassing chapter in CNN's illustrious legacy.

If two is company and three is a crowd, then logic dictates the CaNiNes had a convention on Saturday. Nineteen devout and talented CNN players made the trek to Montgomery County, plus the two deer that pranced across the outfield shortly before game time.

That's more people to turn out for anything at CNN since former Bureau Chief Kathryn Kross celebrated October birthdays four years ago with cake and mint chocolate chip ice cream. Past newsroom speeches by Rick Kaplan, Walter Isaacson, Gerald Levin, and a host of other network execs never came close to creating the buzz now triggered by softball.

D.C. Photojournalist Manager Ben Coyte said 25 people enrolled in his one-hour primer on digital newsgathering last week. A CNN investigation found only half showed up for the class; the remainder went to Starbucks to get iced lattes, enjoy the ambiance of an Internet café, and watch the crew guys transfer video files of the latest shark attack off the Florida coast to the Atlanta server.

For those who thought the new CNN video on demand was the hottest thing going, they should look at what the softball team is accomplishing. Odds makers now say the likelihood of the CaNiNes winning their division is better than 50/50, pushing slightly ahead of predictions that William Rehnquist will resign and Frank Sesno will be nominated to pinch hit for the Supreme Court Chief Justice.

The biggest task against Dow Jones was figuring out how to get 19 CaNiNes into an 11-person lineup. As it happened, Game 1 ended early after the umpire stopped the onslaught. Every CNN person got playing time and free subscriptions to the Wall Street Journal as a parting gift.

It was far from a romp early on. Not even the return of John King, making his first softball appearance in two years, could rouse the team. In front, 1-0, CNN had just one single in three innings. "I haven't seen such a sorry spectacle since going through the script approval process for *NewsNight*," said one sullen reporter.

The second time through the lineup, CNN got things going with one out in the fourth. Howie Lutt and John K singled, followed by a walk to Stephanie Kotuby to load the bases. Willie Lora punched a two-run double. Juan Cabral blistered a two-run triple. After another out, Chris Kenny and Virginia Moubray earned their way on base with big-time walks. Then Matt Guastaferro hit a propitious two-run single, and Greg

Robertson capped the inning with a two-run double. Like that, CNN's stale performance turned into a 9-0 route.

Wholesale substitutions were made in the lineup: Tom Bentz, Bill Tipper, Jessica Rosgaard, Brett Tyler, Jim Barnett, Jacqueline Wilde, and Dave Robinson built the lead to 12-0, helping end the route mercifully in the sixth inning.

The crackerjack defense made one laudable play after another, especially in the third inning after Dow Jones led off with a single. The next three consecutive batters hit ground balls to short, and John K tossed to Stephanie at second for force outs each time.

CNN's whitewashing of Dow Jones marked the third shutout of the season for the CaNiNes.

The frugal defensive effort continued against the Washington Post in Game 2, helped in part by a morale-enhancing appearance by Deep Throat. CNN took a 4-0 lead thanks to a tomahawk home run by crafty Erik Tavcar. He ran around the bases so fast that he almost knocked down John Davis, who got on base with a walk.

That was just enough as the Post closed the gap to 4-3 in the sixth inning. Lindy Royce tried to trick the opposing team by pretending there were three outs when there were only two and walking off the field, but the plot was uncovered by Bob Woodward, hiding in a nearby parking lot. The Post didn't do any more damage as the CaNiNes turned three double plays in the nightcap to preserve the 10th win of the season.

"They may have more Pulitzer Prizes than CNN has Emmys, but at least Janet Cooke never was a network reporter," said former correspondent Peter Arnett during a damaged milk factory tour outside Baghdad.

A happy CNN club then posed for pictures that included Ana and Madeleine Tyler and Noah and Hannah King.

The MMSL is on hiatus until July 9, when CNN plays host to division rivals CBS News and ABC News at Capitalview field. D.C. Bureau Chief David Bohrman has requested all department heads and managers give employees the option of attending the games or facing termination. Come out and root for the team. Tom Cruise will be in attendance, handing out free samples of Adderall and Ritalin.

July 9, 2005

GAME 1	GAME 2
CNN...18	CNN.. 16
CBS NEWS 2	ABC NEWS...8

- **CNN clinches first place! Team to get another trophy.**
- **Broadcast networks don't know what hit them as CaNiNes win 11th straight.**
- **CBS & ABC embarrassed, forced to merge with Christian Broadcasting Network.**
- **ADD 5th graph Hurricane Director Max Mayfield's popularity soars, will host Saturday morning cartoon show alongside Rick Sanchez.**

By Joe Baseball Jr.
Bureau Sports Writer

KENSINGTON, Md. (UPI) — Hurricane Dennis, packing winds of 120 mph, may have grabbed the weekend headlines as it made landfall in Florida, but the storm paled in comparison to CNN's ransacking of softball adversaries CBS and ABC.

The CaNiNes played with sustained wind and fury, signifying everything and sending its opponents scurrying for cover during a relentless volley of singles, doubles, triples, and home runs. It was a clean sweep as CNN cruised to the division title, demolishing CBS News 18-2 and beating up ABC News 16-8.

"It was a Cat 3 in the Gulf and a Cat 16 at Capitalview field," confirmed a rattled Chad Myers from Pensacola. "I've been in the business since the invention of AccuWeather, and I've never seen anything like what our softball players did to the other team."

The ferocity of Hurricane Dennis left everyone equally spellbound. Viewers at home were glued to the riveting live shot of John Zarrella and Anderson Cooper as the two veteran reporters spent more than an hour breathlessly monitoring the fate of a Ramada Inn welcome sign and the roof of a Chevron gas station off Route 12. "I think it's about to go," Zarrella repeatedly yelled as he sought refuge behind Cooper. "Watch out!" cautioned the brave anchor. Cooper reminded viewers just tuning in "around the world" that "leaves are blowing all around us."

Washington Post media critic Tom Shales wrote, "It was gripping television and something not found on the Big Three networks, which were all broadcasting game shows. I don't have much else to say about the softball games except I hope this quote helps you make a transition."

CNN (12-2) scored 18 runs in just four innings in the opener, after which CBS agreed to stick to doing news.

CBS took an early 2-0 lead. But faster than getting a media source number and feeding tape to New York, CNN scored two runs of their own, courtesy of John Davis's two-run homer. The lead expanded to 5-2 in the second with a Bill Tipper single, walk to Jacqueline Wilde, an RBI single by Brett Tyler, a Chris Kenny walk, and a single by Erik Tavcar.

The turning point came in the top of the third when CBS received an automatic out to start the inning for not having enough women. Howie Lutt needed just two pitches, one to each of the next two batters, to retire the side.

"CBS lost its compass. They were clearly distracted by the rumors Connie Chung would sit in for Bob Schieffer," deduced Tom Rosenstiel, director of the Pew Research Center's Project for Excellence in Journalism.

Faced with a mandate to revamp the network's nightly news broadcast, CBS News President Andrew Heyward ordered his players to wave the white flag immediately. "We have a problem. Our audience skews to viewers 85 and older, and we can't play softball."

Willie Lora and Stephanie Kotuby led off the bottom of the third with walks. One out later, Bill, Jacqueline, and Brett singled. Lindy Royce walked, Chris dropped in a hit, Erik and John tripled, and Howie slugged a two-run homer. Stephanie, Juan Cabral, and Bill came up for a second time in the inning and hit safely before the demolition derby ended with 10 runs and 10 hits.

Erik completed the onslaught and hit for the cycle by blasting a monster three-run homer in the fourth inning after singles by Liz Flynn and Chris. Virginia Moubray and Tom Bentz barely had time to break a sweat before the umpire decided he had seen enough and called the contest "out of respect for the game."

In a terse communique, CBS Chairman Les Moonves said, "Our team was wretched. We deserve to be the laughingstock of the Metropolitan Media Softball League. At least we can do great storytelling."

It was obvious CNN was in a hurry to get off the field so players could watch the latest installment of *On the Story*. Company executives corroborated they're reconsidering the current strategy of always pre-taping the program after Christiane Amanpour spent the entire hour talking about the Olympic committee's decision to award the 2012 games to London and never once said anything about the four suicide bombings on London trains that killed 52 people.

"Who knew they'd be breaking news?" said Senior Executive Producer Lucy Spiegel, while grasping at straws. "I hope our devoted viewers were shrewd enough to know our show was taped."

After feasting on Munchkins from Dunkin Donuts between games, CNN was ready for the nightcap against ABC. A win would clinch the Capitalview Division for the CaNiNes. ABC was shut out the last time the two teams faced each other.

This time, ABC put two runs on the scoreboard in the first inning—just a drop in a large bucket. CNN responded by batting around. Chris walked, Erik doubled, John singled, and Howie and Willie tripled. With one out, Juan doubled, and Bill and Liz singled. It was 6-2, and the rout was on.

Howie put the finishing touches on the game with a two-run homer in the fourth and a three-run blast in the sixth. A crowd of three, including Juan's nephew Manuel and Brett's wife Ana and daughter Madeleine, went home happy.

Oddly, one of the most pressing assignments facing CNN all day was keeping the scorebook from turning into an utter mess of lines and chicken scratches. Thankfully, Jessica Rosgaard charted the action with precision. "I made a conscious decision not to put myself in the lineup to spare ABC any further egg on their face."

CNN's 34 runs on the day are the most scored by the team all year. The regular season wraps up with two more games on Saturday. Then come the playoffs on July 23-24 weekend at Cabin John Regional Park. Sources say D.C. Bureau Chief David Bohrman may hand out pom poms in the newsroom.

July 16, 2005

GAME 1	GAME 2
WRC...10	WASHINGTON TIMES..................8
CNN... 5	CNN...5

- **CNN hits brick wall, loses doubleheader to end regular season.**
- **CaNiNes finish with second-best record in MMSL as team prepares for playoffs.**
- **D.C. Bureau to sponsor clinic entitled "How to Succeed in Softball Without Really Trying."**
- **ADD new lede Fledgling network nixes co-anchor format in favor of cardboard cutouts.**

By Joe Baseball Jr.
Bureau Sports Writer

LAYHILL, Md. (UPI) — CNN's unforgettable softball season on Saturday became entirely forgettable as the team got smacked around in a pair of games that didn't matter one iota when all was said and done.

CNN is headed to the postseason at 12-4 as a No. 4 seed, good enough to get a well-deserved bye in the first round.

To be sure, it was not a particularly successful weekend. The effort by players followed the let-sleeping-dogs-lie approach. It worked to perfection. In the opener, WRC hounded CNN, 10-5, ending the CaNiNes 12-game winning streak. The Washington Times invoked the kicking-the-dog-when-it's-already-down theory and put a leash on CNN, 8-5, in the nightcap.

The back-to-back losses, the first time this year, aren't viewed as a setback. The players said it's all part of a master plan. The CaNiNes set out to lower expectations heading into the playoffs. "It's a strategy that has proven effective, especially for our upcoming show," prophesized Sam Feist, executive producer of *The Situation Room*.

CNN will play the winner of the game between Townhall.com and Atlantic Video as the double-loss elimination series gets underway this Saturday at Cabin John Regional Park.

The road to the title on Sunday will likely have to go through this past weekend's opponents, the Washington Times and WRC, if the brackets and seeds hold to form. CNN did its part to give them a false sense of security in case of a rematch. "If the other teams think we're going to roll over and get our tummies scratched like we're real canines, they better think twice," said CNN and the American Kennel Club in a joint statement released over the weekend.

Playing conditions at soupy Layhill Field led to sloppy play. Overnight rains left the infield a mud pit suitable for pigs but not softball. Pre-game field maintenance took over an hour of raking, sweeping, and 10 bags of kitty litter. Both teams faced the same hurdles, though CNN's speed on the base baths took a noticeable hit.

In Game 1, CNN took a 3-0 lead in the first inning thanks primarily to hot-hitting Stephanie Kotuby, who swatted a two-run single with two outs. The rest of the team was AWOL, and WRC, last year's champions, fought back with 10 runs to knock the starch out of any thoughts of a rally. Juan Cabral accounted for the final two runs in the sixth inning when he clobbered a two-run homer, much to the delight of his entire family, who came out to watch, along with Steve Redisch, his girls Lena and Annabel, plus Ana and Madeleine Tyler.

CNN only had two innings with more than one hit. The first two batters in the lineup were hitless. In one sorry stretch, the CaNiNes had three hits in 17 at-bats. We're talking lifeless. Yet they were within five runs, but there was no comeback this day.

The second game against the Washington Times didn't start out much better. Things got so bad even Sun Myung Moon got a base hit as they took a 4-0 lead in the first, a lead it never would let go. Again, CNN went through a horrid stretch where it couldn't marshal anything resembling a rally. Over a span of 21 batters, CNN collected just three trifling hits.

CNN played like it had one foot stuck in the mud all day with a mediocre effort. The CaNiNes came up on the short end of the nightcap against an opponent more unified than the Unification Church.

Each player, including Matt, Greg, John, Howie, Brett, Jim, JC, Steph, Lindy, Chris, Virginia, and Jacqueline, pledged to do better next week. They refused to give their last names to protect their anonymity.

Now, the so-called second season begins with the cream of the crop.

If history is any guide, don't count out the CaNiNes, who won the tournament in 1999 and 2002. If you're one of those statisticians who believes in apophenia and things happen in threes, this could be the year.

Fans can still come out to see the CaNiNes in action and the players who have faithfully represented CNN since those early frosty Saturday mornings in March, when the team started spring training.

Catch the fever and join the playoff hype.

July 23, 2005

GAME 1		GAME 2	
CNN	9	CNN	10
ATLANTIC VIDEO	6	NBC NEWS CHANNEL	6
GAME 3		GAME 4	
CNN	8	WASHINGTON POST.COM	8
WASHINGTON POST.COM	7	CNN	0

GAME 5 (CHAMPIONSHIP)	
WASHINGTON POST.COM	9
CNN	3

- **CNN's singular, sensational softball season comes up short as team loses title game! Damn those scribes!**
- **CaNiNes display their "A" game on Saturday and their "F" game on Sunday in marathon.**
- **Players proudly walk away with two trophies and division-winning T-shirts.**

By Joe Baseball Jr.
Bureau Sports Writer

ROCKVILLE, Md. (UPI) — Too bad the Metropolitan Media Softball League season didn't end on Saturday. If it had, CNN would be the 2005 champions.

Unfortunately, the team could not close the door or seal the deal on Sunday. It was a ginormous disappointment. On the other hand, finishing with the second-best record (16-6) isn't too shabby, either.

Interviews with more than a dozen people with knowledge of the team's inner workings say that despite losing in the title game, the players took meaningful strides to help transform the entire network.

"We see signs of progress and a lucrative cable division," said CNN in a statement released over the weekend. "The future is rosy. We are evolving back to the kind of journalism the network was founded on."

On Sunday, the Washington Post.com completely dominated CNN, beginning with the first pitch. CNN had come into the last day as the only team out of 24 that hadn't lost in the double-loss elimination play-offs. Post.com took care of that by shutting out the CaNiNes 8-0 to force a final winner-take-all showdown.

It wasn't to be. The so-called Bucketheads had the Big Mo, and they road it all the way to the end, defeating the CaNiNes, 9-3, to claim the championship.

Just 24 hours earlier, on Saturday, CNN had defeated Washington Post.com, 8-7, in an extra-inning nail-biter to send Post.com into the loser's bracket, but the Posties would ultimately get sweet satisfaction.

It was a memorable weekend in so many ways at picturesque Cabin John Regional Park: adept hitting, dramatic catches, and three come-from-behind victories against playoff teams.

Since 1999, the CaNiNes have finished in first, second, or third place five out of seven seasons, a success rate other teams can only thirst for.

"CNN's news division would gladly take just one of those accomplishments," theorized Jim Walton, CNN news group president. "We can't all be like Lance Armstrong and win every year. Congrats to the CaNiNes!"

CNN/US President Jon Klein used his Monday 9 a.m. conference call to heap faint praise upon the softball team: "What they have done for the trustworthiness of this network is immeasurable. I've tried every-thing from elevating Rick Sanchez from obscurity in Florida to cancel-ing *Dolans Unscripted* and getting rid of Bill Hemmer, but nothing has worked. Thank goodness we have a softball team in Washington."

CNN started the weekend with half of its squad having never experi-enced a playoff atmosphere. The rust and nerves showed. On top of that, there was little margin for error for a club lacking a deep bench. Two players, Chris Kenny and Virginia Moubray, had to leave early, and Brett Tyler pulled a hamstring. Aaron Lewis played Saturday but had to work Sunday.

Atlantic Video took a 3-0 lead in the first inning of Game 1. CNN returned the favor by scoring four runs of its own. Atlantic Video hung tight and tied the score in the fifth inning. The CaNiNes got down to business in the sixth and took a three-run lead to win, 9-6.

Next up for CNN was division rival NBC News Channel, which had split its previous head-to-head games during the regular season. Again,

CNN fell behind early but bounced back with three runs in the second, four in the third, and three in the fourth to pull ahead 10-3. They hung on for a 10-6 victory.

It only got better Saturday afternoon as CNN's third opponent was Washington Post.com in a battle of the last two undefeated teams.

CNN began the game with four runs on five singles by Greg Robertson, Erik Tavcar, John Davis, Howie Lutt, and Willie Lora. Stephanie Kotuby and Matt Guastaferro each hit into a fielder's choice but got credit for two RBI.

CNN was treading water with a 6-4 lead when Post.com staged a sneak attack in its last at-bat and scored three runs to move in front 7-6. But the CaNiNes, true to form, never say never.

Matt led off with a single. Jacqueline Wilde came up to bat. With the entire CNN intern program riding on her shoulders and Vanderbilt University's stature hanging in the balance, she flew out. Still, it was just deep enough to force the shortstop to fire wildly to first base to get Matt, who darted to third, drawing another throw, this time from first base. The ball sailed over the third baseman's head, allowing Matt to score the tying run.

Neither team could score in the eighth inning. Post.com came close, but Howie tagged out a runner at third to hold them at bay.

In the bottom of the ninth, John led off with a single. Howie moved him up one base with a 270-foot sacrifice fly. With two outs, Stephanie grabbed a bat and smashed a double to drive in John with the winning run. She was swarmed by the CaNiNes who rushed onto the field in ecstasy. It was utter bliss.

The stage was set for Sunday's finals.

Alas, there's not much to say on that score. It wasn't a day to treasure except for what happened after Post.com defeated CNN.

In a postgame ceremony before a throng of media cameras, the CaNiNes received a trophy for winning the Capitalview Division and another for finishing second in the playoff tournament, plus individual fancy T-shirts.

Shout out to Bill Tipper (Total team player and coach), Greg Robertson (One of the best pitchers in the MMSL), Erik Tavcar (Right up there with Willie Mays), John Davis (All-around teammate), Howie Lutt (Heaven-sent midseason addition), Willie Lora (Designated hitter and spiritual leader), Stephanie Kotuby (Most improved), Matt Guastaferro

(Faster than a gazelle), Juan Cabral (Taught everyone how to curse in Spanish), Lindy Royce (Harmony and joy), Tom Bentz (Rookie sensation), Jessica Rosgaard (Number cruncher and statistician), Jacqueline Wilde (Intern extraordinaire) and Skip Nocciolo (Team photographer).

It was then on to Ledo's Pizza, where the CaNiNes celebrated a marvelous year.

The Great Wood Bat Rift

The most defining change to the Metropolitan Media Softball League occurred before the 2005 season. At the league's annual spring meeting, Commissioner Dennis Tuttle announced that high-performing aluminum "superbats" would no longer be allowed for male

Howie Lutt with a firm grip on a wood bat.

players. They would have to swing wood bats. The decision was immediately controversial, and a few teams, including charter member USA Today, threatened to leave the league.

The Commish's response: "Good luck to y'all."

The change followed increased concern nationally about equipment costs and the alarming risk of injuries posed by superbats, which increase the speed and distance of hard-hit balls. Teams that could afford the superbats (around $300 each at the time) were at a significant advantage against those that could not. Wood bats were about $65.

Very quietly, Tuttle had been studying the impact of superbats since they swept into softball leagues in 2003. During the 2004 season, he collected data from each week's MMSL games and consulted with a Cleveland lab that conducted aluminum bat testing across amateur baseball. On a comparably struck ball, the exit velocity off the superbats accounted for around 20-25 feet more distance than a wood bat.

This troubled potentially liable government recreation agencies when it came to line drives at pitchers and corner infielders at such close range. The MMSL also worried about outfielders on adjoining fields crisscrossing to catch deep fly balls.

While the safety factor was the core of The Commish's case, some of the outfields at parks where we played were too small for the superbats, allowing for easy home runs, elevated offense, and slaughter-ruled games when teams had a 12-run lead after 4½ innings—not to mention losing softballs over fences or into the woods.

But he also saw the switch to wood bats as a competitive balance issue between the teams and a fairness issue for female players, who would be allowed to continue using any aluminum bat and increasing their chances for success. Closer games would mean fewer slaughter-rule games, providing more innings for people to play.

"The new-fangled superbats have changed the dynamics of the game. It's now become a contest about physics," I said at the time of the bat switch. "Frankly, some in the league have lost sight of what these Saturday morning get-togethers are all about. It's recreational. It's not professional tryouts."

Despite the grumbling about losing their superbats, teams and players adjusted quickly. Gone were the days of pop-fly home runs and so many lopsided game scores. In their place were bouncy grounders and routine flies to the outfield. Or, as CNN pitcher Greg Robertson said, "A more accurate reflection of the way you actually hit the ball."

At the end of the 2005 season, data showed the significant difference wood bats made to the co-ed game and MMSL. Games went much faster, with only seven of the season's 352 games ending because of the 65-minute time limit. Slaughter-rule games dropped from 65 in 2004 to 46. Shutouts jumped from four to nine. And 61 games were decided by four runs or fewer, compared to 45 the year before. Scoring dropped, and single-digit games became more frequent and competitive. The average game score was 10-7, leveling the playing field.

The move to wood bats brought back a sense of nostalgia for many male players. Softball had not used wood bats regularly since the early 1970s. But the league voted overwhelmingly to keep the wood bats for 2006 and has never looked back. And no teams ever left the MMSL over the squabble.

TOP OF THE 9th

There's No Quitting

April 29, 2006

GAME 1		GAME 2	
CNN	10	CNN	30
NBC NEWS CHANNEL	5	ABC NEWS	1

- **CNN makes alphabet soup of NBC and ABC in sweep of season opener; slew of scoring records set.**
- **Abu Musab al-Zarqawi releases video to CNN Pipeline praising team's killer instinct.**
- **Last year's unmet expectations now just distant memory, much like Lucia Newman.**

By Joe Baseball Jr.
Bureau Sports Writer

KENSINGTON, Md. (UPI) — Taking a page out of the George W. Bush playbook just about three years to the day, CNN proudly announced "Mission Accomplished" on Saturday as the once-delayed, long-awaited 2006 softball season got underway.

The CaNiNes mauled division rival ABC News, 30-1, in the second game of a doubleheader at Capitalview Park. If that was the main course, a 10-5 denunciation of NBC in the opener was the appetizer on a pleasant, chilly day. Twenty-one people, enough to field two quality softball teams, participated in the public kick in the teeth.

For those with short-term memories who don't recall when an average network audience was a point seven, CNN finished runner-up last year in the Metropolitan Media Softball League at 16-6. Of course, winning is nothing new for the CaNiNes.

Since 1999, CNN has won the championship twice, finished second twice, and come in third once. "What's so scary is that CNN didn't play to its full potential on Saturday," shrieked Headline News anchor Nancy Grace, someone who knows all too well what it's like to frighten people every weekday night.

The 30 runs against feeble ABC were the most scored by CNN since entering the MMSL 16 years ago when the price of a gallon of unleaded gas was $1.27; Turner Broadcasting Company stock was $94 a share, and tapings of *World Championship Wrestling* routinely interrupted CNN news broadcasts at 1050 Techwood. The 29-run differential was the fifth-highest margin of victory in the league's history.

"You call that fair and balanced? I call it a failed strategy. It should have been 60-1," raged anchor, commentator and part-time journalist Lou Dobbs. "Trust me, I've seen more people in the past week running across the Mexican border into Texas than touching home plate."

CNN fell behind in the first game against the maligned but far-from-vanquished NBC News Channel. Former CNNer David Shuster, playing his brand of *Hardball*, rapped a three-run homer to give his team an early advantage in the opening frame. The CaNiNes responded by stringing together three doubles and three singles to take a 4-3 lead. Matt Guastaferro led off with a walk. Erik Tavcar singled. John Davis doubled in a run. So did Howie Lutt. Willie Lora singled for an RBI. Lindy Royce grounded into a double play but got credit for a run. Juan Cabral kept the inning going by doubling. Bill Tipper singled him in.

NBC retook the lead 5-4 in the second inning. CNN looked hyperkinetic, "Like the first block of *The Situation Room*," drooled a spokesman for Executive Producer Sam Feist. But the CaNiNes, displaying unflinching resolve not seen since Daryn Kagan dumped Rush Limbaugh, tacked on six more runs in the fourth. Others who figured in the scoring included Lydia Garlikov, David Robinson, and Liz Flynn, who lined a double over the center fielder's head, drawing more laughs than comedian Stephen Colbert at the White House Correspondents' Association dinner.

With time running out in the mandated 65-minute game, CNN started swapping out players in wholesale substitutions. Steve Redisch, Rae Smith, Vilinda Dickerson, Pete Seymour, Greg Robertson, Bill McGraw, Steve Tovarek, and Mike Scheidt entered the game. Mercifully, the umpire, who resembled Grandpa Munster, stopped the contest and affirmed CNN as the obvious winner.

Game 2 was one for the record books and the CNN time capsule. Officially, CNN was the visiting team, but the CaNiNes seemed right at home from the first pitch. If ABC ever needed to have a "Closer Look" about whether to have a softball team, this was the time.

CNN scored 13 runs in the first inning. The team had 11 hits and three walks, including a three-run homer by rookie phenom Quinn Brown, as 17 batters came to the plate. It took so long to play the first inning that Steve Redisch's daughter Annabel graduated from preschool and then high school.

Needless to say, it was a lead CNN would not part with. "Tell Blitzer if he wants to watch the best team at CNN, forget *Inside Politics*. It's right here," tweeted Political Director Tom Hannon, who is reportedly mulling offers to head up Al Jazeera's political coverage for the midterm elections.

ABC did score a run in the bottom half of the first inning. Fearing a possible comeback (just kidding), CNN heaped on 17 more runs. The CaNiNes scored two in the second, four in the third, and 11 runs in the fourth. It was such a runaway that the sub's subs were subbed. Even Jim Barnett pitched in relief. An ABC spokesman summed up the day by saying, "We went down faster than Flight 93."

The CNN offense mass-produced runs, but the defense, already in midseason form, glittered. Liz, Steve R., John, Bill Tipper, Steve T., Matt and Erik stole the show.

CNN, one of only eight teams left undefeated after the opening weekend, heads to Layhill Field on Saturday as it prepares to tee off against company rival AOL and USA Today. It will be a special day as the entire staff of Lou Dobbs Tonight will sing "Nuestro Himno," the Spanish-language version of the national anthem. Go to bed early Friday night and come out to watch.

May 6, 2006

GAME 1		GAME 2	
AOL	10	USA TODAY	18
CNN	4	CNN	3

- **CNN softball team goes on hiatus, swept in games the Motion Picture Association would have rated R.**
- ***Dog Whisperer with Cesar Millan* host summoned to train players how to fetch ball.**

By Joe Baseball Jr.
Bureau Sports Writer

LAYHILL PARK, Md. (UPI) — Mr. Jekyll? Meet Mr. Hyde.

One week after scoring 40 runs in a doubleheader romp, the CaNiNes struggled to find base hits in what might charitably be called a dissociative identity performance. The result was an unnerving pair of losses, 10-4 against corporate nutcase AOL and 18-3 at the hands of USA Today.

You just knew it wouldn't be CNN's day when half the team was delayed getting to northern Montgomery County's Layhill Field because of a backup on the Beltway. The first game was scheduled to start at 10, but the coaches agreed to delay the first pitch for 15 minutes when CNN could not field a complete team.

The umpire generously added another 10 minutes, after which CNN would have to forfeit, something the team had never done. In a godsend, with brownies in hand, Lindy Royce drove up at the last minute thanks to the astute back road driving directions provided by Bill Tipper. Shortly after that, Lydia Garlikov, a game-saver in every sense of the word, arrived, but it was only a reprieve.

CNN had the minimum number of two women. That left CNN penalized for not having three women to avoid an automatic out and a full lineup. The automatic out was waived when Rae Smith arrived without a glove, was forcibly removed from her car, and was transported to the field in the middle of an inning. Since the game was already underway, CNN had to play without two additional men. It's in the rulebook.

The die was cast. It was ugly from the start. Down three runs after the opening frame, CNN's first three batters never even made it to first base. Three up, three down in baseball parlance. Against all odds, CNN tied the game at four in the bottom of the fifth inning. John Davis, Howie Lutt, and Quinn Brown led the way with RBI singles.

The CaNiNes botched a golden opportunity with the bases loaded in the fourth when Pete Seymour left three runners stranded with two out.

AOL poured it on in the top of the sixth inning by scoring six runs. With time running out in the mandated 65-minute game now reduced to 40 minutes because of the late start, CNN went belly up.

The CaNiNes did not fare any better in Game 2 against USA Today. Six continued to be the unlucky number. After giving up six runs to AOL in its last at-bat, CNN allowed USA Today to score six runs in the first two innings of the nightcap. CNN cut into the lead with a ferocious blast courtesy of Willie Lora and a two-run inside-the-park home run by Erik Tavcar. That was the extent of the offense. It was lights out when the Gannetoids put another six runs on the board. It left the umpire no option but to stop the bloodletting.

The rest of the team concurred: Matt Guastaferro, Juan Cabral, Bill McGraw, Jim Barnett, Greg Robertson, and Mike Scheidt.

But here's the good news. It was a doubleheader, not a quadruple-header, and CNN could only lose two games. Where else can you get flogged most unceremoniously and still be in a three-way tie for first place? CNN is statistically on top with a better division record than ABC and CBS.

CNN would have lost to a team from the Lighthouse for the Blind on Saturday. The CaNiNes were outmatched, outcoached, and outplayed. Thankfully, only former CNNer Rebecca Ratliff, who was in town to produce National Geographic's Geography Bee, witnessed the undoing. The rest of CNN's Washington Bureau had something better to do on Saturday, or perhaps they were waiting to read Joe Baseball.

CNN will attempt to get its act together by Saturday when it plays a twin bill against the Discovery Network and Atlantic Video at Layhill Park.

May 13, 2006

GAME 1		GAME 2	
CNN	21	CNN	14
DISCOVERY	3	ATLANTIC VIDEO	2

- **CNN softball squad goes on offensive worthy of a football team.**
- **CaNiNes make like Indonesian volcano, erupt for equivalent of three touchdowns in opener and two in nightcap.**
- **President Bush to address nation, may order National Guard to control fickle performance of softball team.**

By Joe Baseball Jr.
Bureau Sports Writer

LAYHILLPARK, Md. (UPI) — Softball is a simple game. The yellow brick road to success is paved with good pitching, defense, and hitting. When a team does all three, the result is what CNN did on Saturday at a soggy Layhill Park.

The CaNiNes ran rings around the Discovery Network in Game 1, 21-3, and punished Atlantic Video in Game 2, 14-2, both victories coming before they could play seven innings. The two wins put the news network back atop the Capitalview Division alone in first place, one game ahead of ABC and CBS.

CNN (4-2) returned to Layhill Field, the scene of the May 6 massacre, where the team was caned in an off-putting sweep. "They played like a bunch of cloistered nuns last time," sobbed the park superintendent.

Upon hearing the results of Saturday's games, former CNN political reporter and anchor Gene Randall said, "Back in the day, I was urged to bring my innovative ideas, my unique perspective, and my storied career in the field of journalism as a way to fire up the softball team. I'm heartened to see it taking root."

CNN was relentless, piling on runs one after the other. In fact, CNN scored more runs in the second inning (eight) against the Discovery Ducks than in the entire doubleheader the week before. What made the barrage even more remarkable was that an hour before the game, players were not even taking batting practice but sweeping, raking, and shoveling the waterlogged infield to get it in playing condition.

The CaNiNes were also helped by Discovery's pitcher, who walked two batters in the first inning sandwiched around three doubles (Steve Tovarek, Howie Lutt, and Juan Cabral) plus an RBI single by Liz Flynn. Down by five runs, the Duck's coach contacted CIA nominee Michael Hayden to monitor CNN's game strategy.

In the second inning, CNN's patience was rewarded with seven free passes. Bill Tipper received two walks in the same inning as the team batted around. His second walk came with the bases loaded and a woman due up next in the batting order. The result was two RBI. Also in the inning, Willie Lora doubled in two runs, John Davis had an RBI, and Greg Robertson singled in a pair. The score was 13-2 and would have been more, except the umpire, to keep the game competitive, called Steve out when he stepped across the plate before hitting a single.

By the third inning, CNN made substitutions faster than *The Situation Room* changes its rundown. Mike Scheidt came in to pitch, and Vilinda Dickerson spelled first-timer Alexis Perkins in the outfield. Another rookie, Mike Brevner, a standout performer for ABC News, also made his CNN debut at third base and recorded a walk in his first at-bat. Tom Bentz (3-3) returned to the team with an RBI single, much to the delight of wife Patti and son Evan. Bill McGraw played an error-free game at first base as the CNN defense shut down Discovery before they could promote their next summer shark special.

CNN had everything going its way. With two outs in the second, John made a great play in right field by catching a ball on two bounces and firing a missile to JC at first to nip a runner before she could touch the bag. Bill Tipper had an unassisted double play to end the fourth inning.

Another third-place finish for the 2006 CaNiNes.

Game 2 against Atlantic Video was a seamless continuation of sound fundamental softball. Down 1-0, CNN put up six runs in the second inning of the nightcap with seven singles and two walks. Matt Guastaferro had a mission-critical two-out hit to keep the onslaught going.

The CaNiNes escaped a two-out bases-loaded jam in the top of the second when Greg picked up a dribbler near the mound and tossed the ball to Lindy Royce, covering home plate for the force. Another Atlantic Video rally was snuffed out in the third when Matt threw to Howie, who relayed to Greg to tag a runner trying to stretch a triple into a home run. CNN increased its lead to 8-2 in the third when Greg walloped a triple, driving in the fleet-footed Willie, who had led off the inning with a single.

CNN upped the score to 13-2 by piling on five more runs with the help of Steve, John, Tom, Liz, Greg, and Alexis, who sparkled with her first hit for the CaNiNes. The game ended with one out in the sixth when Howie drew a walk, Tom doubled him to third, and Mike singled home the winning run. The only player who didn't see action was Jim Barnett, who was shopping for a shotgun on eBay before his daughter's senior prom that night.

After the game, the team celebrated with pizza at the nearby Stained Glass Pub.

Only seven teams have better records than CNN. Next Saturday, the CaNiNes play two of them, WTTG and Comcast Sports, both 5-1, at Aspen Hill.

May 20, 2006

GAME 1		GAME 2	
CNN	15	COMCAST SPORTS	4
WTTG	13	CNN	3

- **CNN softball team ends day with half a loaf, winning one and losing one.**
- **CaNiNes fall short of sweep as players don new uniforms.**

By Joe Baseball Jr.
Bureau Sports Writer

ASPEN HILL, Md. (UPI) — Here is the question of the day. What is the number 65? It's the length of about a dozen Wolf Blitzers laid end to end. It's how many times Lou Dobbs says the words "illegal immigrants" in one hour. It's the average age of a typical CNN viewer.

Sixty-five also happens to be the number of feet between third base and home plate, which is all that separated the CaNiNes from earning a second W on Saturday at Aspen Hill Park.

CNN (5-3) was on the brink of a massive win against Comcast Sports (6-2) on a chilly, cloudy morning that gave way to sun-soaked skies. However, the CaNiNes lost with a desultory effort, 4-3, leaving the bases loaded, the tying run at third base, and the winning run at second.

It wasn't a total loss. CNN staged a determined comeback in the opener against WTTG (6-2), overcoming a six-run deficit in the last inning and hanging on to outfox the Fox affiliate 15-13.

CNN is in a statistical tie for first place with CBS in the Capitalview Division, with both teams sporting a 5-3 record. The CaNiNes hold the advantage with a better division record.

So far, the 2006 season has been one of extremes. CNN's four previous victories have come by margins of five, 29, 18, and 15, an average of about 17 runs a game. The CaNiNes' two losses were by six and 15 runs. In the world of cliches, it's feast or famine.

What made Saturday's doubleheader not for the timid was that both games came down to the last pitch. It went CNN's way in the opener, but the script didn't work out for the CaNiNes in the nightcap.

In a slugfest that ebbed and flowed against WTTG, CNN took a 5-0 lead in the top of the first inning. Matt Guastaferro led off with a single and galloped home with the first run on a double by David Gracey, making a return to the team after a one-year layoff. Eric Tavcar singled, and Quinn Brown and John King doubled. After an out, Jim Barnett and Tom Bentz singled to knock in RBI.

"I think our performance dispelled any doubts management may have had about our motivation to strike forthwith," sneered John King. "You have my word on it. I'm no Claire Shipman."

The CaNiNes added another run in the second on a double by David Robinson and a single by the other David, David Gracey.

Ahead 6-2, CNN came apart at the seams defensively in the bottom of the third, giving up seven runs to hard-hitting WTTG and falling behind 9-6. It got worse.

The CaNiNes had a couple of great scoring chances. Lindy Royce, the team's most patient batter, twice got picked off first base on line drive outs after getting aboard with walks.

WTTG upped its lead to 11-6 going into the fifth. That's when CNN's run of luck began to kick in. David G. and Erik doubled. Quinn singled in a run. After one out, Alexis Perkins reached safely on a hit. Bill McGraw had an RBI single to drive in the third run to make it 11-9.

Then came the decisive sixth inning. With the mandated 65-minute game limit approaching (there's that 65 number again), CNN players knew this would be it. Pete Seymour led off with the day's only triple. After a walk to Matt, David (4-4 in Game 1 and three RBI) singled, as did Erik and Juan Cabral. John K. smashed a two-run double. Lisa Goddard, making her first appearance for the CaNiNes, walked. Jim singled in a run to add to the lead 15-11. CNN needed all of it.

WTTG, in its final at-bat, tallied two runs, and they had the bases loaded with two outs and a count of three balls, two strikes. A walk would have forced in two runs because a girl batter was on deck. Instead, a grounder to first base ended the game, and the CaNiNes had a well-deserved W with defensive helping hands from Lydia Garlikov and Liz Flynn.

Then, it was time to switch fields and play a second game. CNN came out flat; no two ways about it. The CaNiNes had just two hits (singles) in the first 15 at-bats. Bill Tipper and Josh Rubin pulled themselves out of the game to find a way to energize the troops. Down 4-0 after Comcast netted a pair of runs in the first and third, the CaNiNes got on the scoreboard in the fourth inning and cut the deficit in half.

Down by two, CNN began the bottom of the seventh with two quick outs. But then Peter and Lindy drew walks to make it interesting. Matt singled in a run to cut the deficit to 4-3. Runners were now on first and second. Dave G. singled to load the bases, but Lindy was stopped at third, so she didn't get thrown out attempting to score the tying run. Erik was CNN's last best hope, but he grounded sharply to the shortstop, who raced to third base for the force out to end the game.

It was an emotionally draining day, but at least the CaNiNes looked dapper in their new red uniforms with the distinctive CNN world logo. The shirts are courtesy of the team's most prominent booster outside of Washington, the strategic marketing department at company headquarters.

No games are scheduled for next week, but the second half of the season will resume after Memorial Day with another doubleheader on June 3.

June 3, 2006

GAME 1		GAME 2	
CNN	20	CNN	15
NBC NEWS CHANNEL	8	CBS NEWS	11

- **CNN starts second half of season with pair of wins.**
- **Softball team throttles division rivals NBC and CBS to take over first place.**
- **CaNiNes make defiant statement: "There are known knowns. There are also unknown unknowns."**

By Joe Baseball Jr.
Bureau Sports Writer

KENSINGTON, Md. (UPI) — You had to be there to believe it. Just ask Jayson Blair, the poster child for plagiarism, who provided most of the details for this report.

The CaNiNes showed up at a windy Capitalview field on Saturday to make a statement. They didn't do it in the grammatical sense with ellipses, question remarks, or semicolons. They did it with exclamation points—two of them.

CNN (7-3) moved into sole possession of first place by walloping NBC News Channel 20-8 in the opening game, the third time this season the original cable news network has scored at least 20 runs in a game. The

CaNiNes were not content with the idea of a split, so the team staged a stupendous comeback in Game 2 against CBS and pulled off a 15-11 win to complete the sweep. It was CNN's fifth victory in the past six games.

"It was as if every single player was on a search and destroy mission," said one curmudgeon, who looked eerily like Defense Secretary Donald Rumsfeld. "The Marines in Haditha have nothing on the CaNiNes."

Game 1 against NBC (2-8) was a mismatch from the start, a tune-up for Game 2 and CBS (5-5), which came into the day in a statistical tie with CNN and riding an emotional high since Katie Couric publicized, she might play the clean-up position before the season ends.

A team doesn't score 20 runs without a lot of help up and down the lineup. Erik Tavcar had a memorable day against NBC, going 4-4, including two home runs, two doubles, and five RBI. Not to be outdone, Willie Lora also was nonpareil in the first game. He tripled and pasted two doubles and collected four RBI. When John Davis wasn't making All-Star catches in right field and battling wind gusts up to 20 miles per hour, he was doing it with the bat. He had three hits, two of them doubles and three RBI.

Men weren't the only ones finding success on the field. The women also came to play. And as the women go, so goes the team. Liz Flynn was on fire, hitting safely in every at-bat, drawing a walk, and driving in a pair of runs. Lisa Goddard made a difference by getting a base hit. Lydia Garlikov had a pair of fantastic hits to the outfield to spark scoring opportunities. Behind the plate, Lindy Royce called some great pitches for Greg Robertson to keep the opposition off balance.

Bill Tipper, Tom Bentz, and Howie Lutt employed an unambiguous game strategy by subbing players throughout the day to protect the lead. Mike Scheidt, Vilinda Dickerson, Bill McGraw, Steve Tovarek, Pete Seymour, Alexis Perkins, and Mike Brevner were ready to answer the call when it came knocking.

Game 2 proved to be a gutsy contest. CBS took a 6-2 lead after two innings; the deficit could have been worse if not for two double plays by John Davis, who stepped on second and threw to Quinn Brown at first to quell big innings. In the meantime, CNN kept pecking away. Matt Guastaferro did what leadoff hitters should do by going 4-4, needing just a home run to complete the cycle. David Gracey and Erik made up for that. They homered and roamed the outfields to run down long drives through the trees.

CNN tied the game at seven and took the lead, then held off CBS to win going away 15-11.

The dawg dogs of June continue on Saturday as CNN plays another doubleheader, this time at Veirs Mill Park, against the team with the best record in the Metropolitan Media Softball League, Townhall.com (8-2) and the Washington Post (6-4).

June 10, 2006

GAME 1		GAME 2	
TOWNHALL.COM	13	CNN	13
CNN	8	WASHINGTON POST	12

- **CNN softball team pulls off biggest win of year after staring into abyss.**
- **Company executives say it wasn't an abyss but just dead air on CNN.**
- **CaNiNes maintain two-game lead with four to play in regular season.**

By Joe Baseball Jr.
Bureau Sports Writer

SILVER SPRING, Md. (UPI) — The cardiac kids from CNN proved Saturday there's no shame in losing. They also learned a valuable lesson when faced with one of life's most elusive questions: How should a team (and a news organization) respond to adversity?

The answer came in the form of an edge-of-the-seat, fingernail-biting, last-at-bat against the Washington Post, which saw a three-run lead dissipate in a blink to an unswerving and determined CaNiNes squad.

CNN (8-4) pulled off a Hail Mary-like 13-12 win in Game 2 at Veirs Mill Park after handing a gift-wrapped victory to Townhall.com, 13-8, in Game 1. CNN had an 8-3 lead against the Capitalist Tools but endured a historic letdown in the fifth inning, giving up a jarring 10 runs on five walks, to suffer a stinging loss.

"I guess this proves some of us in *The Situation Room* are human after all," said pitcher Howie Lutt.

The CaNiNes have a two-game lead against ABC News in the Capitalview Division. CBS News lost twice and is now mathematically eliminated, giving them plenty of time to get acquainted with Katie Couric.

Faster than anyone could ask, "What's happening with CNN's *On the Story*," Matt Guastaferro led off the first game with a double. David Robinson (3-3), John Davis (3-3), and Willie Lora singled to stake CNN to a 2-0 lead. After Townhall tied it, David, John, and Willie again figured in the scoring to push the CaNiNes up 4-2.

With CNN clinging to a 4-3 lead, the defense turned in some exceptional fielding. Lindy Royce pounced on a dribbler in front of the plate and threw out a batter like Hall of Fame catcher Johnny Bench. John D. started a double play to end a scoring threat in the fourth.

CNN seemingly had everything going its way against Townhall, the top-ranked team in the MMSL. In the top of the fifth, the CaNiNes scored four runs on five consecutive hits and a walk to lead 8-3. Matt doubled with one out. David doubled in a run. John and Howie both singled to knock in two more runs. Willie capped the scoring with a two-run triple but was tagged out on a close play at home.

Defensive lapses and an inability to find the strike zone opened the floodgates in the bottom of the fifth inning, and Townhall (11-1) took full advantage, leaving CNN players unnerved. What started as a five-run lead abruptly turned into a five-run deficit, and it was lights out; the party was over.

The team was so distraught it briefly considered canceling the rest of the season and seeking solace at Nissan Pavilion to watch Tom Petty and the Heartbreakers. Instead, the players voted, and Liz Flynn, Juan Cabral, Pete Seymour, Lydia Garlikov, Bill Tipper, Vilinda Dickerson, Lisa Goddard, Mike Scheidt, Alexis Perkins, Rae Smith, Sarah Chakales, and Jim Barnett decided CNN needed to persevere.

That drew an ecstatic response from ardent fan Gary Krakower, who brought along a furry canine, Kobe, and the pup, not Gary, was immediately ordained the team's official mascot. Jessica Rosgaard, the team's official scorekeeper, responded by putting Kobe in the lineup and having him bat for Willie.

CNN switched fields, hoping it would bring better luck in the second game. It worked. Matt slugged a leadoff home run to start. David tripled, and John singled him in. The Washington Post moved in front briefly 3-2, and it would have been more except for one of the best plays ever witnessed in Metropolitan Media Softball League history.

John D. made an over-the-shoulder catch of a line drive to left field with two outs and two runners on. The entire team rushed out to exchange hugs with Johnny.

The brilliant catch ignited CNN, which broke out with seven runs in the bottom of the third inning after two outs. Bill singled, and Lisa walked to start the rally. John tripled, Howie singled, Willie doubled, Liz walked, JC singled, Mike singled, and Vilinda came through with a two-run bases-clearing double. By the time the inning was over, CNN held a 9-3 lead, and the Post was re-thinking it might need to spend more time salvaging its softball team and not its waning circulation.

CNN's six-run lead evaporated over the next three innings. The Washington Post retaliated and took a 12-9 lead going into the bottom of the seventh.

The CaNiNes had the last laugh. Left for dead, the players put on their rally caps. Matt and David hit singles. John followed with a double to close the lead to 12-10. Howie doubled to make it 12-11. With the tying run at third, the winning run at second, and no outs, Willie proved his mettle with a single to seal the deal as Howie was mobbed at home plate.

CNN is off next week. The CaNiNes return to action on June 24 when they play a pair of playoff-bound teams, Washington Post.com (8-4) and WRC (8-4), in a critical showdown at Layhill Field.

June 24, 2006

GAME 1		GAME 2	
CNN	16	CNN	8
WASHINGTON POST.COM	2	WRC	7

- **CNN clinches playoff spot with impressive doubleheader sweep.**
- **Stoked CaNiNes come out raging like Sedona wildfire.**
- **Team shines in tune-up for postseason.**
- **Angelina Jolie to join Anderson Cooper as co-host for revamped *AC 360*.**

By Joe Baseball Jr.
Bureau Sports Writer

LAYHILL, Md. (UPI) — The last time CNN faced Washington Post.com was Championship Day weekend in July 2005. The CaNiNes needed to win one of two games to claim the MMSL championship. They fizzled out. CNN couldn't tie its own shoelaces.

Fast-forward to this past Saturday at Layhill Park, with ominous storm clouds on the horizon—perhaps a meteorological metaphor? The same two teams with identical records (8-4) squared off again with much less riding on the game. A win would guarantee a trip to the playoffs for one of them.

CNN doled out a full-fledged facial in a 16-2 conquest of the current champions, providing a tiny bit of redemption for the news network's long winter of discontent.

The win in the first game was no fluke. In the second game, CNN came out strong against WRC and hung on for a hard-earned victory, 8-7. The local NBC affiliate had the tying run on second base in the last inning but could not score.

CNN made only one grave mistake all day, and it happened before the first pitch was even thrown. It absent-mindedly gave home-field advantage to Washington Post.com when, in reality, Post.com should have been the visiting team. No harm, no foul.

For the fifth time this season, the CaNiNes defeated an opponent by double digits. Winners of five of the past six games, they're hitting their stride as the regular season winds to a close in two weeks. It's the fourth time CNN has swept a doubleheader this year.

The CaNiNes never trailed on Saturday in either game. They went ahead 3-0 in the top of the first inning against Post.com. Leadoff hitter Matt Guastaferro lined a triple before fans had even gotten to their seats. Okay, there were no spectators except for coaches Bill Tipper and Jim Barnett. David Gracey singled in Matt to go in front. John Davis followed with an RBI single. Quinn Brown doubled in John.

Washington Post.com chipped away at the three-run lead. Normally sure-handed shortstop John King, fresh off his grilling of Vice President Dick Cheney on the VEEP's front porch, bungled a pair of slow grounders hit by women. But John would make amends the rest of the day when it counted.

CNN stretched its lead to 5-1 in the third inning on a John Davis single and doubles by Quinn and John K. The CaNiNes busted the game wide open with eight runs in the fourth. Lydia Garlikov hit a two-run RBI single to drive in Howie Lutt and Greg Robertson. David Robinson, playing the role of designated hitter, also singled to keep the rally going. With two outs, David Gracey, John D., Quinn, John K., Liz Flynn, and Howie all got on base and scored.

The CaNiNes, who have a deep bench, immediately put in subs Alexis Perkins, Sarah Chakales, and Mike Brevren, who only demoralized their opponent. In the sixth inning, Howie singled in a pair of runs. Alexis closed out the scoring with her first RBI hit.

Game 2 featured another playoff-bound team, WRC, a proficient squad that matches up well against CNN.

Matt did what leadoff hitters are supposed to do. He got on base with a double to start the nightcap. John D. singled him home to put CNN ahead for good.

Softball games, of course, are not just won with lumber. They are also won in the field, where this story picks up. In the bottom of the first, with one out and a man on, a WRC player ripped a line drive to deep right center. The ball was hit in the air so far that the runner on first had rounded second base by the time a streaking David Gracey jolted to his right, fully outstretched, and secured the ball in the webbing of his glove. After rolling over two times, he got up and launched a throw to a cutoff player who doubled up the runner at first. It was one of the best defensive plays ever seen in MMSL history.

The fielding gem roused the CaNiNes and rattled WRC. In the second inning, Greg clubbed a three-run homer to put CNN in the driver's seat, 4-0. What made this inning so special was that each of the "L" women in the lineup hit safely. Liz, Lydia, and Lindy Royce all singled. The men canonized the trio, plus Alexis and Sarah, Queens for the Day.

WRC cut the lead in half and was a play away from evening the score when another defensive gem was turned in. John D. caught a deep fly ball in left. The runner on third tried to tag up, but the throw beat her by 20 feet.

CNN moved out in front 8-2 after four innings. That's when WRC staged a comeback and narrowed the lead to 8-5. They put their first two runners on base in their last at bat with a couple of hits and an error. The score was 8-7 in a blink, with the tying run at second. But the CaNiNes hung on when WRC's batter grounded out.

CNN goes into the July 4th break with a lock on first place in the Capitalview Division, two games ahead of ABC News. The CaNiNes (10-4) have two games left, one against CBS News (6-8) and then ABC News (8-6). And don't forget, CNN beat ABC the opening weekend, 30-1.

July 6, 2006

GAME 1		GAME 2	
CNN	9	ABC NEWS	20
CBS NEWS	4	CNN	2

- **CNN splits doubleheader but still wins division.**
- **CaNiNes take care of business in opener, then lay egg in regular-season finale.**
- **Seven teams finish with identical 11-5 records.**
- **Kim Jong Il dares Wolf Blitzer to arm wrestle in ploy to boost 7p ratings.**

By Joe Baseball Jr.
Bureau Sports Writer

KENSINGTON, Md. (UPI) — CNN rarely gets to say it is number one in the news business, especially when its broadcast brethren NBC, CBS, and ABC are part of the same sentence. But when it comes to softball, hands down, there's no one better in the Capitalview Division.

For the second consecutive year, the CaNiNes showed they are cagey and proven winners, entitled to bring home another trophy for the newsroom, already crowded with hardware from previous years.

On Saturday, the team wrapped up another successful regular season by clinching the division title against CBS News, 9-4, in Game 1 of a doubleheader at Capitalview Park. CNN (11-5, one of seven teams with that record) unveiled its worst game of the year when it mattered the least, losing to a hot-hitting ABC squad in the nightcap, 20-2. That's not a typo. (CNN emasculated ABC the first time the two rivals met six weeks ago, 30-1.)

"I know I'm supposed to put a good spin on everything this company does, but the second game was a debacle," divined a stupefied Edie Emery, public relations manager, who couldn't find anything positive to say about the 18-run drubbing. She felt compelled to state the obvious, "It wasn't even as close as the score might indicate. I want to promote that our sister station TBS will air *Gone with the Wind* Wednesday night at 8."

Poor Jessica Rosgaard, the official game scorer. "I ran out of ink just trying to keep track of all the ABC runs and clunky plays by CNN," she exhaled. "I hadn't seen so many casualties since *Gone with the Wind*."

"I want names," yawped Keith McAllister, former CNN vice president, who hasn't been available for comment since the 2004 season.

"CNN should be ashamed of itself... dragging down the good name of the network. It's more embarrassing than when I did The Whip," marveled former wry CNN anchor Aaron Brown, with his trademark wan smile. "I have no illusions about the vicissitudes of fame. I don't even know what that means. But I am going to host a game show soon."

CNN players were all smiles when the day started. Just 24 hours earlier, the D.C. Bureau hosted a top-notch pep rally and five-star lunch. Each team member also received a $25 gift certificate to the Sharper Image.

Sharp was precisely how the CaNiNes played and looked in their royal blue caps and sporty red jersey shirts.

History of the wrong kind was made in the first inning of the first game. CBS's second player hit a solo home run, the first time a woman has achieved that feat against CNN. It was ruled a double, but a two-base throwing error compounded it.

Matt Guastaferro drew an opening walk for the CaNiNes in the bottom half of the inning. Erik Tavcar singled. Matt came around to tie the score on a sac fly by Quinn Brown.

It stayed close early, thanks to dazzling catches by Lydia Garlikov and Liz Flynn. CNN added to its slim one-run lead in the third. With two outs and John Davis on first, John King (no relation to Larry) singled. Liz walked to load the bases. Howie Lutt lined a single to make it 5-3.

CBS would not go away, much like CNN's Jack Cafferty in his endearing role as the world's angriest man. It was just 5-4 heading to the fifth.

Matt and John Davis opened with singles. Quinn doubled to knock in a run. Then came the human spark plug. John King blasted a back-breaking three-run homer to widen the lead to 9-4. The bench players went crazy. There hadn't been so much hoopla since Nancy Grace told her fanatical viewers she would broadcast live from Aruba as she snorkeled in search of Natalie Holloway.

When the last CBS batter lined out to pitcher Jim Barnett to end the game, CNN players celebrated a well-earned victory. The upstart 24-hour cable channel had beaten Edward R. Murrow's squad like the sad mules in the 20 Mule Team Borax commercials aired by CBS in the 1960s on *Death Valley Days. (Editor's note: There were no mules in the ads.)*

CNN's Domestic Operations President Jon Klein addressed the team on a closed-circuit Pipeline link. "This is what I call winning with substance, not sizzle," said the notoriously upbeat executive, "Something those slackers at Fox News could learn a thing or two about."

There is something to be said for consistency. CNN is heading to the playoffs for the fifth time in six years.

In Game 2, the brain trust for CNN reshuffled the lineup. The CaNiNes made wholesale substitutions. Lisa Goddard, Alexis Perkins, Mike Brevner, Mike Scheidt, Bill Tipper, Dave Robinson, and Steve Tovarek saw action as the news network showed its depth.

Before CNN founder Ted Turner could say, "The news is the star," the CaNiNes were staring at a four-run hole against ABC. Then it was 9-1. By the third inning, 13-1. That was the good part. The final was 20-2. Ouch! So much for the short-lived celebration.

CNN's ad department immediately promised to play Head On ("Apply it directly to the forehead") commercials every 10 minutes. "Oh wait," said one sales exec. "We already do that."

"CNN flamed out faster than a Taepodong-2 rocket," said the official North Korean news agency, which monitors the Metropolitan Media Softball League from a small room in Pyongyang.

John Pike, from GlobalSecurity.org, quipped the missile test was an aberration. "CNN's loss to ABC was a certifiable dud."

The games were played in front of the biggest crowd of the year. Seven people turned out, including Edie Emery.

The playoffs take place at Cabin John Park in Rockville July 22-23. Twelve teams will participate in the double-loss elimination tournament.

July 22, 2006

GAME 1		GAME 2		GAME 3	
CNN	19	COMCAST SPORTS	12	CNN	4
GAZETTE	9	CNN	8	POST.COM	3

GAME 4		GAME 5		GAME 6	
CNN	12	CNN	10	WRC	9
ASSOCIATED PRESS	6	WTTG	9	CNN	3

- **CNN softball team unable to find playoff miracle.**
- **High-octane CaNiNes survive five Saturday games only to run out of gas on Sunday.**
- **Players overcome heat, humidity, and Hezbollah-like opposition to finish 3rd.**
- **Saddam Hussein vows to continue hunger strike until Spring or until U.N. Ambassador Bolton shaves mustache.**
- **ADDS 9th graph Company considers scaling back 24-hour network to 12 hours.**
- **ADDS 12th graph CNN's drumbeat of war sting tops Billboard Top 40.**

By Joe Baseball Jr.
Bureau Sports Writer

ROCKVILLE, Md. (UPI) — Some things in life are guaranteed, for example, Christiane Amanpour reporting from a war zone, Tiger Woods sucking up all the oxygen at major golf tournaments, and Google Earth animation appearing on CNN every few minutes.

When it comes to softball, nothing is a given. That alone makes the accomplishments of CNN's scrappy and unheralded team so remarkable year after year.

The 2006 softball season is officially in the books; another award sits glistening under the newsroom lights, awaiting a new trophy case. It wasn't first place, but it was close, finishing in the top three.

In a timely move, pop singer Britney Spears released her latest album, "Oops! I (Almost) Did It Again," with her iconic lyrics, "I played with your heart, got lost in the game, oh baby baby…"

It wasn't immediately clear whether she was referring to someone in her life or the softball team that came in first in its division and third-best overall out of 24 teams. In the past eight years, CNN has finished either first, second, third, or fourth six times—dynasty, baby.

The CaNiNes ended with a 15-7 record, including three straight sudden-death wins on Saturday, two by just a run. They did themselves and the company proud this past weekend in the Metropolitan Media Softball League tournament.

WRC, which lost to CNN a month ago, took full advantage of a dog-tired and punch-drunk team of CaNiNes to secure a 9-3 win on Sunday when it counted most, knocking out the news network.

The Peacocks had an easy time against AOL, although WRC would lose in the Championship Game to USA Today.

Despite the deflating end to another season, CNN's softball team remains one of the network's redeeming parts and among the elite and most-feared opponents in the MMSL. Three-quarters of the playoff teams publicly declared they would rather spend a day cooped up in a windowless, unventilated room with Larry King than face the CaNiNes on a softball field.

It's not just domestic fearmongering. The Cubans, who scrimmaged against CNN in April, are still under house arrest in Havana for their wishy-washy effort against the CaNiNes. "Fine by me," snapped anchor Lou Dobbs without elaborating.

According to political columnist and Pulitzer Prize-winning commentator George Will, who has written numerous stories about baseball, "CNN, the news network, may have lost a step or two in the competitive world of broadcast journalism, but at least their softball team offers more value than you can find on YouTube."

There's not enough space here to tick through every highlight of six games. But here's some of what happened on Saturday and Sunday.

Shortly after 8:30a, long before most readers of this column were awake and checking their Blackberries, 18 CNN players, many from the far reaches of Virginia, Maryland, and District of Columbia, were already warming up on the manicured fields at Cabin John Park in Rockville.

"Think about it," said D.C. Bureau Chief David Bohrman. "I can't even get people to come here for free pancakes, but our folks on the softball team were willing to go out there and lay it on the line on just a few hours of sleep. They are a special group."

The CaNiNes, the No. 5 seed, were the home team for Game 1 by having a better season record than the Gazette. They danced all over the No. 12 seed. With two outs in the bottom of the first, CNN pushed across four runs on four hits (John Davis, Willie Lora, Juan Cabral, and Greg Robertson) and a pair of walks (Howie Lutt and Liz Flynn.) The Gazette was equal to the competition, and they tied it in the second.

CNN went back out in front in the bottom of the second on a walk to Lindy Royce and another two-out rally with hits from David Gracey, John, Howie, and Willie. The Gazette rallied again to make it even at seven up. In the third, Lydia Garlikov smashed a two-run single. Steve Tovarek also singled. Lindy and Matt Guastaferro walked, and David doubled for an RBI.

With the sun burning off the morning dew, a warmed-up CNN then piled on by pushing across five runs in the fifth and three in the sixth. The CaNiNes scored in every inning except for one, and that's only because they stopped to get group training for NewsDesk 3.0.

Final score: CNN 19, Gazette 9.

Game 2 was against Comcast Sports, and it started swimmingly. Seven of the first eight batters got on base as CNN took a 4-0 lead. Then the steroids kicked in for Comcast, and the SportsNuts, their official moniker, hit two balls over the centerfield fence 275 feet away.

David, Matt, and JC made separate diving catches in the bottom of the fifth inning to keep the score tied at six runs before Comcast broke open the game in the sixth. The final score was Comcast 12 and CNN 8.

CNN was saddled with its first loss in the double-loss elimination tourney. It was on to the loser's bracket, where a second defeat would mean a swift exit and home to shower, leaving time to watch happy-go-lucky Tony Harris anchor the weekend news.

How uncanny that CNN's fate would now be decided in Game 3 by Washington Post.com, the same team that beat the CaNiNes twice last year in the championship.

This time, in one of the lowest-scoring playoff games, CNN gave the Post a taste of its own medicine by escaping with a 4-3 victory. Loyal former players Gary Krakower and Virginia Nicolaidis were there to see it.

Matt led off the first with a single, and John tripled him home. Behind 3-1, CNN tied it in the third when Lydia singled, followed by a David Robinson hit. Matt also had another single and an RBI. For a while, it looked as if CNN wouldn't score again.

With the game tied at three, David R. singled to lead off the sixth. David G. moved him along with a hit. John, CNN's only grandfathered player and the team's MVP of the playoffs, doubled to put CNN in front. It was enough for the win behind the pinpoint pitching of Greg, who only walked two batters in six games. CNN 4, Washington Post.com 3.

It was on to Game 4 and a date with the Associated Press, another team facing elimination with a loss. How would CNN respond in its fourth hour of softball in the oppressive humidity? By scoring in EVERY inning. Two runs in the first and second, a run in the third, three in the fourth, three in the fifth, and one in the sixth.

As CNN kept rolling merrily along, Vilinda Dickerson, Bill Tipper, and Tom Bentz provided fresh legs for a pooped-out team. Jessica Rosgaard also played a vital role, keeping track of where opponents hit the ball and positioning defensive players. Sarah Chakales, on the bench, stuck it out as the CaNiNes' secret weapon. Final score: CNN 12, AP 6.

Did CNN have anything left for Game 5? It was now going on 3p. At least half the players were suffering from dehydration and sore muscles. Courtesy runners were getting courtesy runners.

It didn't take long for CNN to get an answer against WTTG, its third consecutive opponent, which was also facing an end to its season with a loss. Who was going to blink? The Fox Trotters looked like they wanted it more than CNN at the outset, taking a four-run lead in the top of the first. But the CaNiNes sent 10 players to the plate to tie the game.

After the Fox affiliate retook the lead, 7-4, CNN batted around in the bottom of the second with five runs, thanks to four free passes and singles by Lindy, Dave G., John, and Liz. WTTG wasn't done, though. Down by three in their last at-bat, they scored two runs and had the tying run at first base before CNN closed the door in another enthralling squeaker: CNN 10, WTTG 9.

CNN survived to play another day and, at the same time, knocked out two teams. There were now only four left. It would be CNN against WRC on Sunday at the unspeakable hour of 9:15 a.m.

This time, luck would not smile down on the CaNiNes, who were hoping for a few breaks to play again in the finals. Even the addition of Pete

Seymour wasn't enough. After a CNN runner was thrown out at home plate in the first inning, the team never seemed to get on track. Late in the game, the CaNiNes had the bases loaded and no outs but only scored one run. It was that kind of day: WRC 9, CNN 3.

The sting didn't last long. CNN was awarded its second consecutive divisional trophy, and each player received a navy blue shirt adorned with the words Montgomery County Champions. No truer words.

And so, another MMSL season was in the books.

This year's team included 30 people at various times. Some played, some coached, some kept score, and some watched. Many sacrificed their time away from families and friends, while others cut short vacations. They are among the best at CNN.

BOTTOM OF THE 9th

Dynasty in the Making

April 21, 2007

GAME 1		GAME 2	
CNN	10	CNN	22
NATIONAL PRESS CLUB	5	DAILY EXAMINER	1

- **CNN starts season with impressive in-your-face sweep.**
- ***American Idol* singer Sanjaya throws out first ball, then is run over by the Fit Nation Challenge bus.**
- **Note contents 3rd graph Crime wave grips CNN Center; trigger-happy security guards equipped with water pistols to patrol newsroom.**

By Joe Baseball Jr.
Bureau Sports Writer

LAYHILL, Md. (UPI) — Welcome to the start of another Metropolitan Media Softball League season, your go-to source when you want to know what CNN company executives are up to. And how the softball team is doing.

First, the games.

The CaNiNes rolled out of the gate, looking fit and ready for what, in this case, was a doubleheader laugher.

If you were looking for high drama and a catfight, stick with singer Sheryl Crow and political strategist Karl Rove's heated confrontation about global warming at the annual White House Correspondents' Association dinner. The softball games were child's play in comparison.

In the opener, CNN easily defeated the National Press Club, 10-5. The CaNiNes then played smash-mouth ball in the nightcap, annihilating the Daily Examiner, 22-1, in a contest that was no contest and felt much worse than the 21-run margin, especially if you played on the losing team. It mercifully ended under the slaughter rule after five innings.

Embattled Attorney General Alberto Gonzales was reached for comment about the one-sided second game, and he repeatedly said he couldn't recall ever seeing such a weak-kneed performance. "Let's face it, if I had the authority, I would fire every one of the Examiners and every U.S. attorney at DOJ."

With CNN shredding the newspaper team and the outcome never in doubt, the grumpy umpire ordered CNN players to swing at every pitch, even if the toss was six feet off the plate.

"If you thought Alec Baldwin and Virginia Tech shooter Cho Seung-Hui needed anger management training, wait and see what I do," the ump blubbered. "Hurry up and get this over with. I want to get home and watch *Week at War*."

CNN scored at will. The first six batters were a collective 16-18. The CaNiNes were up by a dozen before the Daily Examiner knew what hit them, namely hits.

"The scorebook was a confusing mess with all those baserunners. Watching *The Situation Room* with all its boxes and video is easier to follow," said the official scorer.

The Daily Examiner immediately announced after the game it was changing its name to the Daily Debacle.

Players were in a rapturous mood. The splendid, sunshiny day at Layhill Field provided ideal conditions. The CaNiNes, who finished in third place at 15-7 last year, looked as sharp as a 65-inch Sony HDTV screen.

Company executive Phil Kent, without further ado, updated the Turner Employee Survey: "Dear Colleagues: The CNN softball team rocks, and it's directly responsible for Turner Broadcasting's success. Let me also shout out that tomorrow is Softball Appreciation Day."

The CaNiNes came out swinging against NPC in Game 1. The first four players got on base. Matt Guastaferro (3-4) led off with a single. David Gracey (3-4 2 RBI) followed with a hit. John Davis singled in a run, and Quinn Brown (3-3) kept the slugfest going with a double. It was 4-0 before World Bank President Paul Wolfowitz could interject and recommend his girlfriend, Shaha Ali Riza, apply for a job at the CNN Washington Bureau.

"Look, I know I made a mistake when I recommended my sweetie be promoted and get a pay increase. I hope she gets a VJ job if the OA thing doesn't work out."

A complacent CNN softball team allowed the Press Club briefly back in the game. Trailing 5-4, the CaNiNes scratched together a couple of runs to retake the lead. David Robinson and Liz Flynn singled to open the fourth inning. After one out, rookie Joanna McGuire got her first hit as a member of the CaNiNes. Matt then sealed it with a two-run single to put CNN ahead to stay.

The CaNiNes are not a power team in the conventional sense and don't

CNN team comes up just short in the 2007 championship game.

appear to be candidates for winning a Major League Baseball Home Run Derby. CNN recorded 15 singles and three doubles against NPC. Standout performances in the field by David, Liz, and Quinn kept the Press Club at a safe distance.

Things were a lot easier in Game 2. CNN scored four in the first, six in the second, two in the third, four in the fourth, and six more in the fifth.

Howie Lutt went 3-3, slugging a double and a triple and getting four RBI. Matt was a quintessential leadoff hitter, going 3-3. John was 4-4. Bill Tipper put down the scorebook long enough to get a single and an RBI. Jim Barnett was credited with two RBI after walking with the bases loaded.

Greg Robertson exhibited All-Star pitching form in a brilliant display of control as he kept opposing hitters off stride all day. The "L" women, Lindy Royce, Liz Flynn, and Lydia Garlikov, shined with top-notch play, much to the delight of Lydia's mother, who came to see her daughter in action. Two other rookies, Chris Nowak and Chris Carter, also made impressive debuts.

CNN hasn't had a losing record in 10 years. If this first weekend is any indication, the team is ready to make another run at the championship, which it last won in 2002. Of the 46 teams that have played in the MMSL, only two (the Washington Times and USA Today) have better records than CNN (145-93) after 14 years in the league.

The CNN schedule promises to get much harder next week when last year's champs, USA Today, comes knocking, along with archenemy AOL.

April 28, 2007

GAME 1		GAME 2	
CNN	7	CNN	12
USA TODAY	6	AOL	10

- **CNN remains undefeated for another week.**
- **Police show up at softball field and order everyone to move along, "Nothing to see here."**
- **Company executives jet off to British Virgin Islands to plan next year's Cheeseburger in Paradise spring fling.**

By Joe Baseball Jr.
Bureau Sports Writer

SILVER SPRING, Md. (UPI) — It was surreal. Emergency room doctors at Suburban Hospital in Bethesda were told to prepare for an influx of CNN employees all suffering from heart palpitations on Saturday afternoon. It happened just minutes after CNN's softball team completed a doubleheader trouncing.

Medical experts at first thought the kerfuffle was linked to stunning revelations by the D.C. Madam and her upscale escort service.

"I can assure you that all of our drivers have been thoroughly tested and screened," said John Dunaway, chief of security at the Washington Bureau. "When it comes to escorts to the Union Station garage, we do it by the book. We don't do massages unless you're wearing a CNN ID."

What caused the rush to treat so many people? Was it merely a coincidence or something more troubling, such as cumulative exposure to Head On ads?

The players' symptoms included shortness of breath, hyperventilation, racing pulse, dry mouth, and urges to whoop in ecstasy. Doctors determined it was all caused by CNN's come-from-behind softball wins.

The CaNiNes waited until it was almost too late to pull out two victories. Call it what you want: inherent stubbornness, collective nonchalance, disobedience, or dysfunctional stagnation. It was a revelatory experience. It was enough to invigorate Katie Couric to craft her lead-in without the help of a plagiarist for the first time.

CNN beat last year's MMSL champions, USA Today, 7-6, in the opener by scoring four runs in the bottom of the seventh inning after two outs. In the nightcap, the CaNiNes ceded a seven-run lead against AOL, once a household name, now just a punchline. CNN stormed back with five runs in their last at-bat, again with two outs to complete an amazing daily double, 12-10.

CNN is one of only five teams (out of 24) unbeaten at the season's quarter mark. The CaNiNes are in sole possession of first place in the Capitalview Division.

The team likes to keep its powder dry until the chips are down. That was never more readily apparent than in these two contests.

Reached for comment after the games, Chief National Correspondent John King hissed, "Take your broadband and $165 billion merger and stuff it where the sun doesn't shine. We've got Pipeline and I-Report."

Ask any softball sports writers about their worst nightmare, and they will tell you it's when they can't come up with a storyline. But ask the same sports writers to describe their ultimate journalistic high, and they will tell you it's when a team is down to its last strike and pulls off a one-in-a-million finish. This story writes itself.

On Saturday, at Veirs Mill Park, it didn't just happen once. Lightning struck twice.

The levees broke. We're talking about the Great Deluge. The floodgates opened. Use any cliché you want. It sounded like a freight train. Packing winds. Adding fuel to the fire. Neighbors say he was quiet and kept to himself. Only time will tell. I'm here all week.

Are you looking for unsung heroes? You don't have to wait to see them on Lou Dobbs on Fridays.

"I just launched a CNN global initiative to showcase ordinary people who have accomplished extraordinary deeds," notified Jim Walton, president of CNN Worldwide, a division of Turner Broadcasting System, Inc. "Except for Carol Costello's cut-ins, and my man Rick Sanchez, we often don't have time to tell soul-stirring stories. We're fortunate to have that option on a great softball team."

CNN fell behind USA Today by two runs in the first inning but tied the score on a pair of singles, fielder's choices, and a walk. The Gannetoids pulled out in front with four runs in the second on three Texas League bloopers.

The deficit would have been greater if it hadn't been for Lindy Royce's one-handed catch behind the plate and Greg Robertson's three-pitch inning to get three outs. Bill Tipper plugged up every hole at short and assisted in the season's first double-play. Matt Guastaferro roamed center-field like a cheetah on an African safari. Quinn Brown scooped up throws like a man possessed.

For the most part, the CNN offense was non-existent. It was down-right offensive. Over a span of 26 plate appearances, the CaNiNes had a scant six hits. Like *American Morning*, it was excuse after excuse. "Can't anyone give me some names," wailed a Keith McAllister look-alike.

Jon Klein, the president of CNN's domestic operations, said the soft-ball squad seemed to lack charisma and glitz. "We need kick-ass players willing to step up and show us some leg. I know something about putting winning teams together."

"Don't forget about me," chimed in an effervescent anchor Tony Harris.

So, this was the scene. USA Today 6, CNN 3. Bottom of the seventh.

With one out, Edwin Lora made his first Metropolitan Media Softball League appearance and ripped a triple to right center. Intern assistant Nicole Alberico went down swinging for the second out. The CaNiNes weren't done, not by a long shot.

Matt lined a single to drive home Edwin and make the score 6-4. David Gracey (3-4, 2 RBI) pummeled a two-run homer to tie the game, sending the standing-room-only crowd of Denise McIntosh, Willie Lora (on injured reserve with a cracked rib), and Patrick Davis (brother of John) into a delirious frenzy and group hug.

With the score now knotted at six and USA Today exhibiting more confusion than the 10 o'clock editorial meeting, John D singled. Quinn (3-4) smashed a single to put runners on the corners. Howie Lutt stepped into the batter's box, and after making sure Sit Room contributors Donna Brazile and James Carville were in their locked and upright positions, he lined a game-winning hit to rescue the day.

Klein said, "We need to be better despite the captivating victory. I didn't hire Kieran Chetry or Brianna Keilar to be another pretty face. That's why I signed Larry King to a new 50-year contract. He's all ours until he turns 124. I want to own the 'over 100' demo."

The second game of the doubleheader featured dialup villain and dot com bubble disaster America Online, a team not known to have much love for the CaNiNes. A few years ago, as we have previously reported, CNN knocked AOL out of the playoffs with a game-ending tater that resulted in a scrum among players.

AOL was in no mood Saturday to talk about its dwindling insignificance as a once highly touted Internet service provider.

The team had already forfeited its first game of the day because it didn't have enough players. Still, they somehow fielded nine people by the first pitch against CNN, probably the same way they recruited celebrities years ago to look relevant.

AOL's softball team is a shadow of its former self, much like the business plan that squandered shareholder value. CNN went for the jugular.

Former co-founder Steve Case, the man who brought the once-booming company to Time Warner, sat on the bench shaking his head. "We can only aspire to our past greatness," he sighed.

At least for an inning, the dream was alive. For the first time this season, CNN went down in order. To compound matters, John Davis suffered back spasms and immediately left the game and was driven to the hospital, where he used his senior citizen's discount to receive Valium.

The CaNiNes were undeterred, and they took a 7-0 lead after three innings with the help of the "L" ladies: Lydia Garlikov, Lisa Goddard, and Lindy.

AOL roared back to go ahead 10-7. CNN was in a heap of trouble, as Jed Clampett would say.

Over a span of 12 batters, the CaNiNes scratched out just two singles and a walk. "We failed to show the same patience that we do when waiting for our mail to be sorted by Carlton," said a visibly depleted coach Jim Barnett.

If it hadn't been for the indomitable Lydia, who was 4-4, CNN would have been lost in its own ineptitude. "I know a thing or two about slam dunks and other crap," said former CIA Director George Tenet in a series of encrypted messages while receiving updates about the game. "It looked bleak at best."

Could the CaNiNes come up with a humdinger of an ending? The table was set for another dramatic finish.

Trailing 10-7, Matt lined a double with one out. AOL's left fielder heaved a rocket to the woman standing at second. The ball missed her glove and found her arm instead. It was like a mallet hitting a side of beef. The woman crumpled to the ground in pain. The misplay allowed Matt to take third, angering AOL players, who insisted CNN should have taken a knee. The woman recovered feeling in her arm and stayed in the game. But AOL was about to be knocked senseless.

With a runner on third, David Gracey, the hero of Game 1, grounded out but brought in Matt to close the gap to 10-8. Now there were two outs and no one on base.

Edwin Lora and Jason Sporbert had back-to-back singles. Howie walked to load the bases. Cue Al Michaels in Lake Placid. CNN needed a eureka moment. Greg Robertson, hitless for the game, ripped a two-run single to tie the score. Lydia again singled for the fourth time to put two runners on. AOL was collapsing faster than its stock price. Chris Nowak added the icing on the cake with a go-ahead two-run double. A deflated AOL could do nothing but scratch their heads. They lost internet connection in every sense of the word.

CNN can now enjoy a week off, but it's back to business on May 12 with the season's first round of division games at Capitalview field. ABC News comes calling, followed by the Discovery Channel.

May 12, 2007

GAME 1		GAME 2	
CNN	9	CNN	13
ABC NEWS	7	DISCOVERY	1

- **CNN makes it six in a row as CaNiNes keep rolling merrily along.**
- **Befuddled news executives announce plan to airdrop Rick Sanchez into Florida wildfires to test new flame-retardant jackets.**
- **Al Qaeda takes day off from suicide attacks in Iraq to watch CNN anchor T.J. Holmes update viewers on three-alarm dumpster fire in Tukwila, Washington.**
- **Note nature of 3rd graph: CNN anchors are forbidden from "thanking" reporters after their live shots because reporting is what correspondents are PAID to do.**

By Joe Baseball Jr.
Bureau Sports Writer

KENSINGTON, Md. (UPI) — A plot by ABC News was foiled on Saturday just hours before the CNN CaNiNes were set to play a must-have divisional game. Homeland Security officials confirm ABC "deliberately and with malicious intent" sent CNN a bogus email tease on Friday claiming terrorists were planning to attack U.S. personnel in Germany.

CNN reporters and producers spent the entire day trying to confirm the story, which left many on the softball team cranky and exhausted.

The Washington Bureau was so distracted with "developing news" that Virginia Nicolaidis couldn't even find time to make a Red Phone call to tell everyone that Defense Secretary Robert Gates had an honor cordon with the Namibian minister of defense. "We also missed the start of World War III and the sinking of the Lusitania in 1915," Nicolaidis imparted.

Company President Jon Klein told those listening to the 10 a.m. conference call, "Effective today, we will never believe anything ABC tells us unless they back it up with two sources and a pinky promise. I'm ordering our softball club to kick ABC's ass."

That's precisely what happened. The CaNiNes (6-0) ignored swarming gnats and foot-high grass in the outfield at Capitalview Park to put on a gritty performance against ABC and eked out a well-deserved 9-7 win in the opener.

CNN let the Discovery Channel have it in the nightcap, 13-1, which ended in the fifth inning after the umpire decided he had had enough and ordered Discovery players to go home and watch every *Tarzan* movie starring Johnny Weissmuller, Maureen O'Sullivan, Boy, and Cheeta.

The doubleheader sweep gives CNN a lofty two-game lead in the Capitalview Division.

"It was a relief to get both those wins. A loss would have been costly," said Richard Parsons, the chairman of Time Warner Inc. "Our first quarter revenues only rose 9% to $11.2 billion. I was prepared to outsource the first two hours of *The Situation Room* to India."

Senior Executive Producer Sam Feist energetically piped in, "It's time we lift the veil on how we do our show. Talented people indubitably do a lot of the routine stuff in another time zone at much lower wages. I've hired someone in Mumbai, and I'm paying him $12,000 a year to write things like 'The best political team on television,' 'A picture is often worth a thousand words,' and 'You're in the Situation Room.' I told (Washington Bureau Chief) David (Bohrman) we could take the money we dish out to reporters, writers, and guest bookers and give it to the softball team."

CNN could have used the extra help because the CaNiNes found themselves down by three runs against ABC after just half an inning. But in the bottom of the first, CNN put its first six batters on base and scored four times. Matt Guastaferro and Greg Robertson walked. Howie Lutt launched a towering ground-rule double to produce a run. Then cleanup hitter Quinn Brown cleaned up, smashing a three-run homer. (Quinn also had an RBI triple in the third.) Lydia Garlikov (4-6 on the day) continued her torrid hitting and singled, as did Edwin Lora, but that's where the rally ended.

It was back and forth after that, a seesaw affair with each team taking the lead. The score was knotted at six going into the bottom of the fourth inning. Bill Tipper beat out a single to start the rally. After one out, David Robinson doubled to knock in the go-ahead run. Lindy Royce got a productive hit to advance the runners. Matt brought in a second run that proved to be the game-winner.

ABC closed the gap to 8-7 in the sixth. But Greg, Bill, and Quinn teamed up for a huge double play to keep their opponent at bay.

CNN scratched together an insurance run with singles by Edwin and Juan Cabral and a double by Bill. It would have been more, but Juan ran out of steam and did a never-to-be-forgotten belly flop in a cloud of dirt five feet short of home plate.

ABC had the tying runs on base in its last at-bat, but the CaNiNes hung on for the victory. A peeved ABC player told TVNewser that CNN was squarely to blame. "We saw CNN running ads for Tatermitts and thought they would help us catch fly balls. That's false advertising."

Game 2 against Discovery was the antithesis of the opener. Everyone in the lineup lent a hand. Tom Bentz was adroit as the scorekeeper. He also positioned CNN players defensively. Even Joanna McGuire's canine Max played a role by sharing creative suggestions with the Discovery Channel's players for the next *Dog Whisperer with Cesar Millan* episode. "That show is incontestably on National Geographic," woofed Max.

The CaNiNes broke open the nightcap against the Daffy Ducks in the fourth inning. Already ahead 5-1, CNN put the first eight batters on base. Bill, Liz Flynn, David, Joanna, Matt and Greg singled. Howie hit a bases-loaded triple. Quinn, who just missed hitting for the cycle (he needed a double), rocketed his second homer of the day to end the scoring in a laugher, 13-1.

First-timers Marco Arriaga and Luana Munoz got to swing the bat, and each got on base. Chris Nowak closed out the agony for Discovery by fielding a grounder at third base to end the shortened game.

Next Saturday, CNN faces the Washington Post and the Express in a print versus electronic media battle. If you can't stand reading about it and feel compelled to see the action for yourself, the games will be played at Wheaton Forest.

May 19, 2007

GAME 1		GAME 2	
CNN	25	CNN	12
WASHINGTON POST	8	THE EXPRESS	4

- **CNN is all the rage as winning streak now at eight; CaNiNes shred two print opponents.**
- **Coast Guard uses strident voice of Nancy Grace and her publicity photos to coax whales out of San Fran Bay.**
- **ADD 5th graph Washington Post media critic Howard Kurtz notes he's sometimes unreliable.**
- **ADD 6th graph CNN shelves *Reliable Sources*, fills slot with *News to Me*.**
- **ADD 7th graph There actually is a weekly half-hour show by that name on Headline News.**

By Joe Baseball Jr.
Bureau Sports Writer

WHEATON, Md. (UPI) — Check out the front pages of the Washington Post and The Express. Notice anything unusual? There's not one word about how the CNN CaNiNes eviscerated their two softball teams over the weekend.

Hint. You *can* find the story where it belongs on the obituary page.

CNN (8-0) buried the Posties 25-8 in an abbreviated Game 1 at Wheaton Forest Park. The CaNiNes toyed with The Express in Game 2 before breaking it open late, 12-4. The two wins give the Cable News Network a comfortable three-game divisional lead.

The CaNiNes did not have their usual star-studded lineup. Coping with the deleterious problem of missing 10 players due to weddings, retreats, work assignments, and drunken stupors, the team relied on its deep bench and made it look easy against two inferior opponents.

In the opener, CNN scored 12 runs in the first inning, six in the second and third innings, and one in the fourth. The Washington Post played like a team in need of last rites. When Dr. Sanjay Gupta heard about their performance, he immediately became sick to his stomach. "I'm not sure if it was because of the game or the poor ratings of my poison food special, which I shamelessly teased every other hour last week."

The pitiful effort by the Washington Post brought to mind the legendary words of former CNN executive Keith McAllister, "Amateur hour."

The CaNiNes had 11 hits in the bottom of the first as 16 batters came to the plate. The official scorebook was a mess, complete with misplaced information and mistakes, not unlike the daily editorial decisions made by producers for *American Morning*. "Casting aspersions!" drooled Senior Producer Booker Washington. "At least we corrected the map graphic following the weekend shooting in Idaho. My bad. I thought it was the Moscow in Russia."

With one out and CNN trailing by a run, Pete Seymour and Chris Carter made their first appearances of the year and promptly hit singles. Cagey veteran Greg Robertson doubled in a run. Lydia Garlikov continued to amaze opponents by getting a single. Tom Bentz shook, rattled, and rolled an RBI single, as did Juan Cabral and Spanish intern Luana Munoz. After a second out, Bill Tipper drew a two-run walk. Lindy Royce also walked. Matt Guastaferro came up for the second time in the inning and thrashed a bases-loaded single. Pete and Chris made it two for two by hitting RBI singles. Greg capped the scoring by driving a triple in the gap. CNN 12, Washington Post 1.

The first inning against the Post was no more an accident than beleaguered World Bank President Paul Wolfowitz arranging a hefty pay raise for his girlfriend. CNN also batted around in the second inning. The first seven batters got on base: Tom, Chris Nowak, Bill, Lindy, and Matt, all hit safely. JC smashed a two-run homer.

Ahead 18-2, coach Jim Barnett could barely make substitutions fast enough. One petulant CNN player riding the pine and waiting to partake in the blowout championed, "I've seen faster decisions made by those in charge of news standards and practices, the Row and legal."

The route was on full display by the third inning rolled around. Lisa Goddard, who had already filed for radio 14 times and written a 750-word blog on the origins of mass migration, singled in her first at-bat. Fresh off the political bus, Josh Rubin got a hit, and Jason Sporbert was credited with an RBI as the CaNiNes batted around for the third time, stretching the lead to 24-4. It mercifully ended after four-and-a-half innings when the umpire said he felt lightheaded watching CNN beat up the once venerable newspaper.

There was some nervousness in Game 2 against The Express, a team with just one victory. Consider just a month ago, it lost 44-1. Imagine CNN's rude awakening when they found themselves only ahead 3-1 going into the fourth inning.

The Express played with resoluteness. "We felt like executives at Dream-Works waiting for the release of *Shrek the Third*," said the team's coach. Meanwhile, Time Warner managers were pondering if they had made a mistake selling the Atlanta Braves last week and not the CaNiNes.

CNN extended the lead in the fourth. Tom hobbled to first with a single and, in a macho move, refused to come out for a pinch runner. Lisa walked. Josh, Lindy, and Matt all followed with RBI hits.

The Express came to play and again made it close, 6-3.

Rick Sanchez took time off from making cornbread and teaching Spanish to migrants at the OK Café in Atlanta to give the team a pep talk and turn things around.

In the bottom of the fifth, Jason got his first hit of the day. JC sledge-hammered a two-run homer to build the lead back to 8-3. CNN tacked on four more runs in the sixth inning when Greg doubled in a pair, and Jason launched a two-run tater as CNN put the game away, 12-4.

The second half of the season resumes on June 2 when the CaNiNes face the Gazette and Washington Post.com.

June 2, 2007

GAME 1		GAME 2	
CNN	15	CNN	12
GAZETTE	11	WASHINGTON POST.COM	11

- **CNN wins 10th straight game as club stages two more improbable comebacks.**
- **Pathologist Jack Kevorkian retracts offer to assist team.**
- **"Winning is contagious," says tuberculosis patient Andrew Speaker while flying on crowded airplane.**
- **Note content 11th graph Hustler Magazine offers million dollars to first team to beat CaNiNes.**

By Joe Baseball Jr.
Bureau Sports Writer

ASPEN HILL, Md. (UPI) — A defibrillator has been ordered, and thankfully, there's still one left on the shelf at Costco. We're now in the silly season.

CNN turned in not one but two remarkable, incredible, okay, if you insist, heart-stopping softball games to keep its perfect season blissful.

It took a while, but the CaNiNes, aka the Cardiac Kids, ran over its competition like a car hurtling through a crowded street festival in Washington. It wasn't pretty, yet they got the job done with their fifth double-header sweep of the season.

Only one other team (Team Video) remains undefeated out of 24 in the Metropolitan Media Softball League. The CaNiNes now own a four-game lead in the Capitalview Division over ABC News and CBS News, with six games to play before the postseason.

In the opener at a sticky Aspen Hill Field, a listless CNN (10-0) kept its gunpowder dry most of the day against the Gazette, which held the lead practically the entire game. The CaNiNes' lackadaisical approach was understandable.

"I knew it would be taxing for the softball team to overcome the feeling at the thought of seven hours of wall-to-wall coverage of the Democratic debate in New Hampshire," said Jane Maxwell, director of Special Events. "I don't know which event was more somnolent."

CNN marked this week's D-Day anniversary with a sneak attack against the Gazette by scoring seven runs in the last inning and pulling off a hair-raising 15-11 victory. In the nightcap against Washington Post.com, CNN never led until Quinn Brown singled in David Gracey (minus his wisdom teeth) with the game-winner in the bottom of the seventh, 12-11.

Oh mercy. Bring on the heart paddles.

On paper, the CaNiNes appeared to hold all the cards and have every advantage against its two inferior opponents. But that's why they play the games. CNN was confident before the day started that its undefeated season would continue. Not so fast.

In Game 1, the Gazette came out smoking, while CNN couldn't even mobilize a whiff of get-up-and-go. The CaNiNes had one single among the first five batters. Things got a little better in the second inning thanks to a two-out rally and a promise from Paris Hilton to sit on Larry King's lap when she gets out of prison.

"She's not allowed to use her get-out-of-jail card," said jovial CNN executive Jack Womack. "Those are only for CNN staffers who abuse the Meta Data privileges."

With one down, Greg Robertson doubled, and Willie Lora singled. Liz Flynn brought in a run with a ground out. David Robinson hit a two-out double. Bill Tipper brought in the tying run with a big-time single.

The Gazette didn't flinch, and the weekly paper proceeded to zoom out to an authoritative lead, 10-4, with six runs in the bottom of the third, the biggest outburst in a single inning against CNN all year. Lindy Royce tried unsuccessfully to distract them with some gooey brownies, but nothing worked.

The CaNiNes kept chipping away. In the bottom of the sixth, the Gazette scored what looked like an insurance run to stretch its lead to 11-8.

That's when the umpire announced the sixth inning would be the last of the game under established time rules. CNN needed three runs to tie and keep the contest going. How does seven sound?

Edwin Lora began the rally with a walk as Gazette's pitcher started to whither on the vine like a ripened grape or a CNN primetime show to use a TV metaphor.

Intern Cat Belanger, just two days shy of her 21st birthday, also got aboard with a free pass. Matt Guastaferro loaded the bases with a single. David Gracey flew out but got an RBI. Then, like the 17th Street Canal in New Orleans, the floodgates opened.

John Davis, Quinn, Lydia Garlikov, and Greg earned their stripes with clutch singles. Willie walked to force in a run. Stephanie Kotuby, making a triumphant return to Saturday softball, brought in the final run with a grounder.

A shell-shocked Gazette squad, thinking it had earned bragging rights as the first team to defeat CNN this season, could only watch in disbelief as they unraveled and ended up losing 15-11.

Indeed, Game 2 against Washington Post.com would be easier, right?

In one of the strangest contests all year, CNN looked positively stodgy. Not even the threat of a fuel pipeline attack at JFK Airport and the hope of reporting on something other than poisonous toothpaste from China could energize the team.

CNN scored just a single run in five innings. Between the first and sixth innings, only three CaNiNes touched first base. According to official scorer Tom Bentz, there were at least 10 fly ball outs.

It was as embarrassing as watching Paula Zahn lead with the story about the Alabama boy shooting the wild pig with a revolver. "We were the first prime-time show to confirm the family would get 700 pounds of sausage meat," announced Jacques Grenier, a jaunty executive producer. "It was a natural segue into the compelling drama of the whale story and the Spelling Bee."

Post.com established an 8-1 lead with two innings to play. Coach Jim Barnett's head was seconds from imploding, which would have been apropos since *CNN Newsroom Saturday* was looking for a good implosion for its weekly segment. Some of Barnett's players privately bet he would perform his version of a Lou Piniella dirt-kicking tirade on the field.

The season's largest crowd was also getting antsy. Cat's mother, Diane, John's brother Pat, Steve Bartlett, and Marco Arriaga were not amused.

CNN wasn't quite ready to throw in the towel. With two outs in the sixth, Cat and David Gracey walked. John singled. Quinn knocked in two runs with a single. Lydia walked to load the bases. Greg calmly stepped up and hit a dramatic inside-the-park home run to make it 8-7. Yes, Virginia (Nicolaidis), there is a Santa Claus.

Not so fast. Post.com manufactured three more runs in the top of the seventh. It would have been even more if not for ESPN *SportsCenter* play-of-the-day catches by Cat and Juan Cabral. JC came up lame with a pulled muscle and was replaced by rookie Jamie Gray, who had been regaling the team with his ambition of one day writing a book about the joys of cross-rolling tapes.

Trailing 11-7, CNN had the bottom of the batting order due up in the seventh. With one out, Jamie singled in his first at-bat to drive in an RBI. Cat followed with a single. Matt did the same to load the bases with the tying run at first. David belted a two-run double to make it 11-10. John singled to tie the score. With runners on the corner and one out, Quinn waited for his pitch and bopped a hit through the middle for the game-winner.

Be still my beating heart; thou hast a defibrillator on order.

The CaNiNes rushed onto the field to celebrate and then paused for a group photo looking like participants at a G8 Summit.

CNN has another doubleheader on Saturday against division rivals CBS News and Discovery Channel.

June 16, 2007

GAME 1		GAME 2	
CNN	16	CNN	9
DISCOVERY	4	CBS NEWS	6

- **CNN team makes it 12 for 12 and clinches division title.**
- **Dan Rather commends effort, blasts CBS for "dumbing down and tarting up" all that's good about softball.**
- **District Attorney Michael Nifong withholds evidence proving CaNiNes are legit but says Duke lacrosse players are another story.**
- **Recast lead: Queen Elizabeth and Christiane Amanpour play fungo exhibition.**

By Joe Baseball Jr.
Bureau Sports Writer

KENSINGTON, Md. (UPI) — When was the last time CNN could say it was better than any other media organization?

Maybe in 1984, when TBS launched the Cable Music Channel?

The Big Three television networks, ABC, NBC, and CBS, routinely attract millions of viewers, the kind of audience CNN can only yearn for. The Fox News Channel has been spanking CNN for years, and FNC now boasts ratings twice as large. PBS and *Sesame Street* do pretty well in comparison, especially when Bert and Ernie appear.

It's not just television. Newspapers like the Washington Post and USA Today routinely drive news coverage at CNN.

Well, boys and girls, gather 'round; the days of CNN taking a back seat to anyone are over. There's a new news leader in town on Father's Day Weekend, and it's the CNN CaNiNes. Who's your daddy? Stop the presses. Breaking news.

Let's go to TJ and Carol in the newsroom.

CNN (12-0) sits alone atop the Metropolitan Media Softball League, enjoying the air of first place, sporting a better record than 23 other teams. How does that feel, Katie Couric, Charlie Rose, and Brian Williams?

Poker-faced anchor Campbell Brown said, "Now you know what convinced me to sign with CNN and get off weekends."

"I wish my staff could figure out a way to harness the softball team's can-do attitude," yawned Paula Zahn.

CNN has plowed through the MMSL and swept a doubleheader for the sixth time. The current 12-game win streak is the fourth longest in league history. The gold standard is 16 by the Associated Press in 1997.

The CaNiNes are the only team to have clinched an automatic playoff berth. This is their third straight division title and 11th playoff appearance in 15 years. When you think of sports dynasties, CNN has to be right up there with the Spurs, Celtics, and UCLA Bruins—except those are all basketball teams.

The Discovery Channel quickly learned that all dogs can bite, especially the CaNiNes. CNN barely broke a sweat with an easy win in Game 1, 16-4, at Capitalview Park. In Game 2, CBS put forth a good faith effort, but like its declining audience share, the Tiffany Network came up short, 9-6.

Both teams filed FOIA requests in search of CNN's secret to success.

From the get-go in the opener, CNN had a spring in its step and power to its swing. "Maybe the D.C. Bureau should have an electrical shutdown every Friday night," half-joked former Facilities Manager Kim Linden.

CNN hit three home runs in the first inning. Even the guy who tried to hurdle into the Popemobile was impressed. "Team, good. Players in better shape than I am," he revealed from a mental facility near the Vatican.

After Discovery went down one, two, three in the top of the first, Matt Guastaferro (6-6 on the day) led off with a single. John Davis (4-4, two home runs, triple, eight RBI) (and that's just Game 1) slammed a two-run homer. Howie Lutt lined a base hit. Quinn Brown also blasted a home run. Greg Robertson (3-3, two homers, three RBI) hit the team's third homer of the inning to stake the CaNiNes to a five-run advantage.

To say there were holes in the Discovery outfield would be like saying CNN can't get enough of Angelina Jolie, missing people stories, and Apple iPhone commercials.

Ahead 5-1, CNN kept the pressure on. It was like a Texas flood; there was no stopping the torrent. Chris Nowak singled. Bill Tipper and Lindy Royce hit into fielder's choices. Matt singled. John then clubbed a bases-clearing triple to jack up the lead to 7-1. Discovery players begged for compassion and Boniva samples, but no relief was coming.

The CaNiNes made complete substitutions. David Robinson, Juan Cabral, Pete Seymour, Stephanie Kotuby, Chris Carter, Jamie Gray, and Cat Belanger made their presence felt as they generated more power than the fickle International Space Station.

Even mailroom clerk Carlton Downer got caught up in the excitement and promised to sort the 4,500 pieces of backlogged mail this week.

In the fifth inning, John hit his second two-run homer, bringing in Matt, who had singled. Stephanie whacked a ball clear over the center field's head to drive in a run. Greg followed with his second two-run homer to make it 12-2.

The rout continued in the sixth with consecutive hits by Jamie, Pete, Lindy, and Matt. John completed the massacre with a game-ending two-run single, leaving Josh Rubin in the on-deck circle as the only sub who did not get his name in the lineup. Under league rules, the game ends when a team leads by 12 runs after the fifth inning.

The nightcap against CBS proved a much more challenging contest. Defense was the name of the game. Lydia Garlikov, who singled in the first inning to drive in a run, made an out-of-this-world catch in the outfield to keep the game close. Liz Flynn repeatedly forced base runners at second. Bill was a human vacuum at short. Matt roamed the field like a cat hunting for rodents. The CaNiNes turned a pair of double plays and also gunned down a runner at home plate on two bang-bang relay throws from Edwin to Bill to Greg.

CNN erupted in the third, helped by three walks and a two-run homer by Greg. The CaNiNes added single runs in the fifth and sixth innings to provide enough breathing room.

The doubleheader brought out a multitude, including Carly Walsh and Hua Hua (pronounced Wah-Wah), as in chihuahua, Edwin's son Danny, Lindy's nephew and her father Randy, John's brother Patrick, Marco Arriago and former interns Sarah and Meredith.

CNN faces its biggest test of the season this week when it faces the third and fourth-best teams in the league: WRC (9-3) and WTTG (11-1). It will have all the makings of a playoff atmosphere.

If truth be told, the most arduous part for the CaNiNes in the coming weeks will be figuring out how to fit CNN's latest division title trophy into an already jam-packed trophy case.

June 30, 2007

GAME 1		GAME 2	
CNN	7	CNN	21
CBS NEWS	2	ABC NEWS	0

- **CNN finishes regular season with sweet sweep.**
- **Threat level raised to 'Code Red' as team punishes CBS and ABC.**
- **Gen. David Petraeus reports new surge not on battlefield but on softball field.**
- **Eds: Joe Baseball returns from one-week hiatus after CaNiNes lose two games last week.**

By Joe Baseball Jr.
Bureau Sports Writer

KENSINGTON, Md. (UPI) — Just before the start of this year's Metropolitan Media Softball League season, CNN prognosticators were adamant that if the CaNiNes were going to compete for a title run, they would need to throw out the old game plan and bring in the new.

What would CNN, a trusted institution and a journalistic mega brand, do? Maintain the status quo or start over and leave no stone unturned?

Prickly coaches for the CaNiNes, laggard though they may be, held a séance and decided the team would not become the laughing stock of the MMSL. They would not bench their veteran players, who have over 250 years of collective softball experience, and insert young studs willy-nilly. It would be a combination.

"There was no sense of urgency, no thought whatsoever of writing off the season," mulled coach Jim Barnett. "From the start, it was a matter of using what we had, giving a little extra, a soupcon if you will.'"

Three months and 16 games into the season, the CaNiNes are right where they want to be in a three-way tie for the best record.

On the strength of tiebreakers, CNN has earned the No. 3 seed (behind Team Video and WTTG) and a first-round bye. The CaNiNes will face the winner of the CBS/AOL game.

CNN (14-2) put the finishing touches on a superb regular season by basting division rivals ABC News and CBS News on Saturday at Capitalview Park in Kensington.

The CaNiNes never trailed on the day as they dispatched CBS, 7-2, in the opener, and then, in the nightcap, they conquered ABC for no reason other than they could, 21-0, CNN's first shutout of the year. What's even more remarkable is that ABC began the game fighting for the last playoff spot but couldn't even score a run.

"CNN hasn't seen that kind of domination since former Political Director Tom Hannon slugged a producer in the face 25 years ago," said a hardened sentinel in a posting on MediaBistro.com.

CBS Chairman Sumner Redstone and CEO Les Moonves, shrugging off any lingering residue of ill will following their power-sharing showdown, let on they want to "loan" Katie Couric to the viewer-challenged *Paula Zahn Show* in exchange for a few CNN softball players. "We're poring over their offer," responded a CNN spokeswoman in a flash of candid enlightenment.

Coming off two disconcerting losses last week, which this reporter regretfully missed, the CaNiNes made a statement in advance of the playoffs. The next league champion will have to go through CNN.

Game 1 started slowly, a pitcher's duel. After the first two innings, CNN was nursing a meager 1-0 lead.

Despite the CaNiNes doddering offense, their defense was on full display. Liz Flynn, Bill Tipper, and Chris Nowak (no relation to Lisa Nowak, the former diaper-wearing astronaut charged with kidnapping) combined on a scintillating double play to end the second. In addition, Lydia Garlikov made a run-saving catch by stabbing a scorching fly ball off the bat of CBS' best player.

CNN took charge in the bottom of the third when they scored four runs. It was the veterans leading the way.

David Gracey hit an inside-the-park homer to start the inning. Howie Lutt got on base with one of his three singles, to the delight of his parents, who were on hand. Willy Lora, who didn't make an out all day (4-4 in both games), slapped a single. And it kept going from there with hot-hitting Lydia (2-4, two RBI), Greg Robertson, David Robinson (2-3), Cat Belanger, Chris, Bill (2-3), Lindy Royce, and Matt Guastaferro (2-4).

Contacted for comment, reporter David Mattingly vouched, "It reminded me of that flying fish story I filed a few weeks ago. The CBS players could do nothing but stand there and get hit in the face like I did by Asian carp."

There's no question the hit-happy CaNiNes are on a roll, not counting last week's slight doubleheader reset, and the impact is being felt across the network.

"They have redefined *American Morning*'s catchy phrase, 'Quick Hits,'" said a CNN executive imbued with authority to cut through bureaucracy.

Washington Bureau Chief David Bohrman ordered special correspondent Frank Sesno to include CNN's odds for another softball title run in his next "What If" installment.

Every batter got on base except for Joanna McGuire. "Let's face it," she said, "My main responsibility was restraining Max, our unofficial canine mascot, from dragging the cooler onto the field."

The defense again proved to be the difference. Bill Tipper made an exquisite leap at short on a soft fly, briefly snagging it in the webbing of his glove, but he couldn't quite hold the snow cone as it popped out when he hit the ground. Play was briefly stopped as CBS players near second base attempted to unsuccessfully cajole Tip into inking a two-year contract.

Greg Robertson was Greg Maddux-like on the mound, striking out three hitters, nailing 92% of his pitches for strikes, and assisting on four putouts. The CaNiNes sealed the deal in the first game when David Gracey caught a line drive to deep right field on the run and catapulted a laser throw to Chris at first base to beat the runner. It left official scorer Tom Bentz downright baffled. "I've never recorded a 9-3 play. Very cool."

How times have changed. For years, CNN, the nascent news operation, has always asked CBS for favors. On Saturday, the players for the Tiffany network begged CNN to beat ABC in Game 2, as that was the only way CBS could claw its way to the postseason.

Meanwhile, division rival ABC also had playoffs on its mind. In their opener, they pulled off a last-at-bat victory against the Discovery Channel on the adjoining field and seemed to have the momentum.

Momentum is a funny thing in softball. There's a surefire way to stop it: outscore your opponent.

In Game 2, CNN scored five runs in the first inning, two in the second, nine in the third, and five more to boot in the fifth and final frame to build a football-like lead, 21-0. For the fourth time this year, the umpire invoked the mercy rule.

Hitting stars included Jamie Gray (2-2, four RBI), Liz (2-2), Willie and Greg (4-4), Matt, David, and Howie (each 3-4 and three runs), Lydia and Chris (2-3 plus two runs), Bill (2-3), Lindy (single and a run), and Tom, who put the scorebook down long enough to smack a single.

Along the way, CNN had three innings where ABC batters went three up and three down. This game also had its defensive marvels, including a falling backward catch by Matt in center and a throw to the infield to start a rundown involving Cat, Tom, and Howie, who tagged out a runner.

And what better way to cap off the day than with pizza and beer at the Stained Glass Pub, where Sir Willy generously picked up the tab.

CNN finished the regular season 6-0 in the division and 14-2 overall, the best ever by the CaNiNes, including the championship runs in 1999 and 2002.

The beer and skittles continue with the top 12 teams squaring off in a double-loss elimination tournament at Cabin John Park, July 14-15.

July 14, 2007

GAME 1

AOL.....................................8

CNN.....................................5

GAMES 2, 3 & 4

CNN drops to loser's bracket and beats Associated Press, Washington Post, and Comcast Sports.

GAME 5	GAME 6 (CHAMPIONSHIP)
CNN.....................................17	USA TODAY 11
WTTG 7	CNN.....................................7

- **CNN makes remarkable 2007 playoff run after opening loss in tournament.**
- **CaNiNes respond with FIVE straight wins but come up short in championship.**
- **Team finishes in second place, receives two trophies, and respect from MMSL.**

By Joe Baseball Jr.

Bureau Sports Writer

ROCKVILLE, Md. (UPI) — Remember synergy?

That was the buzzword a few years back, and it set CNN apart from every other news organization on this side of the Mississippi.

Well, synergy went the way of the Edsel, *Inside Politics*, and pterodactyls. We all know what happened to AOL after the merger.

CNN and AOL are inexorably linked, not only in the world of broadcasting but also in the world of sports.

It was only fitting that the CNN CaNiNes would find themselves playing AOL again, this time in the opening game of the Metropolitan Media Softball League tournament.

CNN was the No. 3 seed thanks to its 14-2 regular season record. AOL, 12-4 and a No. 6 seed, had to get by CBS in the first round of the Big Dance for a date with destiny and CNN. And that's how the script unfolded.

AOL drew first blood on Saturday, beating CNN. But by Sunday afternoon, CNN would have the final say, and it was not, "You've Got Mail, bitch." No need to dredge up those skeletons. Let sleeping canines lie. We'll hold off on that for another day.

CNN brought its best to the immaculate fields at Cabin John Regional Park, where the team played seven tension-filled games over two days in the double-loss elimination tourney, losing the first and then rebounding with five sudden death victories in a row before letting the championship slip through its worn-out fingers with the tying run on base and two outs.

As dawn broke on Saturday, CNN players gathered miles away to have a practice so the team would be ready when the first pitch was thrown.

"We should have stayed in bed," said one sleep-deprived CaNiNe. The strategy of stretching and warming up only works in Hollywood movies and Carol Buckland romance novels.

What happened in Game 1 against sworn enemy AOL was not pretty. It was a car wreck. To paraphrase the overly used Las Vegas slogan, what happened on field six should have stayed on field six.

CNN came out with so little octane the chairman of Exxon Mobil called for hearings on Capitol Hill. The team was operating on no cylinders. CNN had one base runner through the first three innings. It was a sitcom without the laugh track. AOL was ahead 5-0 in a blink.

True to form, the CaNiNes found their legs and never gave up. That's their trademark. It's been that way all year. Back they came slowly, methodically, to tie the game in the bottom of the sixth.

AOL had some hits in the nick of time to break the tight contest open in the last inning to take an 8-5 lead. It was too much to handle, like watching a full hour of Nancy Grace. AOL held on to win and move on, while CNN dropped into the loser's bracket.

That's not a customary place for the CaNiNes, as readers of this column know well. Since 1999, CNN has won the championship twice, finished second twice, and ended up in third, fourth, and fifth place. Darn near a dynasty. To reach the top again in 2007, CNN would have to navigate the hard way, winning every remaining game after the opening debacle. And the CaNiNes came this close to doing it.

CNN shrugged off the first loss and ran off wins against the Associated Press, Washington Post, and Comcast Sports the rest of the day. Saturday was in the books.

It was on to Sunday with the near-impossible task of winning four more games to become champions.

WTTG was waiting. The Fox Trotters were the No. 2 seed and, by most accounts, the MMSL's most impressive regular-season squad. But they also had one loss in the tournament.

The CaNiNes blew the gates open late and ended WTTG's valiant run with a 17-7 thrashing. Greg Robertson continued his crafty pitching. The bats of Howie Lutt, Quinn Brown, John Davis, and Willie Lora led the way. The incomparable defense of Cat Belanger, an intern at George Washington, had people talking about her range and throwing arm all weekend. She also worked opposing pitchers for several grade-A walks, her diminutive frame posing a challenging strike zone.

"She was the catalyst for us and the missing ingredient," said coach Barnett. "Opposing teams saw this tiny lady way out in right center and found the target irresistible. Cat routinely called off veteran outfielders and caught everything that came her way."

CNN then squared off against AOL to decide who would move on from the loser's bracket and face USA Today. The CaNiNes did what they had to do with an ultrafast dispatch of their corporate pain-in-the-ass opponent.

And just like that, it was on to the finals.

USA Today had a 4-1 lead after three innings when the Gannetoids broke the game open with six runs in the fourth. They did it with a series of excuse-me hits and an occasional liner mixed in for good measure. The frustration was evident on the faces of the CaNiNes, who scored twice in the sixth and seventh and had the tying run at the plate with two outs but couldn't close the gap any further.

"We had more bloopers against USA Today than all the bloopers on the CNN Blooper Reel on YouTube," said the CNN team in a statement.

Just like that, it was over. A not-too-shabby second-place finish in 2007… with time to meditate and refocus.

The CaNiNes will be back.

Top, Mark Guastaferro takes a big rip and, well, you see the mighty drive; Left, sure-handed third baseman Darrin White tracks a pop fly; Above, Tom Bentz and his scorebook in 2012.

In 2012 CaNiNes action, Billy Holbert (above) has eye on the ball and bat in the right position; Right, Matt Guastaferro and Peter Lanier converge on a liner, but the ball squirted free.

Top left, Matt Guastaferro makes a running grab in 2015; top right, Matthew Vossekiul and his trusty bat at Aspen Hill Park. Above, unidentified CNN intern from summer 2012.

Top, Bill Tipper was with the CaNiNes through the thick and thin years; Above, pitcher Shannon Gillece in 2016; Right, Katie Lobosco on the pivot in 2022.

Top, Sheena Wilson takes a big rip during the CaNiNes' 2022 MMSL Championship run; Above, Scott Volmer (left) and Ben Krolowitz play a little "I got it. nope, you got it."

Top, CaNiNes jump for joy after defeating Discovery for CNN's first MMSL title in 20 years. Right, Katie Lobosco plays a slick second base.

EXTRA INNINGS

Epilogue

Aristotle, the ancient Greek philosopher, scientist, and writer, is credited with the catchphrase, "The whole is greater than the sum of its parts." He was talking about metaphysics 2,400 years ago, but it could have easily been softball. It's a good way to describe my news career at CNN and writing about the CaNiNes.

Softball was more than a weekend pastime. It was also a counterpoint to the seriousness of reporting on world events. I liked the mix of being a newsman during the week and a softball writer on the weekend. It was the total package. I often arranged family vacations around the softball schedule. The game write-ups published on Monday mornings were an unspoken part of my job, or at least that's how I felt.

It has been a pleasant journey revisiting these softball summaries.

I equate it to opening a time capsule, reconnecting with old friends, and stirring up great memories about *Playing Games at CNN*.

In writing this book, I reached out to current and former colleagues. One of the questions I asked them was what they enjoyed most about playing softball on Saturday mornings. There was unanimity. It was all about our connection.

After the network did some corporate house cleaning, CNN and I, aka Joe Baseball Jr., parted ways. Maybe company executives figured out Joe's real name and pushed him out. Some surmised the higher-ups were miffed when they visited the Washington Bureau and saw the trophy case teeming with more softball trophies than news awards.

After capturing the 2022 championship, CNN players show off their new hardware through a live stream with teammates who had to work in the office.

Not long after my departure, I landed as a news editor at Al Jazeera English, where, along with Chris Sheridan, I helped shepherd a Metropolitan Media Softball League team from the ground up in 2013 called the Al Jazeera Islanders. I was later hired by China Global Television Network as a news editor, where I briefly played for the CGTN Pandas.

Meanwhile, across town at CNN, the softball legacy did not exactly go according to script. The CaNiNes dissolved after the 2013 season. Without Joe, enthusiasm waned, recruitment dried up, and the employees found other things to do on Saturday mornings in the summer. Over the next couple of years, there were attempts to get the group back together, but the newsroom response was always tepid. Finally, in the spring of 2016, CNN hired Ben Krolowitz, who previously worked at ABC News and used to play softball.

He helped resurrect a team that was a cross between the 1899 Cleveland Spiders and the CaNiNes circa 1999. The rejuvenated CaNiNes had the perfect person to lead the way: longtime booster Lindy Royce-Bartlett, part of the 2002 championship squad. She became the new skipper and team mom, ensuring everyone knew where to be, how to behave, and, best of all, how to enjoy game days.

A cross-section of employees jumped on the bandwagon, including the control room, assignment desk, digital unit, editors, producers, show bookers, podcast editors, security, and an occasional spouse. But just as things were gaining momentum, COVID-19 came along.

The pandemic led to the cancellation of the 2020 season. It was a scary and uncertain time for all of us. The MMSL survived, a testament to its staying power, as players craved a return to normalcy and life without surgical face masks.

In 2021, Lindy became the 19th recipient of the Dale Solly Award for Sportsmanship and Camaraderie, the league's highest honor. She was showered with applause from the many players and family on hand to see the presentation—and those who played with her through the years.

"We genuinely like each other. People want to come out," Lindy reflected about the team and her softball journey.

"We're making memories again," said Paul Miller, a 24-year veteran on the CaNiNes and a self-described bench warmer, third base coach, right fielder, and designated hitter.

They no longer have weekly write-ups poking fun at the network. However, game results are now posted on Facebook with stats and minimal commentary. It's mostly a new generation of players with no institutional memory of what came before.

Still, CNN management is doing its part. In addition to paying the annual entry fee, approaching $800, the Washington Bureau continues to pony up for the uniforms and softball equipment. They also sponsor pizza and beer outings and a barbecue at the end of the season.

CNN had a respectable showing in 2021, riding Lindy's enthusiastic coattails and finishing in third place. That, as it turned out, was just an amuse-bouche.

In 2022, the energized CaNiNes scored more runs than anyone else during the regular season and even had an unassisted triple play in a game. They entered the playoffs at Wheaton Regional Park as the No. 5 seed— a scrappy team no one wanted to face.

The big story was the weather. For the first time in the MMSL's 31-year history, the entire playoffs were rained out and had to be rescheduled for the following weekend. And it was worth the wait for the CaNiNes. Call it *Lady Luck*. Two of CNN's best female players, previously unavailable because of wedding commitments, were back in town.

In the first round, CNN dusted Bloomberg, a three-time league champion, 13-2. Then they beat the top-seeded Washington Post, 9-5, a team that had only lost twice all season. CNN made it three-for-three and steamrolled over parent company Discovery, 9-1, to conclude the first day of the playoffs. But CNN and Discovery would meet again less than 24 hours later for all the marbles.

The CaNiNes were making their sixth trip to the finals, but their first time since 2007. The Discovery Sharks had never made it this far. They were the last two teams standing: experience versus unbridled enthusiasm. It was no contest. CNN won the championship in a blowout, 13-1.

Looking back on the two-decade drought, Miller said, "Winning felt familiar, but it was not as dramatic this time. It was more of a statement."

It was an all-around effort of pitching, great defense, and a mighty offense like the CaNiNes of old. Lindy delivered an inspiring speech to her players, referencing the team of today and yesteryear. She captured the celebratory moment fittingly on a Facebook Live event back to the newsroom, where their teammates who had to work were jubilant.

The CaNiNes were again champions 20 years after their last title—a fitting bookend to this nostalgic visit down softball memory lane.

2022 MMSL Champion CaNiNes! Bottom row (L-R) Sheena Wilson, Katie Lobosco, Lindy Royce-Bartlett, Haley Thomas, Hiram Gonzales. Top row: Andrew Cotton, Adam Wollner, Michael Kim, Paul Miller, Ben Krolowitz, Tom Ebel, Devin Garbitt, and Chris Cross.

THE DALE C. SOLLY AWARD

The highest honor of the Metropolitan Media Softball League is the Dale C. Solly Award for Sportsmanship and Camaraderie, presented annually at the playoffs. The award was created after Dale, the beloved softball coach, anchor, reporter and colleague at WJLA-TV, died of a heart attack during the 2002 season. He was 53 years old.

Recipients of the Solly Award are selected on the basis of Dale's immense spirit of camaraderie on softball Saturdays and his enthusiasm, fairness, selflessness, and sportsmanship. I was honored to be the first recipient at an emotional ceremony that included Dale's family. Here is a list of Solly winners through the 2024 season:

2002	Jim Barnett, CNN
2003	Jonathan Salant, Associated Press
2004	Carolyn Hong, WTTG
2005	Laura Ingle, Discovery
2006	Chris Cicatelli, WJLA
2007	Don Collins, USA Today
2008	Rob Terry, The Gazette
2009	Eric Wray, ABC News
2010	Darren Ziegenbein, WRC
2011	Ken Giglio, National Press Club
2012	Cathy Hekimian, The Gazette
2013	Langdon Johnson, Discovery
2014	Peter Brewington, USA Today
2015	Dick Shinnick, Umpire
2016	Mark Hayes, USA Today
2017	Bruce DePuyt, WJLA
2018	John Vagnetti, WJLA
2019	Christina Jamieson Mozaffari, Alumni Team
2020	No season due to pandemic
2021	Lindy Royce-Bartlett, CNN
2022	Scott Moore, Washington Post
2023	Adam Mendelson, Sirius XM
2024	David and Ellen Sands, Alumni Team

Lindy Royce-Bartlett, 2021 Solly Award winner.

ALL-TIME LIST OF MMSL TEAMS

(Through 2024)

ABC News
Allbritton VoSox
Allbritton Philibusters
Al-Jazeera
Alumni
America's Most Wanted
America's Voice
AOL
Associated Press
Atlantic Media
Atlantic Video

British Broadcasting Corp.
Bloomberg

CapitalView News
CBS News
China Global Television Network
CNN
City Paper
Comcast SportsNet
C-SPAN

DCI Publications
Digital Ink
Discovery Channel
Dow Jones

Energy Now
Fox News
Los Angeles Times/Times Mirror
Montgomery Sentinel

National Geographic Channel
National Journal
National Public Radio
National Press Club
NBC News Channel

NBCSports Washington
NewsChannel 8

Political News Network
Politico
Potomac Almanac
PVS Speer

Real Clear Politics
Reuters

Scripps Howard
Silver Spring Express
Silver Spring Record
Sirius XM

Team Video
The Gazette Papers
The Journal Papers
Townhall.com

Voice of America
Vox Media

Wall Street Journal
Washington Examiner
Washington Post
Washington Post.com
Washington Times
WJLA
WJLA-NewsChannel 8
WUSA
WRC
WTOP
WTTG

United Press International
USA Today
U.S. News

ACKNOWLEDGMENTS

Thanks to all the past, present, and departed CNN colleagues who have been part of this softball odyssey. A high-five to Dennis Tuttle, the brains behind the MMSL, who held my hand throughout this project, and Jenine Zimmers for wrapping the words into a beautifully designed cover. Shout-outs also go to Lindy Royce-Bartlett, David Shuster, and Paul Miller for their contributions. Kudos to photographers Mike Ahlers, Michelle Brooke Poley, and Skip Nocciolo for capturing the action over the years.

A special tip of the cap to Faye Elkins, my wife and biggest fan, who has shown the patience of a saint and encouraged me throughout the writing process. I'll never forget the time when only eight CaNiNes showed up for a pivotal MMSL game. Faye played to prevent a forfeit. At age 66, she became the oldest woman to ever start in right field and score a run.

ABOUT THE AUTHOR

Born and raised in New Orleans, Jim Barnett attended Phillips Exeter Academy in New Hampshire before getting broadcast journalism degrees from Syracuse University and Boston University. In addition to his career in television news, his work has been published in The Times-Picayune, Associated Press, Boston Globe, Boston Herald American, Sunbelt Executive Magazine, The Courier, and Bethesda Magazine. This is his first book. Jim lives with his wife in Bethesda, Maryland, and near their four grandchildren.

Made in the USA
Columbia, SC
21 December 2024

50276943R00188